Boris Pasternak's
Translations of Shakespeare

Boris Pasternak, Chistopol', winter, 1942. Photo by V. Avdeeva.

ANNA KAY FRANCE

Boris Pasternak's Translations of Shakespeare

University of California Press
Berkeley · Los Angeles · London

University of California Press
Berkeley and Los Angeles, California

University of California Press, Ltd.
London, England

Copyright © 1978 by
The Regents of the University of California

ISBN 0-520-03432-5
Library of Congress Catalog Card Number: 76-52027
Printed in the United States of America

1 2 3 4 5 6 7 8 9

For Denis

Contents

Acknowledgments

I AM DEEPLY grateful to Lowry Nelson, Jr. and Victor Erlich for their advice, assistance, and encouragement during the writing of this book. Their generosity has been beyond repayment. I am indebted also to Laurence Michel, Marvel Shmiefsky, and Pierre Hart for reading individual sections of the book and making a number of important suggestions, to Emilia and Konstantin Hramov and to Richard Menn for invaluable assistance with English translations from Russian, to Alexis Rannit for his help with the early research, to Cathleen Carter for aiding with more than the typing of the manuscript, and to friends and members of my family for much needed support and understanding.

I particularly want to thank Evgenii Borisovich Pasternak, Lydia Pasternak Slater, and Ann Pasternak Slater for their interest and their kindness in providing information about Boris Pasternak's translations, which I could not have obtained otherwise.

Portions of this book have already appeared in print. A shorter version of the chapter on Pasternak's *Othello* appeared in *Shakespeare Quarterly* (Winter 1977), copyrighted by the Folger Shakespeare Library; the chapter on "Prosody and Verse Structure" was published in somewhat different form in *Canadian-American Slavic Studies* (Fall 1975); and the chapter on Pasternak's *Hamlet* appeared originally in *Russian Literature Triquarterly* (Fall 1973).

I wish to thank the editors of these journals for permission to reprint the articles. Finally, I appreciate the support provided toward preparation of the manuscript through the Julian Park Fund of the State University of New York at Buffalo.

Introduction

THE STATUS of translation among the arts has long been subject to speculation, and the translator has frequently been looked upon as an inferior craftsman at best, not as a genuine artist. Boris Pasternak stands among those who are most emphatic in asserting that literary translation is an art, and that freedom from the demands of literal exactitude is necessary if the translator is to capture the force of the original work. In his "Notes of a Translator" he remarks characteristically:

We have already said that translations are impossible because the principal charm of the work of art lies in its uniqueness. How then can a translation repeat this?

Translations are conceivable, because ideally they too should be works of art and, in sharing a common text, should stand on a level with the original, through their own uniqueness.[1]

It would be easy to contrast his point of view with that of some of his contemporaries in the Soviet Union and abroad. Vladimir Nabokov has been outspoken in defending the necessity for literal accuracy in translation, arguing that scholarly and even scientific exactitude should be employed in translating the original text. The translator's concern with literal meaning is to precede, and even preclude,

1. *Sochineniia,* ed. G. P. Struve and B. A. Filippov (Ann Arbor: University of Michigan Press, 1961), III, 184. This first appeared in *Znamia,* Nos. 1-2 (1944), pp. 165-66. Subsequent quotations from the Michigan edition of Pasternak's works will be followed simply by volume and page number.

any consideration of prosodic features or matters of style in general. Any latitude for freedom of expression in reproducing the original work is out of the question.[2] A.V. Fedorov, a major figure in translation theory in the Soviet Union, is more concerned with questions of style and tone, but only slightly less strict in his demand for a careful evaluation of the means of obtaining equivalence in translation. In his view, meaning is recognizably determined by context, and style is subject to objective analysis. The task of the theorist is to determine principles and set regulations by which the translator may be guided in reproducing the meaning and tonal quality of any work in a foreign language.[3]

However, Pasternak is only one of a number of theorists and translators in the Soviet Union and abroad who emphasize that artistic translation cannot be a wholly objective or impersonal process. Such leading critics as K. I. Chukovsky and E. Etkind have pointed out indications of personal style and viewpoint in the work of some of the major Russian translators. Chukovsky, for example, has traced evidences of puritanism and sentimentalism in Zhukovsky's translations from Schiller, Homer, and other poets; he has pointed out the personal idiosyncrasies which appear in various translations of the *Raid of Prince Igor* and works of Shevchenko and of Shakespeare.[4] The au-

2. See Nabokov's essays "The Servile Path," in *On Translation*, ed. Reuben Brower (New York: Oxford University Press, 1966), pp. 97–110; "The Art of Translation," *The New Republic*, 105, No. 5 (Aug. 4, 1941), 160–62; "On Translating Pushkin," *The New York Review of Books*, 2, No. 6 (Apr. 30, 1964), 14–16.

3. See in particular the opening chapter of Fedorov's *Vvedenie v teoriiu perevoda* (Introduction to the Theory of Translation) (Moscow: Izdatel'stvo literatury na inostrannykh iazykakh, 1958).

4. K. I. Chukovsky, *Vysokoe iskusstvo* (The High Art) (Moscow-Leningrad: Gosudarstvennoe izdatel'stvo khudozhestvennoi literatury, 1941), p. 18ff.

thors of *Shekspir i russkaia kul'tura* (Shakespeare and Russian Culture) (Moscow–Leningrad, 1965), analyzing and evaluating various pre-Revolutionary translations of Shakespeare into Russian, often give evidence of individual interpretation, textual distortion, or personal affinity of the translator for certain works.[5] In his work on poetry and translation, *Poeziia i perevod* (Moscow–Leningrad, 1963), Etkind has devoted an entire chapter to the translator as poet, to the manifestations of individual artistic style and technique in the works of such major Russian translators as Samuel Marshak, V. V. Levik, Nikolai Zabolotsky, and Pasternak himself.

The writings of numerous translators attest further to the imaginative probing necessary to the act of translation, through their descriptions of attempts to render within their own language the complex and elusive patterns of meaning and tonal nuance found in foreign works of literature. It is not uncommon to find such outstanding Soviet translators as Marshak and Levik openly asserting that translation constitutes a form of interpretive art, and that it cannot be carried out effectively without considerable latitude for the play of the individual imagination.[6] Pasternak may be extreme in his assertion of the artistic validity of translation, but he is not alone in his beliefs, and indeed seems part of a broad current of opinion in the Soviet Union today.

Among Western European and American theoreticians

5. See, for example, the discussions of Druzhinin, Weinberg, and Satin, pp. 390–93, 477–83, 506–09.

6. S. Marshak, "Iskusstvo poeticheskogo portreta" (The Art of Poetic Portraiture), in *Masterstvo perevoda 1959* (Moscow: Sovetskii pisatel', 1959), pp. 245–50; V. Levik, "O tochnosti i vernosti" (On Exactness and Faithfulness), in ibid., pp. 255–75, and "Vernoe slovo—na vernoe mesto" (The Right Word in the Right Place), in *Masterstvo perevoda 1963* (Moscow: Sovetskii pisatel', 1964), pp. 90–106.

and poet-translators, many have held an equally high opinion of the creative or re-creative role of the translator. D. S. Carne-Ross has written that

at its highest, a translation comes into existence in the same way as a work of original literature: a man experiences something—in this case, a foreign text—which he has got to find words for if he is to have any peace.[7]

In his introduction to Ezra Pound's *Translations*, Hugh Kenner comments that

translating does not, for [Pound], differ in essence from any other poetic job; as the poet begins by seeing, so the translator by reading; but his reading must be a kind of seeing . . . A good translation seems like a miracle because one who can read the original can, so to speak, see the poem before the poet writes it, and marvel at the success of his wrestle to subdue his own language to the vision.[8]

In the preface to his translation of the *Eclogues* of Virgil, Paul Valéry describes the experience of translating these poems from Latin into French:

I had, before my Virgil, the sensation (which I knew well) of the poet in labor; and I debated absentmindedly with myself off and on about this famous work, fixed in the glory of millennia, as freely as I would have done about a poem I was working on at my table.

He writes of approaching Virgil's poem not as something finished and "crystallized in its glory," but of returning, in his imagination, to its source, to the state of the poet when the work was first coming into being, and resolving

7. *The Craft and Context of Translation*, ed. W. Arrowsmith and R. Shattuck (Austin: University of Texas Press, 1961), p. 5.
8. Introduction to *Translations*, by Ezra Pound (New York: New Directions, 1963), p. 10.

this experience in "a work in a language other than the original."[9]

From such a point of view, the confrontation of two creative personalities through the action of translation may be seen as an extraordinary and revelatory event. The extent to which the translation represents a sensitive recapturing of the style and meaning of the original or becomes a vehicle for the translator's own expressive statement or stylistic formulations is a matter of considerable interest and significance. Boris Pasternak's translations of poems and plays of William Shakespeare are of a scope and sensitivity which provide a revealing view of the conflict of creative personalities, the nature of the functioning of a highly original writer in the role of interpretive artist.

Pasternak translated with varying degrees of success Goethe's *Faust*, Schiller's *Mary Stuart*, much Georgian poetry, many of the works of the Hungarian poet Petöfi, and scattered works of such writers as Keats, Shelley, Byron, Ben Jonson, Walter Raleigh, Verlaine, Johannes Becher, Hans Sachs, Rilke, Rafael Alberti, Calderón de la Barca, Juliusz Słowacki, Vitězslav Nezval, Ondra Lysogorskiĭ, Taras Shevchenko, Maksym Ryl's'kyĭ, and Rabindranath Tagore, among them English, French, German, Spanish, Polish, Czech, Ukrainian, and Indian poets. But the focus of this study will be upon his translations of works of William Shakespeare, illuminated by his references to them in poems and essays. These translations include four poems: Sonnets 66 and 73, "Music" (from III.i of *Henry VIII*), and "Winter" (from V.ii of *Love's Labour's Lost*), all published in his *Collected Translations*, in 1940[10]; and

9. Paul Valéry, *Oeuvres*, ed. Jean Hytier (Paris: Gallimard, 1957), I, 214–16.

10. Pasternak's correspondence with Grigorii Kozintsev in 1953–54,

eight plays: *Hamlet* (1940), *Romeo and Juliet* (1943), *Antony and Cleopatra* (1944), *Othello* (1945), *Henry IV, parts 1 and 2* (1948), *King Lear* (1949), and *Macbeth* (1951). The translations are not even in quality, but this in itself seems to reveal the degree of sensitivity Pasternak had for various aspects of the mind and manner of expression of the original author. To a certain extent, Pasternak's motivation in producing this extraordinary body of translations may have been purely practical. The playwright Afinogenov wrote of conversations with Pasternak in 1937, at a time when the latter was deeply absorbed in his own creative work, already engaged on his novel:

It's hard for his wife, they have to get money and live somehow, but he doesn't know anything about it, only sometimes when the money problem gets really severe, he starts some translations, "But I'd do just as well being a travelling salesman . . ."[11]

Still, as Vladimir Markov has pointed out, Pasternak's translations served him as a means of personal creative expression, through the very choice of subject and through changes introduced into the wording of the original text, at a time when other avenues of artistic self-expression were closed to him, when he could not express himself freely or hope to have his own work published in the Soviet Union.[12] Further, there are numerous indications in his writings that he did not look upon translation as an

---

when Kozintsev was working on a stage production of *Hamlet*, using Pasternak's translation, also contains a translation of Sonnet 74, made by Pasternak at Kozintsev's request. See "Pis'ma o *Gamlete*" (Letters about *Hamlet*), ed. E. Pasternak and V. Kozintseva, in *Voprosy literatury*, No. 1 (1975), pp. 218–21.

11. From *Stat'i, dnevniki, pis'ma* (Essays, Diaries, Letters) (Moscow: Iskusstvo, 1957), p. 152.

12. See "An Unnoticed Aspect of Pasternak's Translations," *Slavic Review*, 20, No. 3 (Oct., 1961), 503–08.

inferior artistic endeavor. In a series of notes and comments published in 1922 under the title of "Several Positions," Pasternak refers to the experience of translating Swinburne's drama *Chastelard* as a means of illuminating his view of the inherent power of poetry, and he indicates that to be able somehow to re-create a work of art is as extraordinary as to produce it initially:

What constitutes the miracle? That there once lived in the world a seventeen-year-old girl named Mary Stuart, and that somehow in October, by a window behind which the Puritans were hooting, she wrote a poem in French, ending with the words:

> Car mon pis et mon mieux
> Sont les plus déserts lieux.

Or, second, that once in his youth, by a window behind which October caroused and raged, the English poet Charles Algernon Swinburne completed *Chastelard*, in which the quiet plaint of the five stanzas of Mary became the terrible drone of five tragic acts.

Or, third, finally, that when sometime about five years ago, a translator glanced through the window, he did not know what to marvel at the most.

At the fact that the Elabuga snowstorm knew Scottish, and that, just as on that day, it still troubled itself about a seventeen-year-old girl, or that the girl and her sympathizer, the English poet, had managed so well, so sincerely well, to tell him in Russian what continued to trouble them both as before, and had not ceased to pursue them. (III, 153–54)

The process of translation is not seen here as a self-conscious, analytical, or mechanical one; the original work is viewed not as a set of words, phrases, or stylistic and prosodic devices, but as a living voice, a vital presence which transmutes itself into the translator's own language as if under its own power. Pasternak shows here his sense of the continuing vitality of the work of art, its existence as a living reality ("a book is a living being") not delimited by words and literary devices.

The translation of Swinburne's drama, inadvertently destroyed near the beginning of World War I, was probably not a masterpiece; but the attitude toward translation displayed in this passage remained much the same through the period of Pasternak's finest work as a translator. Two decades later, in the "Notes of a Translator" which accompanied the publication of his translation of *Hamlet*, Pasternak insisted that a translation is not a copy but an outgrowth of the original work, and can be produced only when the original work has entered into the consciousness of the translator and has become a part of his own experience.

The relationship between the original and the translation should be like the relationship between what is fundamental and what is derived from it, between a trunk and a cutting. The translation must come from an author who has experienced the influence of the original long before beginning his work on it. It should be the fruit of the original, and its historical consequence. (III, 183)

Pasternak never pretended that the original work would not be transformed in the process; on the contrary, he asserted that the translation should possess its own "uniqueness." As Andrei Siniavsky has put it:

It was Pasternak's conviction that the translator must not take a mold of the object he is copying but must transmit its vital and poetic force, thus transforming a copy into an original creation, living on a level with the original in another linguistic system.[13]

13. From "Poeziia Pasternaka," Siniavsky's introductory article to *Stikhotvoreniia i poemy* (Poems), by B. Pasternak, ed. L. A. Ozerov (Moscow–Leningrad: Sovetskii pisatel', 1965), p. 51.

Articulating this point of view in the introduction to his *Hamlet*, Pasternak insisted that his translation "must be judged as an original Russian dramatic work" (III, 191), a statement for which his critics frequently took him to task.

Pasternak's translations of Shakespeare's works, particularly *Hamlet*, were given considerable attention in the Soviet Union, and from the very beginning he received severe criticism for the free approach he took in making them. To be sure, his translations met with enthusiastic praise in some quarters, and the very frequency with which they have been published and performed attests to their popularity and wide acceptance. Even Pasternak's critics have acknowledged their poetic merits. But few critics or theoreticians, at the time of their publication or more recently, have held them to be ideal or flawless. Few have shared Pasternak's own view of the latitude to be allowed the translator. Many have criticized evidence of carelessness, deliberate or accidental departures from the meaning of the original work, as well as a failure to suggest the style of the original. Some have complained that the translations sound too little like Shakespeare, and too much like Pasternak, and that certain stylistic characteristics have carried over from his own work into his translations—expressions peculiar to twentieth-century Russian poetry, or the persistent use of contemporary, colloquial Russian, which markedly alters the rhetorical flights of the newly enraptured Romeo, for example, and affects the tone of speech of many of the other characters.[14] Before Pasternak's

14. For a discussion of these various points, see, for example, the essays (in Russian) by Iu. Gavruk, "Is a New Translation of *Hamlet* Needed in Russian?"; V. Levik, "Are New Translations of Shakespeare

translations of the plays were even published, they were
subject to the criticism of the prominent Shakespearean
critic Mikhail Morozov, and their correspondence on the
subject reveals a clash of two fundamentally opposed
views on the nature of translation.[15] Morozov, while appreciative of the poetic qualities of Pasternak's work,
insisted that the genius of Shakespeare would be best conveyed through as complete and accurate a translation as
possible. (He wrote of some minor omissions Pasternak
had made in *Romeo and Juliet*, "Why is this abridgement
necessary? The theater can do its own cutting, and the
reader needs to be given the full text. This is intolerable.
Why, this is Shakespeare!"[16]) Pasternak, however, while
acknowledging the range and depth of Morozov's knowledge and his distinction as a scholar, remained convinced
that the most accurate translation was not necessarily the
best, that the attempt to translate with literal exactitude
might well result in an exact but lifeless copy, with none
of the vital power of the original.

In published comments on translation, he admitted that
recent Soviet translations of Shakespeare were more accurate than those made in the nineteenth century, that
"they acquaint one with the verbal structure of the Shakespearean texts, with their lexicon."[17] And at various times

---

Necessary?"; E. Etkind, "On the Conventional-poetic and the Individual"; and A. Finkel', "The 66th Sonnet in Russian Translation," all
in *Masterstvo perevoda 1966* (Moscow: Sovetskii pisatel', 1968).

15. See "K perevodam shekspirovskikh dram" (On Translations of
Shakespeare's Dramas), ed. Evgenii Borisovich Pasternak, in *Masterstvo
perevoda 1969* (Moscow: Sovetskii pisatel', 1970), pp. 341–63. This
contains previously unpublished correspondence between Pasternak and
Morozov, and others, on the subject of Pasternak's translations.

16. Ibid., p. 354.

17. B. Pasternak, "Notes on Translation," in *Masterstvo perevoda*

he acknowledged the particular virtues of such individual translators as Lozinsky, Radlova, and T. Shchepkina-Kupernik. But he nonetheless held literal translation to be a "chronic, constantly disappearing, overcome and constantly returning delusion."[18] In a personal letter to one of the editors of his work, he acknowledged at one point that "the works of Lozinsky, Radlova, Marshak and Chukovsky [among the most distinguished of Soviet translators] are distant from me and seem artificial, superficial and soulless."[19] He repeatedly made clear his own preference for the work of nineteenth-century translators such as Druzhinin and Kroneberg, who looked on a translation as being in itself a work of literature, and who took numerous liberties in pursuing their goal.

In translating the plays in his turn, Pasternak knew English well enough to work by himself "with a dictionary and a small publisher's commentary." After completing an initial draft of a translation of *Hamlet*, Pasternak compared it with other Russian translations of *Hamlet* and found himself dissatisfied because it was too literal, filled with "likenesses and coincidences" with those earlier versions, contributing little that was new or useful to the Russians' understanding of Shakespeare. And so, as he states himself, he set himself a new task, turning "from the translation of words and metaphors to the translation of thoughts and scenes," allowing himself that "freedom without which there is no approach to great things."[20] He

---

1966 (Moscow: Sovetskii pisatel', 1968), p. 108. Though published only in 1968, these notes were actually written during World War II.

18. Ibid., p. 108.

19. "On Translations of Shakespeare's Dramas," *Masterstvo perevoda 1969*, p. 342.

20. "From the Translator," preface to the 1940 edition of Pasternak's translation of *Hamlet*, reprinted in *Sochineniia*, III, 191.

made concessions to Morozov and his editors, but unwillingly, and insofar as he was able he tried to maintain the integrity of his own work.

For those, then, who seek a scrupulously accurate Russian translation of Shakespeare's works, Pasternak's relatively free translations have serious drawbacks and may be frustrating and unsatisfying, even though Pasternak's own countrymen are divided on this matter. But these very departures from the original text are of interest in themselves, for they serve as evidence of a reinterpretation of Shakespeare's works by one of the major Russian poets of this century, revealing much about his insights, proclivities, tastes, and ultimately, the nature and limitations of his understanding of Shakespearean tragedy. The very changes he introduced into the texts of the plays often place Shakespeare's work in an unexpected and revealing perspective and may illuminate some characteristics of the original itself.

At the same time, it should be kept in mind that Pasternak's willfulness and freedom as a translator can be, and sometimes have been, exaggerated. One Western editor had been led to believe that Pasternak "had changed the historical events, had transposed them into Russian history . . . and had rewritten entire scenes to provide their equivalent in the popular Russian language of one province or another."[21] This simply is not true. In certain respects Pasternak was remarkably careful, sensitive, and faithful to the original. His interest in Shakespeare was deep and of long standing, and he was obviously concerned with communicating the essence of Shakespeare's work, not

21. Roger Caillois, in *Translation and Translators*, A "Round Table" Discussion in Rome, Nov. 1–4, 1961, ed. L. Gara, P. Tabori, T. Zavalani (International P.E.N.), p. 93.

simply making the translation a vehicle for his own self-expression. Even his departures from the letter of the original were done in the interests of a deeper faithfulness, in an effort to recapture the immediate power and life of the Shakespearean originals. Indeed this body of translations serves to illustrate the essential dilemma of the literary translator who, even as he seeks to recreate faithfully the work of another writer in his own language, must call upon his own creative and imaginative resources and ultimately manifests his own artistic personality.

Some of Pasternak's more dramatic departures from Shakespeare will be brought out in the first section of this study. The possibility that Pasternak used his translations as a means of making a political statement or commenting on conditions in the Soviet Union has been suggested and may have some validity, as will be pointed out in a few instances in the following chapters. But Pasternak was obviously not using Shakespeare's works simply as a means for topical comment. They held for him a more far-reaching significance, providing the profoundest possible insight into the realities of man's nature and the workings of individual artistic genius. Six of the eight plays Pasternak translated were tragedies, and in commenting even on *Henry IV, parts 1 and 2,* he emphasized not the humor or the comic aspects of Falstaff, but the way in which the tavern scenes reflect Shakespeare's own preparation for the graver, more serious work to come (III, 206–07). This is not to say that the translations are humorless or relentlessly heavy-handed, but that Pasternak chose to translate works in which the comic element does not predominate. Accordingly, I shall begin my analysis of Pasternak's translations of Shakespeare's plays with individual studies of four of the major tragedies—*Hamlet, Othello, King*

Lear, and *Macbeth*—published in Pasternak's translation in 1940, 1945, 1949, and 1951, respectively. In all of these, my primary concern will be with the nature of Pasternak's handling of Shakespearean tragedy, particularly his tempering of its more pessimistic strain. I am assuming that deviations from the Shakespearean texts are consistent and distinctive enough to reveal the translator's bias, his own interpretation of the plays.

The second section will focus on Pasternak's "realism" as a translator, a matter of some importance since Pasternak insisted repeatedly on the essential realism of Shakespeare, and on the necessity of recapturing the impact of reality, life itself, in any work of art, including translations. On the most obvious level, this attitude is reflected in his highly controversial use of the language of common everyday life, colloquial Russian. He often makes Shakespeare's characters sound natural and lifelike, but he frequently changes them in the process, and the nature and implications of these transformations will be given close attention, particularly since they appear to reflect Pasternak's own views on "realism" in art and man's ability to transform, evade, or transcend the ordinary conditions of human life. *Romeo and Juliet, Henry IV, parts 1 and 2,* and *Antony and Cleopatra* will be examined most closely in this section.

The translator's style and details of linguistic usage will not be ignored in the first two sections of the book, particularly in the part on Pasternak's use of colloquial Russian. But the final section will focus on two matters of fundamental importance only touched on earlier: first, Pasternak's handling of the mechanics of prosody and verse structure, his ingenious, sensitive, and highly expressive use of patterns in sound; and second, his tendency to transform the involutions and baroque complexities of the original poetry into lucid, pithy, and often classically simple verse. In examining the "classical" style of these translations, I will be concerned in part with phrasing and verbal constructions, in part with Pasternak's handling of allusions to time and space, particularly in narrative and descriptive passages.

Pasternak's translations of Shakespeare must ultimately be considered within the larger context of his creative work. Siniavsky has noted that

Pasternak bore his best translations within himself for years, while he prepared himself for them by the very process of his inner development. . . . "The influence of the original" (not, of course, always a direct one but often complicated, refracted in the various phenomena of world culture) in this case began long before his actual work on Shakespeare's tragedies and to some extent coincided with the artist's own interests and plans. This is why Shakespeare took root so deeply in Pasternak's poetic soil, and why his translating work, which was influenced by his individual tastes, predilections, and manner as a poet, had in its turn an influence on his original work.[22]

The very intricacy and profundity of the relationship between Pasternak's work with Shakespeare and his own artistic creation make it difficult to probe this matter adequately, even in a study focussed on his translations of Shakespeare's plays. Among the many considerations which might arise is the question of Pasternak's view of tragedy in general: its evolution, the relationship between the tragic and Christian elements in such works as *Doctor Zhivago*, and possible analogies to the imagery and implications of the Shakespearean tragedies in the latter,

22. Siniavsky, p. 52.

such as the references to dark, fundamentally destructive impulses in human nature, on the one hand, and the consciousness, on the other, of an impetus toward regeneration and resurrection, and the ultimate affirmation of life. Relevant to Section II are Pasternak's views on reality and realism, and displacement and transformation in artistic creation, presented in such works as *Safe Conduct*. With respect to Section III, there is the extremely complicated matter of defining and explaining the stylistic changes in Pasternak's work over a period of five decades, the growing simplicity of his style, and the relationship this may have to the often classical simplicity of the translations themselves. To probe all of these matters fully is beyond the scope of this study. But they will be touched upon and explored briefly, and the larger context of Pasternak's creative work kept in mind throughout.

With few exceptions, literal English prose translations of Russian passages are provided throughout, although they cannot convey the exact meaning of the original or demonstrate fully the Russian translator's sometimes ingenious or masterful use of his own language. The nature of colloquialisms, diminutives, and other peculiarly Russian expressions and usages is particularly difficult to convey in English, and some aphoristically terse and pithy comments fall flat in literal English translation. On the other hand, some of the shortcomings of the Russian translation may be less obvious in an English version of the text. The clumsier passages may actually improve and appear more graceful when translated from polysyllabic Russian into monosyllabic English. The problem is particularly acute when style itself is the subject, that is, in the very beginning of the section on realism, and also in the

final section, in the chapter on prosody and verse structure, and to a lesser extent, in the one on the classical
simplicity of the translator's style. The chapter on prosody
and metrics, more than any other, necessitates some reading knowledge of Russian, and I have not even attempted
to provide translations of long passages here, although
translations of some individual words and phrases are
supplied.

As far as possible, however, this study is meant to be
accessible to the reader who has little or no knowledge of
Russian, but who may be interested in the perspective
provided here on the work of Pasternak and of Shakespeare, and on some of the problems of translation.

A Russian edition of selected works of Shakespeare,
Izbrannye proizvedeniia (Moscow: Gosudarstvennoe
izdatel'stvo khudozhestvennoi literatury, 1953), the only
volume in which all of Pasternak's translations of Shakespeare's plays appear together, will be used throughout
as a basic text. Unless otherwise indicated, all quotations
from Pasternak's translations will be taken from this edition. Variant wordings from earlier or, in a few instances,
later editions will be provided in footnotes, and occasionally referred to in the body of the text. In translations of
most of the plays, the variations to be cited in this study
are generally of minor significance, and it would matter
relatively little which edition was used. Pasternak's son,
Evgenii Borisovich, has confirmed that Pasternak himself
made all changes and revisions in the text. But he was
often put under pressure, particularly by the Shakespearean scholar Morozov, to revise and bring his translations
closer to the wording of the original text, a matter which
led to painful altercations and compromises. The number

of revisions in the various editions of Pasternak's *Hamlet* makes this translation particularly difficult to analyze or assess, and some of the textual problems involved will be considered in the Appendix. Material from Pasternak's archives may eventually shed more light on the pressures Pasternak was under and the concessions he was forced to make in preparing his translations for publication. Some of it has already appeared in print.[23] But a number of the radical changes which were made in the texts are difficult to account for at present except as expressions of Pasternak's own taste and preference. Accordingly, although I account for variations in all the editions, I have chosen to work from the 1953 text, even in examining Pasternak's *Hamlet.*

It is not known at present which English editions of Shakespeare's plays Pasternak worked with in making his translations, and it seems unlikely that this can be established at all. Ann Pasternak Slater, the poet's niece, reports that only one edition of Shakespeare's plays was found in the library left by Pasternak at the time of his death: *Shakespeare's Tragedies,* Everyman edition (1906: rpt. 1913). She points out that this is relatively unmarked and only slightly worn, and there is little reason to believe that Pasternak used it in making his translations.[24] Because of the uncertainty as to which edition he did employ, I have

23. In "On Translations of Shakespeare's Dramas," cited extensively above, beginning with n. 15.

24. From private correspondence, dated 6 August 1974 and 10 November 1974. Also found in his library were: *A Companion to Shakespeare Studies,* ed. Harley Granville-Barker and G. B. Harrison (Cambridge, 1934; rpt. 1941), which is extensively marked and underlined; C. T. Onions, *A Shakespeare Glossary* (Oxford, 1911; rpt. 1941); and E. M. W. Tillyard, *The Elizabethan World Picture* (London: Chatto & Windus, 1943).

chosen to use the New Arden editions of Shakespeare's plays, in order to keep all possible variant readings before me. All quotations will be from the following editions unless otherwise noted: *Othello*, ed. M. R. Ridley (Cambridge: Harvard University Press, 1964); *King Lear*, ed. Kenneth Muir (New York: Random House, 1964); *Macbeth*, ed. Kenneth Muir (Cambridge: Harvard University Press, 1957); *The First Part of King Henry IV*, ed. A. R. Humphreys (Cambridge: Harvard University Press, 1961); *The Second Part of King Henry IV*, ed. A. R. Humphreys (New York: Vintage, 1967); *Antony and Cleopatra*, ed. M. R. Ridley (Cambridge: Harvard University Press, 1956). Where the New Arden edition is not yet available I have employed the New Variorum edition: *Hamlet*, ed. H. H. Furness (1877; rpt. Philadelphia: J. B. Lippincott Co., 1918); *Romeo and Juliet*, ed. H. H. Furness (1871; rpt. Philadelphia: J. B. Lippincott Co., 1913).

Unless otherwise indicated, all quotations from Pasternak's own writings are taken from the four-volume University of Michigan Press edition of his *Sochineniia*, ed. G. P. Struve and B. A. Filippov (Ann Arbor, 1961).

pessimistically than Pasternak did, emphasizing the difficulty, if not the impossibility, of Hamlet's retaining his
integrity amid the evil and corruption of the Danish court.
In an article published in the Soviet Union in 1961, A.
Anikst wrote that Hamlet "senses in himself the poten-
tiality for the same evil that has poisoned the souls of
others," and he continues:

The real problem of Hamlet's character concerns not his pro-
crastination, but rather the fact that living in a world where evil
reigns, he finds himself every moment in danger of succumbing
to the general infection. Even while preparing to carry out an
act of justified vengeance, he causes, in the process, unwarranted
pain. How to remain pure in circumstances where evil is unavoidable—here is one of the major human problems rising from
the tragedy.[4]

Such a critic as G. Wilson Knight takes a much darker
view of Shakespeare's protagonist, seeing in Hamlet's own
actions a negation of life, a source of evil:

He has seen the truth, not alone of Denmark, but of humanity,
of the universe: and the truth is evil. Thus Hamlet is an element
of evil in the state of Denmark. The poison of his mental existence
spreads outwards among things of flesh and blood, like acid
eating into metal. They are helpless before his very inactivity
and fall one after the other, like victims of an infectious disease.
. . . Not till it has slain all, is the demon that grips Hamlet satisfied. And last it slays Hamlet himself.[5]

Pasternak's view, however, seems to be closer to that
of Robert Ornstein, who in 1960 argued that despite the
brutality of some of his actions, Hamlet remains "the most
noble, pure-minded, and blameless of Shakespeare's tragic
protagonists." "Shakespeare creates within us a sympathy

4. Cited by Arthur P. Mendel in "Hamlet and Soviet Humanism,"
Slavic Review, 30, No. 4 (Dec. 1971), p. 740.
5. *The Wheel of Fire* (1930; rpt. London: Methuen, 1949), pp. 38–39.

with Hamlet which becomes almost an act of faith—a confidence in the untouched and untouchable core of his spiritual nature."[6]

The bent of Pasternak's interpretation may be suggested by a passage which he translated quite faithfully (and in a translation as free as his, faithfulness itself may be revealing). As Rosencrantz and Guildenstern persist in their efforts to penetrate Hamlet's defenses and learn the secrets he is hiding from them, Hamlet tries to persuade Guildenstern to play one of the players' pipes, and is told "I have not the skill." He replies with, in effect, a defense of his own integrity:

Why, look you now, how unworthy a thing you make of me! You would play upon me; you would seem to know my stops; you would pluck out the heart of my mystery; you would sound me from my lowest note to the top of my compass; and there is much music, excellent voice, in this little organ; yet cannot you make it speak. 'Sblood, do you think I am easier to be played on than a pipe? Call me what instrument you will, though you can fret me, you cannot play upon me. (III.ii.347–55)

Pasternak may make the attempts of Rosencrantz and Guildenstern seem even more demeaning to Hamlet, who begins not "how unworthy a thing you make of me," but "s kakoiu griaz'iu vy menia smeshali" (what filth you have sullied me with). But he closely reproduces the lines which follow:

Смотрите же, с какою грязью вы меня смешали. Вы собираетесь играть на мне. Вы приписываете себе знание моих клапанов. Вы уверены, что выжмете из меня голос моей тайны. Вы воображаете, будто все мои ноты снизу доверху

6. *The Moral Vision of Jacobean Tragedy* (Madison: University of Wisconsin Press, 1960), p. 235.

вам открыты. А эта маленькая вещица нарочно приспособлена для игры, у нее чудный тон, и тем не менее вы не можете заставить ее говорить. Что ж вы думаете, со мной это легче, чем с флейтой? Объявите меня каким угодно инструментом, вы можете расстроить меня, но играть на мне нельзя. (Р. 271)

(See, what filth you have sullied me with. You are preparing to play on me. You ascribe to yourselves knowledge of my stops. You are sure that you will wring from me the voice of my mystery. You imagine that all of my notes from bottom to top are open to you. And this little thing is fitted on purpose to be played, it has a wonderful tone, and yet you cannot force it to speak. Do you think that it is easier with me than with a flute? Declare me to be what instrument you will, you are able to upset[7] me, but not to play on me.)

Soviet critics writing during the "thaw," after Stalin's death, referred repeatedly to this passage, probably with special reason for admiring Hamlet's stand:

Never will he let himself be turned into a will-less "flute" from which others can sound wrong notes.[8]

He is not at all a gentle young man, but an aggressive heretic, burning with the joy of struggle, drunk with struggle—with an unequal struggle: against him is force, his only weapon—thought.

But thought won, echoing through the centuries, and we rapturously proclaim again: "Man is not a pipe."[9]

The passage may seem particularly appropriate to Pasternak's situation as a poet who refused to allow himself to

7. The Russian verb "rasstroit'" means "to upset, disorder, disturb, unsettle," as well as "to untune, put out of tune." Pasternak makes use of a play on words similar to the original one.

8. Cited in Mendel, "Hamlet and Soviet Humanism," p. 743.

9. Ibid.

be made the instrument of the state in Stalinist Russia. It might also be pointed out that in his translation it is not the "heart of my mystery" which Hamlet refuses to have wrung from him, but "golos moei tainy," the voice of my mystery.

Perhaps in keeping with this, Pasternak has markedly changed another passage, in which Hamlet implies that not even the best of men possesses defenses against the spreading effects of evil and corruption. Awaiting with Horatio the arrival of the Ghost on the battlements, Hamlet speaks of the Danes' reputation for drunkenness, which lowers them in the general esteem and "takes / From our achievements, though perform'd at height, / The pith and marrow of our attribute":

> So, oft it chances in particular men,
> That for some vicious mole of nature in them,
> As, in their birth,—wherein they are not guilty,
> Since nature cannot choose his origin,—
> By the o'ergrowth of some complexion,
> Oft breaking down the pales and forts of reason,
> Or by some habit that too much o'er-leavens
> The form of plausive manners; that these men,—
> Carrying, I say, the stamp of one defect,
> Being nature's livery, or fortune's star,—
> Their virtues else—be they as pure as grace,
> As infinite as man may undergo—
> Shall in the general censure take corruption
> From that particular fault; the dram of eale[10]
> Doth all the noble substance of a doubt
> To his own scandal.   (I.iv.23–38)

The passage is much altered in Pasternak's translation:

> Бывает и с отдельным человеком,
> Что, например, родимое пятно,

10. In many editions this appears as "the dram of evil"; presumably this was the case with the edition Pasternak was using.

В котором он невинен, ибо, верно,
Родителей себе не выбирал,
Иль странный склад души, перед которым
Сдается разум, или недочет
В манерах, оскорбляющий привычки,—
Бывает, словом, что пустой изъян,
В роду ли, свой ли, губит человека
Во мненье всех, будь доблести его,
Как милость божья, чисты и несметны.
А все от этой глупой капли зла,
И сразу все добро идет насмарку.
Досадно ведь.[11]   (P. 245)

(It sometimes happens to a particular man that, for instance, a birth mark for which he is not to blame since of course he did not choose his own parents, or a strange cast of soul, before which the reason gives way, or a defect in manners, offensive to custom,—it happens, in a word, that an empty flaw, either inherited or his own, ruins the man in the opinion of all, even if his virtues are innumerable and pure as the mercy of God. And all from this stupid drop of evil, and right away everything good goes to pot. It's really annoying.)

The crucial change lies in the fact that Pasternak leaves out the reference to "corruption," the suggestion that an individual's virtues, "be they pure as grace," will "take corruption" from a single drop of evil. Pasternak's Hamlet still states that a single flaw is enough to ruin a man's reputation in the eyes of the world, but he speaks of "that particular fault" as "pustoi iz"ian," an empty flaw,

11. In the 1940 edition, lines 5–6 are

Иль смуглый цвет, который разбивает
Все крепости рассудка, или штрих

(Or a dark color, which breaks down all the strongholds of reason, or a trait . . .);

and Hamlet speaks of a "plevaia kaplia zla" (trifling drop of evil), rather than a "glupaia" (stupid) one.

de-emphasizing its actual, innate harmfulness. In earlier
lines, the "mole of nature" is no longer "vicious," but
simply "rodimoe piatno," a birth mark or mole; there is
no reference to "the o'er-growth of some complexion, /
Oft breaking down the pales and forts of reason," but
rather to "strannyi sklad dushi, pered kotorym / Sdaetsia
razum" (a strange cast of soul, before which the reason
gives way), which may seem an apt and effective translation in a way, but which does not pick up the allusion to
something growing, spreading until it can break down a
stronghold. The final lines of the passage, difficult and
unclear in the English text which has come down to us,
are reduced virtually to insignificance in the translation:

> the dram of evil
> Doth all the noble substance of a doubt
> To his own scandal.

> А все от этой глупой капли зла,
> И сразу все добро идет насмарку.
> Досадно ведь.

(And all from this stupid drop of evil, and right away everything
good goes to pot. It's really annoying.)

The "dram of evil" has become a "stupid" (glupaia) "drop
of evil," and the final "dosadno ved'" (it's really annoying;
it's a nuisance) implies that Hamlet has been talking of
something vexatious, no more. The disturbing possibility
that evil may be able to infect and overcome even the
virtuous does not come out so strongly in Pasternak's
translation.

Few critics, particularly since Caroline Spurgeon's de-
tailed study of Shakespeare's imagery, have failed to notice
the pervasive allusions to spreading corruption, rotten-

ness, and disease to be found throughout the play. Grigorii Kozintsev notes that

Metaphors for gangrene, decay, and decomposition fill the tragedy.

Researches into the poetic images show that concepts of sickness—unto death—and decomposition dominate in *Hamlet*.[12]

Pasternak by no means expunged such imagery in his translation (which Kozintsev himself used in his film version of the play), but some of it is eliminated, particularly the references to the spreading of contamination. In the scene in the Queen's closet, Hamlet forces his mother to compare the portrait of Claudius with that of her first husband:

> Here is your husband; like a mildew'd ear,
> Blasting his wholesome brother.   (III.iv.64–65)

In Pasternak's translation:

> Он—словно колос, пораженный порчей,[13]
> В соседстве с чистым.   (P. 274)

(He is like an ear, spoiled by rot, next to a wholesome one.)

There is only a comparison of the corrupted ear with the good one, no imputation that the "mildew'd ear" would "blast" the wholesome one, that the rot would spread to the model of virtue. After the play has newly aroused his sense of guilt, Claudius speculates whether one may "be pardoned and retain th' offense":

---

12. Cited in Mendel, p. 736. This is taken from Kozintsev's *Nash sovremennik Vil'iam Shekspir* (Our Contemporary William Shakespeare) (Moscow: Iskusstvo, 1962), p. 173.

13. In the 1940 edition, this line is: "Kak kolos, zarazhennyi sporyn'eiu" (Like an ear, contaminated with ergot).

> In the corrupted 'currents of this world
> Offence's gilded hand may shove by justice,
> And oft 'tis seen the wicked prize itself
> Buys out the law.   (III.iii.57–60)

Pasternak leaves out "the corrupted 'currents of this world," though the sense of the original is otherwise retained:

> У нас нередко дело заминает
> Преступник горстью золота в руке,
> И самые плоды его злодейства
> Есть откуп от законности.[14]   (P. 272)

(Among us the criminal often hushes up the deed with a handful of gold, and the very fruits of his wickedness buy off the law.)

After witnessing Ophelia's madness, Claudius says,

> Oh, this' the poison of deep grief; it springs
> All from her father's death.   (IV.v.72–73)

In translation,

> Скорбь об отце свела ее с ума.[15]   (P. 281)

(Grief about her father has driven her mad.)

And of Laertes' return:

14. In the editions appearing from 1940 to 1951, the first two lines are:

> У нас не редкость, правда, что преступник
> Грозится пальцем в золотых перстнях

(Among us in truth it is not unusual for a criminal to threaten with a finger wearing gold rings.)

15. This is more literal in the editions of 1940, 1941, and 1942: "Vot iad glubokoi skorbi" (This is the poison of deep grief). In the editions of 1947, 1951: "Ee kruchina glozhet ob ottse" (Grief over her father gnaws at her).

> Her brother is in secret come from France,
> Feeds on his wonder, keeps himself in clouds,
> And wants not buzzers to infect his ear
> With pestilent speeches of his father's death.
>   (IV.v.84–87)

In translation, there is nothing about "pestilent speeches" which "infect his ear," although

> Живет молвой и верит болтунам,
> А те ему все уши прожужжали
> Про смерть отца.   (P. 281)

(He lives on rumor and believes the gossips, and they keep dinning in his ears about the death of his father.)

In the closet scene, Hamlet warns his mother not to attribute his words to madness:

> Lay not that flattering unction to your soul,
> That not your trespass but my madness speaks;
> It will but skin and film the ulcerous place,
> Whilst rank corruption, mining all within,
> Infects unseen.   (III.iv.145–49)

The translation is in this instance fairly faithful:

> Такая мазь затянет рану коркой,
> А скрытый гной вам выест все внутри.   (P. 275)

(Such an ointment will cover the wound as with a scab, while the hidden abscess will corrode everything from within.)

But in translating

> Repent what's past, avoid what is to come,
> And do not spread the compost o'er the weeds,
> To make them ranker   (III.iv.150–52)

Pasternak again avoids the allusion to something rotten, "rank," "the compost on the weeds," having Hamlet advise Gertrude simply:

> Траву худую вырывают с корнем.[16]   (P. 275)

(They tear out weeds by the root.)

Earlier in the play, Hamlet speaks to Rosencrantz and Guildenstern of "this most excellent canopy, the air, look you, this brave o'erhanging firmament, this majestical roof fretted with golden fire," which "appears no other thing to me than a foul and pestilent congregation of vapours" (II.ii.291–95). In translation the last phrase is "prosto-naprosto skoplenie voniuchikh i vrednykh parov" (p. 257). The Russian "voniuchyi" (stinking, giving off a foul, putrid smell) may seem an apt translation for the original "foul," but it applies primarily to a physical smell, and is not used so commonly in describing moral evil and corruption: "foul deeds," "murder most foul." And "vrednyi" (harmful, unhealthy) is not only a milder term than "pestilent," but fails to pick up the allusions to spreading disease which fill the play. Reuben Brower has pointed out that Pasternak's translation of the Ghost's warning to Hamlet, "Taint not thy mind . . ." (I.v.85), "Ne oskverniai dushi" (Do not profane your soul), "with its religious overtones, hardly permits the links with melancholy and disease to develop as they do in the original."[17] Throughout the play there is a preoccupation with sexual

16. In the 1940 edition this is "I sornykh trav ne mnozh'te udobren'em" (And don't increase the weeds by using fertilizer).
17. "Poetic and Dramatic Structure in Versions and Translations of Shakespeare," in *Poetics*, ed. Donald Davie, Kazimierz Wyka, Roman Jakobson, et al. (The Hague: Mouton, 1961), p. 667.

corruption as well, which is not so evident in the translation. Pasternak's tendency to bowdlerize the text, which
might appear to reflect no more than personal taste, a
reticence in speaking of certain matters, significantly alters
the play. By the time of the 1942 edition, many of the
bawdy, indecent, or suggestive comments or allusions
made to, by, or about Ophelia in particular had been
modified or omitted. From the 1942 edition on, Pasternak
completely omitted the least innocent of the songs Ophelia
sings in her madness:

> By Gis, and by Saint Charity,
>   Alack, and fie for shame!
> Young men will do't, if they come to't;
>   By Cock, they are to blame.
> Quoth she, before you tumbled me,
>   You promised me to wed.
>
> *He answers:*
>   So would I ha' done, by yonder sun,
>   And thou hadst not come to my bed.
>
> (IV.v.56–63)

After the 1941 edition, sexual innuendoes were left out of
the conversation which takes place between Hamlet and
Ophelia before the presentation of the play. One exchange was completely deleted:

Hamlet: I could interpret between you and your love, if I could
see the puppets dallying.
Ophelia: You are keen, my lord, you are keen.
Hamlet: It would cost you a groaning to take off my edge.
Ophelia: Still better, and worse.
Hamlet: So you must take your husbands.   (III.ii.235–40)

Other comments were modified. Hamlet's "Lady, shall I
lie in your lap?" (III.ii.105) becomes "Ledi, mozhno k vam

na koleni?" (p. 266) (Lady, may [I place myself] on your
knees?). And "That's a fair thought to lie between maids'
legs" (III.ii.111) becomes completely innocent: "A ved' eto
chudnaia mysl'—lezhat' u nog devushki!" (p. 266) (But
what a wonderful thought that is—to lie at a young girl's
feet!). Polonius' warning to Ophelia to be more wary of
Hamlet's tenders of affection,

> *Tender* yourself more dearly;
> Or—not to crack the wind of the poor phrase,
> Running it thus—you'll *tender* me a fool.
>
> (I.iii.107–09)

becomes more innocuously general: "ostanesh'sia ty v
durakh" (p. 244) (you will be made a fool of, duped).
And, after the 1941 edition, Pasternak simply omitted part
of Hamlet's warning to Polonius about his daughter: "Let
her not walk i' the sun; conception is a blessing; but not
as your daughter may conceive:—Friend, look to't" (II.ii.
183–85). In translation: "Ne puskaite ee na solntse. Ne
zevaite, priiatel'." (p. 255) (Don't let her into the sunlight.
Be careful, friend.).

Bowdlerization of texts is not unknown or altogether
uncommon in Soviet editions of literary works, but there
is reason to believe that Pasternak made these changes
himself, without undue pressure from his editors or critics
(as demonstrated in the Appendix). These changes help
to maintain the suggestion of Ophelia's innocence, weakening the implication that she too possesses sexual knowledge, is vulnerable to seduction, may be drawn into the
corrupted ways of the world.

The task of Hamlet, of course, is not only to avoid
"succumbing to the general infection" but also to root out
its causes, a task that might well lead to despair. And the

way in which Hamlet goes about the matter of purgation
is also somewhat changed by Pasternak. Some of the
strongest language in the translation comes in the scene
in which the Ghost entrusts Hamlet with the cause of
revenge, telling him of evils he had previously only sensed:
the foul lust which brought Gertrude and Claudius together, and the poisoning of the King, hideous in its effects, which left them free to marry. He says in particular
of Gertrude's fall from grace:

> But virtue, as it never will be moved,
> Though lewdness court it in a shape of heaven,
> So lust, though to a radiant angel link'd,
> Will sate itself in a celestial bed,
> And prey on garbage.   (I.v.53–57)

> Но так же, как не дрогнет добродетель,
> Каких бы чар ни напускал разврат,
> Так похоть даже в ангельских объятьях
> Пресытится блаженством и начнет
> Жрать падаль.   (P. 247)

(But just as virtue will not waver, whatever the charms depravity
puts on, so lust even in an angel's embraces will be sated with
bliss and begin to gorge carrion.)

But Hamlet's sense of the loathesomeness and bestiality
of his mother's actions does not emerge so clearly elsewhere. His pitiless effort to make the Queen recognize
the foulness of her relationship to Claudius is weaker in
Pasternak's translation of the closet scene:

> Nay, but to live
> In the rank sweat of an enseamed bed,
> Stew'd in corruption, honeying and making love
> Over the nasty sty,—   (III.iv.91–94)

Валяться в сале
Продавленной кровати, утопать
В испарине порока, любоваться
Своим паденьем...[18]   (P. 274)

(To loll about in a greasy, crushed bed, to wallow in the per-
spiration of vice, to take pleasure in your own downfall...)

The last line is completely euphemized; and the allusions
to "salo" (grease, fat, suet, tallow), "prodavlennaia kro-
vat'" (a crushed bed), and "isparina poroka" (the per-
spiration of vice) may not match the original "rank
sweat," "an enseamed bed," "stew'd in corruption," in
suggesting the physical grossness, the rankness, that
Hamlet is forcing the Queen to see in herself. Pasternak's
Hamlet no longer reminds Gertrude so clearly and uncompromisingly that she has allied herself to a source of
rottenness and corruption. And his last, sardonic piece of
advice to her is handled discreetly, much of it cut:

Queen: What shall I do?
Hamlet: Not this, by no means, that I bid you do:
          Let the bloat king tempt you again to bed;
          Pinch wanton on your cheek; call you his mouse;
          And let him, for a pair of reechy kisses,
          Or paddling in your neck with his damn'd fingers,
          Make you to ravel all this matter out,
          That I essentially am not in madness,
          But mad in craft. 'Twere good you let him know;
          For who, that's but a queen, fair, sober, wise,
          Would from a paddock, from a bat, a gib,
          Such dear concernings hide? who would do so?
          No, in despite of sense and secrecy,
          Unpeg the basket on the house's top,

18. In the 1940 edition, the last phrase is translated "kumit'sia /
Sredi navoza" (to gossip amidst the dung); in the 1941 and 1942 editions,
"tselovat'sia / Sredi navoza" (to kiss amidst the dung).

>   Let the birds fly, and like the famous ape,
>   To try conclusions, in the basket creep,
>   And break your own neck down.   (III.iv.180–96)

>   Еще вы спрашиваете? Тогда
>   И продолжайте делать, что хотите.
>   Ложитесь ночью с королем в постель
>   И в благодарность за его лобзанья,
>   Которыми он будет вас душить,
>   В приливе откровенности сознайтесь,
>   Что Гамлет вовсе не сошел с ума,
>   А притворяется с какой-то целью.[19]   (P. 276)

(You still ask? Then go on doing what you want to. Go to bed at night with the king and out of gratitude for the kisses he will smother you with, in a surge of frankness, confess that Hamlet has not gone mad at all, but is pretending for some reason.)

Gone are "the bloat king," "pinch wanton on your cheek," "reechy" kisses, "paddling in your neck with his damn'd fingers," and all that follows "but mad in craft": the analogy of the King to "a paddock, . . . a bat, a gib," and of the Queen to an ape about to break its neck. This Hamlet is less cruel in imagining the baseness and bestiality his mother might still be capable of. Earlier in the same scene, Shakespeare's Hamlet asks,

>   O shame! where is thy blush? Rebellious hell,
>   If thou canst mutine in a matron's bones,
>   To flaming youth let virtue be as wax
>   And melt in her own fire; proclaim no shame
>   When the compulsive ardour gives the charge,
>   Since frost itself as actively doth burn,
>   And reason panders will.   (III.iv.82–88)

19. This is translated much more literally in the 1940, 1941, and 1942 editions. No major cuts appeared until 1947.

This may be part of his attempt to bring his mother to an awareness of the enormity of her guilt and the repulsiveness of her alliance with Claudius, as the prelude, perhaps, to purification, purgation. But it is perilously close to being a call for the release of the forces that would bring man to ruin. Recognizing the overmastering of reason by appetite, Hamlet calls for this evil to run its course unchecked: "To flaming youth let virtue be as wax / . . . proclaim no shame / When the compulsive ardour gives the charge." Pasternak's Hamlet, however, simply asks how restraint can be expected of a younger woman, if his mother displays none herself. The lines cited above are completely omitted:

> Стыдливость, где ты? Искуситель-бес!
> Когда так властны страсти над вдовою,
> Как требовать от девушек стыда?
> Какой пример вы страшный подаете
> Невестам нашим![20]

(P. 274)

20. This passage evidently gave Pasternak difficulty, and he made substantial changes twice. In the 1940 edition:

> Стыд, где огонь твой? Греховодник-ад,
> Когда таков ты в матерях семейства,
> Прощай девическая чистота.
> Пусть млеет, воском тая. Нет позора,
> Когда встают от жара на дыбы,
> Раз бесятся и в холод, и хмелеют
> От умозрений.

(Shame, where is your fire? Sinner-hell, when you are such in the mothers of families, farewell maiden purity. Let it die away, melting like wax. There is no shame when they rear up because of ardor, if some begin to rage in the cold, and grow tipsy on speculation.)

In the editions of 1941 and 1942:

> Стыдливость, где ты? Искуситель-бес,
> Когда ты так могуч во вдовьем теле,
> Как девственности быть с ее огнем?

(Modesty, where are you? Tempter-devil! When passions have such power over a widow, how can we demand shame from young girls? What a terrible example you set for our brides!)

There is no longer the possible implication that Hamlet at this moment actually desires that free rein be given to appetite, and man brought to destruction.[21]

None of these passages, so drastically altered by Pasternak, is in keeping with the rather Christ-like Hamlet he refers to in his own work, or with the implication there of the possibility of redemption, the emphasis on the self-sacrificial nature of Hamlet's actions rather than their violence. In his essay he refers only once to the cruelty of Hamlet, making no excuses for his treatment of Ophelia:

In the scene in which Hamlet sends Ophelia to a nunnery, he speaks to the girl who loves him, and whom he tramples underfoot, with the ruthlessness of an egotistical, post-Byronic renegade. His irony is not justified even by his love for Ophelia, which he painfully suppresses at this moment. (III, 197)

But he mentions this only to point out the redeeming effect of the "To be or not to be" soliloquy, which immediately

---

Пускай, как воск, растает. Нет позора
В разнузданности от избытка сил,
Когда и лед пылает, и рассудок
Дурманит волю.

(Modesty, where are you? Tempter-devil, when you are so powerful in a widow's body, how will it be for virginity with its fires? Let it melt, like wax. There is no shame in licentiousness from an abundance of energy, when even ice burns, and reason stupifies the will.)

21. Compare Timon's bitter imprecations against the city of Athens: "Piety and fear, / Religion to the gods, peace, justice, truth, / Domestic awe, night-rest and neighbourhood, / Instruction, manners, mysteries and trades, / Degrees, observances, customs and laws, / Decline to your confounding contraries, / And let confusion live! . . . / . . . Lust and liberty / Creep in the minds and marrows of our youth, / That 'gainst the stream of virtue they may strive, / And drown themselves in riot!" (Timon of Athens, IV.i.15–21, 25–28).

precedes the scene, producing an effect of almost ritualistic absolution over that which follows:

No wonder that the monologue is prefaced to the cruelty of the dénouement which is beginning. It precedes it as the funeral service does the burial. After it may come any inevitability. Everything is redeemed, washed, and exalted, not only by the thoughts of the monologue, but by the ardor and purity of the tears which ring in it.

Yet Hamlet's cruelty to Ophelia in this scene lies largely in his harsh and embittered insistence that in this world she cannot escape untainted, untouched by at least the suspicion of corruption:

If thou dost marry, I'll give thee this plague for thy dowry: be thou as chaste as ice, as pure as snow, thou shalt not escape calumny. Get thee to a nunnery, go; farewell. Or, if thou wilt needs marry, marry a fool; for wise men know well enough what monsters you make of them. To a nunnery, go; and quickly too. Farewell. (III.i.135–40)

And it might be pointed out that although there are no major cuts or dramatic reversals of meaning in Pasternak's translation of this scene, he has made Hamlet's diatribe far less forceful:

Если пойдешь замуж, вот проклятье тебе в приданое. Будь непорочна, как лед, и чиста, как снег,—не уйти тебе от напраслины. Затворись в обители, говорю тебе. Иди с миром. А если тебе непременно надо мужа, выходи за глупого: слишком уж хорошо знают умные, каких чудищ вы из них делаете. Ступай в монахини, говорю тебе! И не откладывай. Прощай.²²   (P. 264)

22. In the 1940 edition, instead of "govoriu tebe" (I tell you), Hamlet says twice "govoriat tebe" (they tell you); instead of "stupai v monakhini" (become a nun), "v obitel'" (to a cloister); and instead of the final "proshchai" (farewell), he repeats "idi s mirom" (go in peace) a second time. In the 1956 edition, the colloquial "napraslina" (tales, a lot of nonsense) is replaced by the more formal "kleveta" (calumny, slander).

(If you marry, here is a curse for your dowry. Be as chaste as ice, and as pure as snow—you will not escape from slander. Shut yourself up in a cloister, I tell you. Go in peace. And if you absolutely must have a husband, marry a stupid one: wise men know all too well what monsters you make of them. Become a nun, I tell you! And do not put it off. Farewell.)

Instead of a "plague," Pasternak's Ophelia receives for her dowry "prokliat'e" (a curse)—which is strong enough in itself but does not pick up the allusions to spreading disease in the original text. The seriousness of the "calumny" which Ophelia will not escape is perhaps not recaptured by the colloquial "napraslina." And instead of "go; farewell," Pasternak's Hamlet says, "Idi s mirom" (Go in peace), which hardly seems to be in keeping with the spirit of the original diatribe. But perhaps the greatest problem with the translation is its clumsiness. The repeated "get thee to a nunnery" takes on different forms in the translation: in an earlier passage, it appears as "stupai v monastyr'" (enter a nunnery); in this particular one, "zatvoris' v obiteli" (shut yourself up in a cloister), and finally "stupai v monakhini" (become a nun). In adding "govoriu tebe" (I tell you) to the latter two, Pasternak may have been trying to re-create the effect of the original repetition, but he succeeded only in making the phrase more unwieldy. And my largely monosyllabic English translation does not suggest the clumsiness of the Russian version of the final phrase: "slishkom uzh khorosho znaiut umnye, kakikh chudishch vy iz nikh delaete" (wise men know all too well what monsters you make of them). Some of the virulent force of Hamlet's invective is lost, simply because of the ineptness with which it is phrased.

In general, the virulence and the bitterness with which Hamlet responds to evidence of depravity and corruption are much mitigated in translation. Pasternak sometimes

manages to suggest the anguish of Hamlet, confronted
with disillusionment and loss, as in his version of the
soliloquy beginning "O, that this too too solid flesh would
melt" (particularly in the 1947 edition); but here, too,
Pasternak has omitted Hamlet's most damning statement
about his mother: "Oh, most wicked speed, to post / With
such dexterity to incestuous sheets!"[23] (I.ii.156–57). Pasternak is more faithful and perhaps more successful in
dealing with passages which suggest the nobility and generosity of Hamlet, and finally the dignity and pathos of his
situation when he has completed the act of revenge and
must face his own death. At the very end of the play,
Hamlet may well be seen as Pasternak describes him in his
essay, as a man who has sacrificed his own life to carry
out the mission entrusted to him. Laertes dies, asking that
Hamlet's death not be visited upon him. Hamlet responds,

> Heaven make thee free of it! I follow thee.—
> I am dead, Horatio.—Wretched queen, adieu!—
> You that look pale and tremble at this chance,
> That are but mutes or audience to this act,
> Had I but time (as this fell sergeant, death,
> Is strict in his arrest) oh, I could tell you—
> But let it be.—Horatio, I am dead;
> Thou livest; report me and my cause aright
> To the unsatisfied.   (V.ii.319–27)

> Прости тебя господь.
> Я тоже вслед. Все кончено, Гораций.
> Простимся, королева! Бог с тобой!
> А вы, немые зрители финала,
> Ах, если б только время я имел,—
> Но смерть—тупой конвойный и не любит,

23. These lines—"S takoiu bystrotoi / Nyriat' pod prostyniu krovos-
meshen'ia!" (To dive with such swiftness beneath the sheet of incest!)—
were omitted after the 1941 edition.

> Чтоб медлили,—я столько бы сказал...
> Да пусть и так, все кончено, Гораций.
> Ты жив. Расскажешь правду обо мне
> Непосвященным.[24]   (P. 299)

(God forgive you. I follow after as well. All is finished, Horatio. Farewell, queen! God be with you! And you, dumb witnesses of the finale, ah, if only I had the time,—but death is an obtuse escort and does not like for people to delay—I would tell you so much... But let that be, all is finished, Horatio. You are alive. You will tell the truth about me to the uninitiated.)

Hamlet's bitter, sometimes vicious condemnation of evil does not come through so strongly in Pasternak's translation as does the suggestion of the pathos of the situation of the victim; and Pasternak was perhaps at his best in his handling of the most innocent victim of the tragedy, Ophelia, in describing that which still remains beautiful, regarded with wonder, arousing grief when it is lost. One of the finest passages in the translation is the Queen's account of the death of Ophelia:

> There is a willow grows aslant a brook,
> That shows his hoar leaves in the glassy stream;
> There with fantastic garlands did she come
> Of crow-flowers, nettles, daisies, and long purples,
> That liberal shepherds give a grosser name,
> But our cold maids do dead men's fingers call them;
> There, on the pendent boughs her coronet weeds
> Clambering to hang, an envious sliver broke;
> When down her weedy trophies and herself

24. In the 1940 edition, the third line is "prostimsia, koroleva-prostata!" (farewell, queen-simplicity!). And lines 6-7 are

> Но смерть—исправный вахтер и не терпит
> Отлыниванья,—я б вам рассказал—

(But death is an industrious porter and will not endure shirking,—I would tell you—)

Fell in the weeping brook. Her clothes spread wide,
And, mermaid-like, a while they bore her up;
Which time she chanted snatches of old tunes,
As one incapable of her own distress,
Or like a creature native and indued
Unto that element; but long it could not be
Till that her garments, heavy with their drink,
Pull'd the poor wretch from her melodious lay
To muddy death.   (IV.vii.168–85)

Над речкой ива свесила седую
Листву в поток. Сюда она пришла
Гирлянды плесть из лютика, крапивы,
Купав и цвета с красным хохолком,
Который пастухи зовут так грубо,
А девушки—ногтями мертвеца.
Ей травами увить хотелось иву,
Взялась за сук, а он и подломись,
И, как была, с копной цветных трофеев,
Она в поток обрушилась. Сперва
Ее держало платье, раздуваясь,
И, как русалку, поверху несло.
Она из старых песен что-то пела,
Как бы не ведая своей беды
Или как существо речной породы.
Но долго это длиться не могло,
И вымокшее платье потащило
Ее от песен старины на дно,
В муть смерти.[25]   (P. 287)

(Above the river a willow lowered its grey foliage into the stream. Here she came to weave garlands of buttercups, nettles, water lilies, and the flowers with red tufts, which shepherds call by such a coarse name, but young girls, dead man's fingernails. She wished to twine the willow tree with grasses, she took hold of a

25. In the 1941 and 1942 editions, the next to last line is "ee s vysot melodii, na dno" (. . . her from the heights of melody, to the bottom). In the earlier 1940 edition, it is the same as in the 1953 edition.

bough, but it gave way, and, as she was, with her sheaf of flowery trophies, she fell into the stream. At first her clothing held her up, billowing out, and like a water sprite, it bore her along the surface. She sang something from the old songs, as if not knowing her distress, or like a creature of the river breed. But this could not last long, and her drenched clothing dragged her from her songs of olden times to the bottom, to muddy death.)

Here, too, Pasternak seems ready to protect Ophelia's innocence. The "long purples" which she had included in her collection of flowers have become "flowers with red tufts" or "dead man's fingernails"; the phallic allusions have disappeared. (In the early poem "Uroki angliiskogo" [English Lessons], published in 1917, Pasternak wrote of Ophelia as going to her death "s okhapkoi verb i chisto-tela" [with an armful of willow and celandine], the latter consisting of "chisto-," which means "pure, clear, clean," and "-telo," "body.")

Apart from this, the translation is close to the original, simple, and far more graceful and musical than my prose translation would suggest. Pasternak has found ready equivalents for "mermaid-like," "old tunes" (in some editions, "old lauds"), and "her melodious lay," in the Russian "rusalka" (rusalka, waternymph, mermaid—a creature of Russian mythology), "starye pesni" (old, olden songs), "pesni stariny" (songs of olden times, antiquity); and "like a creature native and indued / Unto that element" becomes "kak sushchestvo rechnoi porody" (like a creature of the river breed). Ophelia has become something altogether wonderful in the moments before she is drawn "to muddy death," "v mut' smerti." And Pasternak has recaptured this suggestion of loveliness far better than he does Hamlet's description of a corrupt world, possessed by "things rank and gross in nature."

Just as there are entire groups of allusions and images which tend to be omitted or played down in the translation —spreading contamination, plague, pestilence—so there are others—references to flowers and music—that are emphasized and brought out, suggestive of something ineffably beautiful, precious, yet fragile, soon destroyed, lost.

At Ophelia's funeral, the Queen scatters flowers over her grave:

> Sweets to the sweet; farewell!
> I hoped thou shouldst have been my Hamlet's wife.
> I thought thy bride-bed to have deck'd, sweet maid,
> And not t' have strew'd thy grave.   (V.i.231–34)

> Нежнейшее—нежнейшей.
> Спи с миром! Я тебя мечтала в дом
> Ввести женою Гамлета. Мечтала
> Покрыть цветами брачную постель,
> А не могилу.   (P. 292)

The word with which Pasternak's translation begins is not "sweet" or "sweets" ("sladkii," or possibly "milyi"), but rather the superlative of "nezhnyi" (tender, delicate, loving)[26]; and the passage continues:

(Sleep in peace! I had dreamed of bringing you into the house as Hamlet's wife. I dreamed of covering your marriage bed with flowers, and not your grave.)

This translation, too, is simple, graceful, but instead of saying "I hoped thou shouldst have been my Hamlet's wife," Pasternak's Gertrude envisions even more specifically her part in a celebration that now will not take

26. In the 1940 edition, the passage begins "sladchaishee, sladchaishei," (the most sweet to the most sweet); in the 1941 and 1942 editions, "prekrasnoe prekrasnoi" (the beautiful to the beautiful).

place: "Ia tebia mechtala v dom / Vvesti zhenoiu Gam-leta" (I had dreamed of bringing you into the house as Hamlet's wife).

Further, although Pasternak has omitted one of Ophe-lia's songs in which there are open sexual allusions, sug-gesting perhaps a loss of innocence in Ophelia herself, he has translated with sensitivity and imagination those in which she alludes to the death of her father.

> White his shroud as the mountain snow,— . . .
> Larded with sweet flowers;
>   Which bewept to the grave did go
> With true-love showers.   (IV.v.34–38)

> Белый саван, белых роз
> Деревцо в цвету,
> И лицо поднять от слез
> Мне невмоготу.   (P. 281)

(A white shroud, a tree of white roses in blossom, and I have no strength to raise my face from weeping.)

In many editions, the last lines read "Which bewept to the grave did not go / With true-love showers." If this was true of the edition Pasternak used, he has left out the possible allusion to the hasty and secretive burial of Polonius—a cause, perhaps, of bitterness—and instead provides only the indication of grief: "I litso podniat' ot slez / Mne nevmogotu" (And I have no strength to raise my face from weeping). Another change is even more remarkable. Rath-er than singing of the white shroud "larded with sweet flowers," Pasternak's Ophelia simply passes from the white shroud ("belyi savan") to the tree of white roses in bloom ("belykh roz / Derevtso v tsvetu"). An association is thus made between the shroud and the tree of living flowers, and there may even be a suggestion of a trans-formation, one passing into the other.

Much earlier in the play, Laertes warns Ophelia:

> For Hamlet, and the trifling of his favour,
> Hold it a fashion, and a toy in blood,
> A violet in the youth of primy nature,
> Forward, not permanent, sweet, not lasting,
> The perfume and suppliance of a minute;
> No more.   (I.iii.5–10)

> А Гамлета ухаживанья—вздор.
> Считай их блажью, шалостями крови,
> Фиалкою, расцветшей в холода,
> Недолго радующей, обреченной,
> Благоуханьем мига и того
> Не более.[27]   (P. 243)

(But the attentions of Hamlet are nonsense. Consider them a whim, tricks of the blood, a violet that bloomed in the cold, not long giving joy, doomed, the fragrance of an instant, and no more.)

Shakespeare's Laertes imputes a certain lightness to Hamlet's expressions of love; they are "trifling," "a fashion," "a toy," "sweet," but "not lasting." The translator may try to recapture this with "schitai ikh blazh'iu, shalostiami krovi" (count them a whim, tricks of the blood). But the description of Hamlet's love acquires greater seriousness in the translation, where the original "sweet, not lasting" becomes "nedolgo raduiushchei" (not long giving joy); the "violet" that is "forward, not permanent," becomes "fialkoiu rastsvetshei v kholoda" (a violet that bloomed in the cold). And Pasternak's Laertes adds that it is "obrechennoi" (doomed). In this context, the final "no more," "ne bolee," may acquire new seriousness and pathos.

Pasternak seems to have little to say about the forces

27. Until the 1953 edition, the fourth line read "nezhdannoi, gibloi, sladkoi, obrechennoi" (unexpected, wretched, sweet, doomed).

which strike down those who are regretted or mourned, for some reason "doomed." One may miss in his interpretations and translations of Shakespeare's plays the original sense of intimacy with the nature of evil in man, the sources of savagery, violence, the impulse to destroy, the consciousness of an innate depravity. In his "Notes on Translations of Shakespeare's Tragedies," only Pasternak's mention of the ghost who "commands Hamlet to exact vengeance" ("trebuet ot Gamleta mshcheniia") in any way recalls that Hamlet himself is called upon to commit an act of violence, or that he does indeed cause anyone's death. Instead, in both his essay and his poem "Hamlet," Pasternak emphasizes the self-sacrifice which Hamlet reluctantly but voluntarily agrees to undertake. There may well be some curious parallels between Pasternak's Christlike "revenger" and some of his revolutionary heroes, in particular the idealistic Lieutenant Schmidt, who appears in the long poem bearing his name published by Pasternak in 1926. Condemned to death for his part in an abortive mutiny in Odessa during the 1905 revolution, Schmidt addresses his executioners:

> Напрасно в годы хаоса
> Искать конца благого.
> Одним карать и каяться,
> Другим—кончать Голгофой.
>
> Как вы, я—часть великого
> Перемещенья сроков,
> И я приму ваш приговор
> Без гнева и упрека.
>
> Наверно, вы не дрогнете,
> Сметая человека.
> Что ж,—мученики догмата,
> Вы тоже—жертва века.   (I, 171–72)

(It is useless in years of chaos to seek a good end. To some it falls
to punish and repent, to others, to die on Golgotha. Like you,
I am a part of the great upheaval of the times, and I will receive
your sentence without anger or reproach. Probably you won't
shudder, wiping out a man. What of it, martyrs of dogma, you
are also the victim of the age.)

There is no call to overcome and obliterate the oppressor,
the enemy. On the contrary, the death sentence is received
"without anger or reproach," and even the executioner is
regarded as being a "victim of the age," "zhertva veka."
There is a suggestion not only that he is not altogether
responsible for the evil he has done, but also that he is
himself caught up in a process that will lead to expiation,
atonement. Some are destined "to punish and repent,"
"karat' i kaiat'sia"; they are "martyrs of dogma," "victims
of the age." (In Russian, "zhertva" can mean either "victim" or "sacrifice"; in this particular context, the possible
religious connotations are not to be ignored.)

   The very ability of some at least to act in a Christ-like
manner implies a surviving goodness in human nature, and
whatever the immediate sufferings of Schmidt and of
others fated "to die on Golgotha," the outlook is ultimately
an optimistic one. Schmidt has the triumphant assurance
of the coming of a new era:

> Я знаю, что столб, у которого
> Я стану, будет гранью
> Двух разных эпох истории,
> И радуюсь избранью.   (I, 173)

(I know that the post by which I'll stand will be the border
between two different epochs in history, and I am glad that I have
been chosen.)

This is not a tragic conclusion, and it may seem that Pasternak has lessened some of the tragic implications of Shakespeare's *Hamlet* as well, emphasizing Hamlet's readiness to carry out a difficult and exalted task, while not conveying a sense of the full enormity of the evils he is confronted with, which threaten to produce in him a response of despair, paralysis of will, and desire for annihilation, and which make innocence and integrity almost impossible to maintain, and regeneration or redemption anything but inevitable. One might assume from Pasternak's very association of Hamlet with the figure of Christ that he tended to look beyond the hard assumptions of tragedy to the Christian promise of redemption, atonement, and resurrection. Indeed allusions to rebirth, resurrection, appear in many of the poems which follow "Hamlet" in the Zhivago cycle; and the final one, "The Garden of Gethsemane," ends with Christ's own prophecy of the Resurrection which will follow his death and burial. But in this first poem, "Hamlet," there is no anticipation of such an event, only resignation to a bleak and comfortless necessity.

> Но продуман распорядок действий,
> И неотвратим конец пути.
> Я один, все тонет в фарисействе.
> Жизнь прожить—не поле перейти.

(But the order of the acts has been thought out, and the end of the path is inevitable. I am alone, everything is drowning in pharisaism. To live through life is not like crossing a field.)

There may be a note of exultation in Lieutenant Schmidt's realization that "Ia zhil i otdal / Dushu svoiu za drugi svoia. / Vysshego net." (I have lived and given my soul for my friends. There is nothing higher.) (I, 162). But Pasternak makes it clear that at the time of the uprising, the sacrifice he was called upon to make caused him great anguish.[28] Even in some of his more optimistic, ultimately affirmative works, Pasternak touches on tragic possibilities, the situation of Christ in the Garden of Gethsemane, confronted with the necessity of self-sacrifice, unable for the moment at least to look beyond to the Resurrection. And though he has emphasized the essential nobility of Hamlet and the beauty and purity of Ophelia in his interpretation, Pasternak does not minimize their vulnerability to suffering, or to the pain of loss.

OTHELLO

LIKE ALL of his translations, Pasternak's *Othello* has flaws, but it is interesting because of its very unevenness, its strengths and weaknesses, which do not seem to result simply from chance felicities or difficulties in phrasing. Pasternak's greatest problem seems to have been with the character of Iago, who emerges in the translation of the play as a mechanically contrived and unconvincing villain. Yet the tragedy retains much of its power. Pasternak was far more successful in working with Othello and, above all, Desdemona. I shall examine here several aspects of the play as reinterpreted and represented by Pasternak:

28. Schmidt writes from prison to the woman he loves:

> О, как рвался я к тебе! Было пыткой
> Браться и знать, что народ не готов,
> Жертвовать встречей и видеть в избытке
> Доводы в пользу других городов.   (I, 163)

(Oh, how I longed for you! It was torture to begin and know that the people were not ready, to sacrifice meeting and to see in abundance arguments in favor of other cities.)

first, his handling of the references to bestiality and monstrosity which occur throughout the play; second, his modification of evidence of the power Iago exercises over others; third, his portrayal of Othello and his relationship to Iago, the tendency to make Othello view Desdemona more sympathetically than he does in the original, to minimize his disgust at her apparent perversity; and fourth, the way in which Pasternak establishes and brings out the tragedy of loss, the desolation of the central characters.

In his comments on *Othello* in "Notes on Translations of Shakespeare's Tragedies," Pasternak refers to Iago as "an untransformed prehistoric animal" ("neobrashchennoe doistoricheskoe zhivotnoe"), and the comment may be a significant one. Underlying many of Shakespeare's plays, including *Othello*, is the implication that a potential for brute savagery remains even in civilized man, waiting to be released under conditions of anarchy and chaos. The theme is far less common in Pasternak's work, perhaps not appearing at all until *Doctor Zhivago*, where he describes the complete breakdown of the amenities and conventions of civilized society near the end of the civil war.

That period justified the ancient saying, "Man is a wolf to man." Traveller turned off the road at the sight of traveller, stranger meeting stranger killed to avoid being killed. There were isolated cases of cannibalism. The laws of human civilization had come to an end. Those of the beasts were in force. Man dreamed the prehistoric dreams of the cave age. (IV, 388)

In his translation of *Othello*, however, this element is muted at times to the point of unrecognizability. Allusions to bestiality and monstrosity fare badly at the translator's hands throughout the play. Pressed by Othello for confirmation of his jealous suspicions, Shakespeare's Iago reminds him of the difficulty of taking Desdemona and

Cassio in the act, even if they behave with the unrestrained lust of animals:

> It is impossible you should see this,
> Were they as prime as goats, as hot as monkeys,
> As salt as wolves, in pride.   (III.iii.408–10)

With only a slight change in phrasing, Iago himself in the translation denies their bestiality:

> Как их поймать? Они
> Не пара обезьян, не волк с волчицей.   (P. 331)

(How can you catch them? They are not a pair of monkeys, not a wolf and she-wolf.)

From the opening scene of the play, the union of Desdemona and Othello is described by Iago as something not simply bestial, but monstrous, grotesque. Here, too, Pasternak is not at his best. Much of the horror of a liaison between woman and beast, for example, disappears when the directly copulative image of the original text ("you'll have your daughter cover'd with a Barbary horse" [I.i. 110–11]) is replaced by a more nicely euphemistic term:

Вам хочется, чтоб у вашей дочери был роман с арабским жеребцом, чтобы ваши внуки ржали. (P. 303)

(You want your daughter to have an affair with an Arabian stallion, and your grandchildren to neigh.)

And Iago's warning to Brabantio that "your daughter, and the Moor, are now making the beast with two backs" (I.i.115–17) is given a clumsily literal translation into multisyllabic, much inflected Russian:

Ваша дочь в настоящую минуту складывает с мавром зверя с двумя спинами. (P. 303)

(Your daughter, at the present moment, is composing with the Moor the beast with two backs.)

It is not only the direct allusions to sexual activity that are modified in translation. True, Othello's account of the savages and monsters he had encountered on his travels in distant lands—"the Cannibals, that each other eat; / The Anthropophagi, and men whose heads / Do grow beneath their shoulders" (I.iii.143–45)—remains intact in Pasternak's translation. But references to a monstrosity that lies within, ultimately escaping Othello's control, tend to remain unmentioned in Pasternak's translation. Pasternak does occasionally use the adverb "chudovishchno" as a direct translation for "monstrous" (see III.iii.433; p. 332 of the Russian text), and he translates directly one exchange between Othello and Iago:

> *Othello*: A horned man 's a monster, and a beast.
> *Iago*: There's many a beast then in a populous city,
>   And many a civil monster.   (IV.i.62–64)

But more often references to such "monsters" ("chudishcha") are omitted in translation, and the cumulative effect of the repeated allusions is diminished. For instance, Shakespeare's Othello responds to the first oblique intimations that his wife is involved with Cassio:

> *Othello*: Is he not honest?
> *Iago*: Honest, my lord?
> *Othello*: Honest? ay, honest.
> *Iago*: My lord, for aught I know.
> *Othello*: What dost thou think?
> *Iago*: Think, my lord?
> *Othello*: Think, my lord? Why dost thou echo me,
>   As if there were some monster in thy thought,[1]
>   Too hideous to be shown.   (III.iii.104–12)

1. In the New Arden edition, the line reads "By heaven, he echoes

Othello's readiness in recognizing this monstrosity is obscured in Pasternak's translation, where he only questions Iago, still uncomprehending, and the "monster in his thought" remains unrecognized or unmentioned.

> Да что с тобою? Что ты задолбил
> И повторяешь все за мной, как эхо?
> В чем дело? Так ли мысль твоя страшна,
> Что ты ее боишься обнаружить? (P. 326)

(What is wrong with you? Why do you parrot and repeat everything after me, like an echo? What is the matter? Is your thought so terrible that you are afraid to reveal it?)

Similarly, "the green-ey'd monster" that Iago warns Othello against, after doing his utmost to deliver him into its power (III.iii.170), becomes in Pasternak's translation a "zelenoglaz[aia] ved'm[a] . . . / Kotoraia smeetsia nad dobychei" (p. 327) (a green-eyed witch who laughs at her prey), a less brutish figure than her Shakespearean counterpart. And the same "monster," which Emilia recognizes in Othello after his first jealous outbursts ("'tis a monster, / Begot upon itself, born on itself." "Heaven keep that monster from Othello's mind!" [III.iv.159–61]), remains unmentioned or is converted into a "bich" (scourge):

> *Эмилия*: Сама собой сыта и дышит ревность.
> *Дездемона*: Да обойдет Отелло этот бич! (P. 336)

(*Emilia*: Jealousy breathes and is replete with itself.
Desdemona: May that scourge pass Othello by!)

Taken by themselves, these changes may seem slight, relatively unimportant; but the consistency with which Pas-

---

me, / As if there were some monster in his thought," based on the first Quarto version rather than the second Quarto version, which was evidently used in the text Pasternak worked with.

ternak makes them may suggest a reluctance, inability, or
failure to deal with certain implications of the play.

The very suggestion of the power impelling men to such
monstrous actions is weakened in translation. Even as he
encourages Roderigo's desire for Desdemona, Shakespeare's Iago speaks of lust as being potentially dangerous,
difficult to control and capable of leading to strange ends:

If the balance of our lives had not one scale of reason, to poise
another of sensuality, the blood and baseness of our natures
would conduct us to most preposterous conclusions. But we have
reason to cool our raging motions, our carnal stings, our unbitted
lusts; whereof I take this, that you call love, to be a sect, or scion.
(I.iii.326–33)

Если бы не было разума, нас заездила бы чувственность.
На то и ум, чтобы обуздывать ее нелепости. Твоя любовь
—один из садовых видов, которые, хочешь—можно воз-
делывать, хочешь—нет. (Р. 311)

(If it were not for reason, sensuality would wear us out. But
that's why we have an intellect: to curb its absurdities. Your
love is one sort of garden which you may cultivate or not, as
you wish.)

In translation, love is no longer equated with lust; there
is no mention of "the blood and baseness of our nature";
and "our raging motions, our carnal stings, our unbitted
lusts" are reduced to "chuvstvennost'" (sensuality) with
"ee neleposti" (its absurdities). The latter does little to
suggest the possible unnaturalness of the "preposterous
conclusions" to which unbridled lust would lead.

If the dark power Iago attributes to lust and appetite
seems diminished in Pasternak's translation, so is the force
of Iago's presence, his persuasiveness, his ability to manipulate and control others to suit his own purposes. A number of major Shakespearean critics, including A. C. Bradley and Harley Granville-Barker, have considered Iago as

an artist in his ability to arouse and manipulate the imagination and passions of his subject. Examining him as such,
Stanley Edgar Hyman has written of "Iago's great rhetorical triumphs in Act III, scene 3, when he first arouses
Othello's suspicions by the most economical of means, the
smallest whispers of hints."[2] In Pasternak's translation,
however, Iago becomes more crude and unconvincing in
his efforts to arouse the imagination of his victim through
provocative suggestions. As he first inflames Othello's suspicions about Desdemona's fidelity, for instance, Iago
stresses the unnaturalness of appetite that would lead to
an act of miscegenation, reminding Othello that his wife
had the perversity to marry a man not of her own race:

> Ay, there's the point: as, to be bold with you,
> Not to affect many proposed matches,
> Of her own clime, complexion, and degree,
> Whereto we see in all things nature tends.
>
> (III.iii.232–35)

Where Shakespeare's Iago insinuates and suggests, Pasternak's Iago comes out with a straightforward comment and
question, not even preparing the way with "to be bold with
you":

> Вот именно. Примеры под рукой.
> Естественно ли это отчужденье
> От юношей ее родной страны?   (P. 328)

(That's it exactly. There are examples right at hand. Is this
estrangement from the young men of her own country natural?)

And he makes no reference to a concept of natural order,
against which the unnaturalness of Desdemona's choice

---

2. *Iago: Some Approaches to the Illusion of His Motivation* (New
York: Atheneum, 1970), p. 64.

may be judged. Having laid the groundwork, Shakespeare's Iago immediately draws his foul conclusions, dealing a sudden blow:

> Fie, we may smell in such a will most rank,
> Foul disproportion; thoughts unnatural.

Pasternak's Iago simply continues to ask questions of his
listener, expressing astonishment that such things could
be; and there is no allusion to a foulness, a corruption in
Desdemona that can be "smelt," almost physically de-
tectable:

> Не поражают ли в таких примерах
> Черты порока, извращенья чувств?

(Don't the traits of vice, the perversion of the feelings astonish
one in such instances?)

Having made his point, directly and tellingly, Shakespeare's Iago immediately retreats, as if out of deference
to Othello, though not altogether freeing Desdemona from
suspicion:

> But pardon me: I do not in position
> Distinctly speak of her.

In translation, there is no longer the suggestion that he is
saying this only to spare Othello's feelings; on the contrary, he announces flatly and directly:

> Я это отношу не к Дездемоне,
> О ней определенных данных нет.

(I do not apply this to Desdemona. There is no definite information about her.)

And though the final lines are translated fairly directly,

there is no reference to "the will," meaning here "lust, desire" (as in the earlier "will most rank"):

> though I may fear
> Her will, recoiling to her better judgement
> May fall to match you with her country forms,
> And happily repent.

> Но есть опасность, как бы, отрезвевши
> И сравнивая вас и земляков,
> Она не пожалела.

(But there is a danger that, once she has grown sober and compares you with her countrymen, she may repent.)

In general, the persuasiveness and cunning with which Iago works upon his victims is conveyed ineffectively by Pasternak. His Iago is often as blunt and lacking in subtlety as the other characters in the play would expect "honest Iago" to be, and he is less convincing as a manipulator because of this.

Throughout the play, the power of self-assertion, the will to dominate and control, the readiness and the ability to use other people, is weakened in Pasternak's Iago. As Iago first attempts to bend Roderigo to his will, he professes for him a deep and abiding friendship, which may make escape seem impossible and even undesirable:

I profess me thy friend, and I confess me knit to thy deserving, with cables of perdurable toughness. (I.iii.337–39)

In translation this is replaced by the brief and innocuous "Ia poklialsia pomoch' tebe" (p. 311) (I have sworn to help you); Iago's hold over his victim is not so marked. Upon Roderigo's departure, Shakespeare's Iago speaks of him virtually as a personal possession: "Thus do I ever make my fool my purse" (I.iii.381). This, too, is subtly changed:

"Mne etot duren' sluzhit koshel'kom" (p. 312) (This simpleton serves me as a purse). The repeated "my" is left out; and there is nothing to replace the original "ever," which had indicated that Iago's ability to exercise such power is virtually to be taken for granted.

The very assertion of the power of the individual to mold his life according to his desires loses force in translation. In the first act of the play, Iago counsels Roderigo not to drown himself for love of Desdemona but to find the means to satisfy that love, which he defines as "merely a lust of the blood, and a permission of the will" (I.iii. 335–36):

Virtue? a fig! 'tis in ourselves, that we are thus, or thus: our bodies are gardens, to the which our wills are gardeners, so that if we will plant nettles, or sow lettuce, set hyssop, and weed up thyme; supply it with one gender of herbs, or distract it with many; either to have it sterile with idleness, or manur 'd with industry, why, the power, and corrigible authority of this, lies in our wills. (I.iii.319–26)

Не в состоянии! Скажите пожалуйста! Быть тем или другим зависит от нас. Каждый из нас—сад, а садовник в нем—воля. Расти ли в нас крапиве, салату, исопу, тмину, чему-нибудь одному или многому, заглохнуть ли без ухода или пышно разрастись—всему этому мы сами господа. (Р. 311)

(Not in a position [to do that]! Come on now! To be one thing or another depends on us. Each of us is a garden, and the gardener in it is the will. Whether there will grow in us nettles, lettuce, hyssop, or caraway, one or many of anything, whether we will go to seed for lack of care or grow luxuriantly—of all this we ourselves are masters.)

Pasternak has shortened Shakespeare's elaborately developed garden metaphor; more significant, the "will" ("volia") is mentioned only once in translation, not twice as in

the original; and although Pasternak's Iago asserts that
with respect to our "gardens" we are "gospoda" (the masters), there is no mention of "the power" which resides "in
our wills." Pasternak used the word "sila" (power) repeatedly in other contexts, particularly in discussing the
nature of artistic creation, but he leaves it out of the speech
of Iago.

The very process by which Iago evolves his plans for
the undoing of Othello, Cassio, and Desdemona is made
by Pasternak to seem mechanical and rather contrived. In
the first act, Iago begins to work out a strategem for
having Cassio discredited and deprived of the position he
desires for himself:

> Cassio's a proper man, let me see now,
> To get this place, and to make up my will,
> A double knavery...how, how?...let me see,
> After some time, to abuse Othello's ear,
> That he is too familiar with his wife.   (I.iii.390–94)

> Ведь Кассио для этого находка!
> Во-первых, с места я его сшибу,
> А во-вторых... Ура! Ура! Придумал!
> Начну Отелло на ухо шептать,
> Что Кассио хорош с его женою.   (P. 312)

(Why Cassio is a godsend for this! In the first place, I will knock
him down from his position, and in the second... Hurray!
Hurray! I've figured it out! I'll begin to whisper into Othello's
ear that Cassio is on good terms with his wife.)

Iago's determination "to make up my will," his deliberate
intention of perpetrating "a double knavery," are not mentioned in translation. The mulling over of the problem
("let me see now . . . how, how?...let me see") is gone;
and there is instead an enthusiastic setting forth of a plan

which seems fully developed from the very beginning. (Iago lists his moves, "Vo-pervykh . . . vo-vtorykh," in the first place . . . in the second.) And in Pasternak's version, Iago's delight in his own cleverness ("Ura! Ura! Pridumal!" Hurray! Hurray! I've figured it out!) may make him seen ingenuous, boyish, naive, not a man plotting a deadly scheme. The suggestion of process, the evolution of a malevolent idea, is deprived of naturalness and credibility. Further, the implicit analogy between the inception of Iago's plans and the process of gestation and birth disappears in translation. Iago's assurance to Roderigo that "there are many events in the womb of time, which will be delivered" (I.iii.369–70), an implicit promise that Desdemona will betray her husband and become his mistress, is simply left out in translation. Iago's exclamation on first working out his malevolent plans ("I ha't, it is engender'd" [I.iii.401]) is altered to a more businesslike expression: "Tak po rukam!" (So, it's done; it's a bargain). And the "monstrous birth" which, according to Iago, "Hell and night / Must bring . . . to the world's light" (I.iii.401–02) becomes simply a "zamysel" (project, plan, scheme):

> Кромешный ад и ночь
> Должны мне в этом замысле помочь.   (Р. 312)

(Hell and night must help me in this project.)

Metaphorical allusions to gestation and birth are not uncommon in Pasternak's own poetry, often related to the process of poetic creation, as in "Tak nachinaiut" (So They Begin), but Pasternak does not allow them into the vocabulary of Iago. In translation, Iago's very villainy may seem a convention, his malevolence deprived of vitality and disassociated from living process.

On the whole, Pasternak has produced a peculiarly weak Iago, and this may be in keeping with the views set forth in an early essay on the play:

In Othello and Desdemona everything, without admixture, is real. When their fullness and truth collide with the fake and fictitious world of Iago, they perish from the abundance of their own authenticity; from their internal wealth.

In place of Iago-the-villain, one could imagine another Iago, who really is that sincere well-wisher he made himself out to be. And all the same he would be the curse of Desdemona and Othello and the instrument of their destruction. It is important not that Iago is a slanderer and criminal, but that he is an extinguisher of life, that in proximity to the blazing crucible of originality he is threateningly fruitless and ungifted.

Because of this there are no bounds to the fabrications and machinations of Iago. He has nothing of his own, he is bound by nothing and in his actions he makes use of unlimited freedom. Meanwhile Othello and Desdemona are not in command of themselves. They are constrained by their own unambiguous essence, they are not free and are obedient to its laws.[3]

It is curious and surely significant that evil is defined here in negative terms, strictly as an absence of good. Pasternak holds it irrelevant that Iago is a "villain," "slanderer," and "criminal"; what is important is that, in contrast to Othello and Desdemona, he is "fruitless and ungifted," "has nothing of his own," and "is bound by nothing." Pasternak has played down the significance and effectiveness of what might be considered active evil, the "malignancy" (motiveless or otherwise) many have recognized in Iago; and such an interpretation would seem to be reflected in the translation, where Iago does not display the

3. "Notes on Translation," in *Masterstvo perevoda 1966* (Moscow: Sovetskii pisatel', 1968), p. 107. These notes, first published in 1968, date back to World War II.

active force or power of the original character. But in this passage Pasternak nevertheless describes Iago as dangerous and destructive, "threateningly" ungifted, "an extinguisher of life." And that which makes him so are characteristics which make it possible to identify him with the artist—his capacity for creating fictions, illusions, fabrications. His is a "fake and fictitious world." Not bound as Othello and Desdemona are to "reality" (and presumably goodness), he "exercises unlimited freedom" and there are "no bounds to his fabrications and machinations." But in his translation, Pasternak often denies Iago these perverse and destructive gifts. He departs from the original text wherever Iago employs language he uses himself in describing the creative process. He fails to suggest Iago's subtlety in arousing the imagination of his primary victim; he recreates only mechanically and unconvincingly the genesis of a scheme for destruction; and although he has allowed Iago his connection with "hell and night," he has not associated them with birth and creation. In his translation of *Othello*, Pasternak has not used his own powerful poetic and imaginative gifts to suggest their perversion to evil uses by another.

In this early passage, Pasternak sets up a diametric opposition between the "reality" of Othello and the "fictitious world" of Iago, and uses this to explain Othello's vulnerability to Iago. In his "Notes on Translations of Shakespeare's Tragedies," first published in 1956, he argues that the means by which Iago arouses Othello's jealousy in the third act of the play are lacking in credibility, and that this unrealistic, unconvincing section constitutes the major flaw in the play:

But here with a few turns of the key, Iago in the middle section winds up, like an alarm clock, the credulity of his victim, and the phenomenon of jealousy, with a wheeze and a shudder, like an antiquated mechanism, begins to unwind before us. (III, 200)

Like Pasternak, a number of critics have viewed the readiness with which Othello accepts Iago's insinuations as unconvincing and unrealistic, insufficiently motivated. Others, like F. R. Leavis, have found, on the contrary, that "Iago's power . . . in the temptation-scene is that he represents something that is in Othello."[4] Agreeing with this point, A. P. Rossiter asserts that "Othello and Iago are not only antithetical types, noble and base: they have correspondences."[5] Evidence for such an argument would be harder to find in Pasternak's translation. There is nothing in Pasternak's notes on the play to suggest that Othello is anything other than a good and noble man, the "victim" of another's machinations. In his early essay, Pasternak even insists that Othello decides to kill his wife "not with the aim of vengeance, but in order to save the soul of Desdemona, since he believes that his violence to the body of Desdemona in this world will spare her spirit from heavenly retribution in the next" (p. 107). This may be reflected in the translation as well. Othello's words as he proceeds to the murder of Desdemona in the final act, "Thy bed, lust-stain'd, shall with lust's blood be spotted" (V.i.36), are made more circumspect and guarded, and there is a suggestion that purification and not simply brute revenge is about to ensue:

> и все, тобою
> Совершенное, твоею кровью смою.   (P. 351)

(and all that you have done, I will wash away with your blood.)

4. *The Common Pursuit* (London: Chatto & Windus, 1952), pp. 140–41.
5. *Angel with Horns*, ed. Graham Storey (New York: Theatre Arts Books, 1961), p. 203.

Othello's language at this point in the final act reflects the language of Iago much earlier in the play; and Pasternak's tendency to bowdlerize the original text (evident here and throughout his translations of Shakespeare's plays) serves to weaken the indication that the noble Othello is capable of sounding much like Iago. The similarity is further attenuated by the removal or modification of many allusions to monstrosity and bestiality, and by the weakening of the insistence that even Desdemona is governed by foul and base impulses, voiced by Iago and then increasingly by Othello as he comes under Iago's influence. It might be pointed out further that Shakespeare's Othello anticipates his "ancient" in acknowledging the bond between them. When Iago expresses concern that the first intimations of Desdemona's unfaithfulness have disturbed Othello deeply, Othello's reassurance carries an ominous suggestion of a new closeness: "I am bound to thee for ever" (III.iii.217). And at the close of the scene, after Othello has responded with horror, but with great readiness, to the insinuations of Iago and has made him at last his lieutenant, Othello's earlier words are echoed by his officer: "I am your own for ever" (III.iii.486). In translation, the first of these is replaced by a simple expression of thanks ("Net, net, spasibo" [p. 328], No, no, thank you), and the second by a phrase somewhat more conventional, less suggestive of a special bond between the two: "Vash naveki" (p. 333) ([I am] yours forever).

Pasternak does not fail completely to recapture Othello's outbursts of rage, the expression of his desire for revenge, the cruelty of his direct accusations of Desdemona. (See III.iii.460–67, "Never, Iago. Like to the Pontic sea . . ."; or IV.ii.73–83, "Was this fair paper, this most goodly book, / Made to write 'whore' on?") But Othello's growing sense of the foulness and gross depravity of his wife, and the bitterness and disgust which this arouses in him, are often attenuated, nearly lost from view. Where the original Othello, enraged with jealousy, responds to Desdemona's protestations of innocence,

> I cry you mercy,
> I took you for that cunning whore of Venice,
> That married with Othello   (IV.ii.90–92)

Pasternak translates:

> Ну, виноват. А я предполагал,
> Что ты—дитя венецианских улиц
> В супружестве с Отелло.   (P. 345)

(Why, pardon me. I supposed that you were the child of the streets of Venice, wedded to Othello.)

Pasternak has not effected simply a flat bowdlerization here. "That cunning whore of Venice" is transformed into a "child of the streets of Venice," which may call to mind not a prostitute but an orphaned child. It is out of place for Othello to express anything of the pathos of Desdemona's situation at this moment, but Pasternak seems unable to sustain Othello's cruelty here, and at this moment in the play his own sympathies may be showing through.

Though Pasternak has altered the character significantly, Othello remains powerfully drawn; above all, the intensity, the poignancy of his love for Desdemona is communicated in the translation. After the first of Iago's attempts to convince Othello of Desdemona's liaison with Cassio, Othello already anticipates his separation from her:

> if I do prove her haggard,
> Though that her jesses were my dear heart-strings,

> I'ld whistle her off, and let her down the wind,
> To prey at fortune.   (III.iii.264–67)

Pasternak has him say instead,

> Если это правда
> И будут доказательства, что ты
> Дичаешь, мой неприрученный сокол,
> Прощай, лети, я путы разорву,
> Хотя они из нитей сердца сшиты.   (P. 329)

(If this is true and there are proofs that you are running wild, my untamed falcon, farewell, fly away, I will break your fetters, though they are sewn from the threads of my heart.)

Pasternak's Othello uses not the impersonal third person "she," but the intimate second person singular "ty" (thou), addressing Desdemona as if she were actually present, referring to her not as "haggard" (that is, a "wild, not properly trained hawk"), but as "moi nepriruchennyi sokol" (my untamed falcon), which may seem here virtually a term of endearment. He does not suggest that Desdemona might act as a bird of prey (presumably upon men) once released from her bonds. ("I'ld whistle her off, and let her down the wind, / To prey at fortune.") Rather than implying that he would release her to follow out her depraved course, he reveals only that he would give her her freedom, however painful the separation might be for him. It seems to be not the recognition of evil propensities in her, but simply the prospect of losing her, which is a source of anguish to him.

In many instances, Pasternak's Othello shows greater delicacy than Shakespeare's in speaking of Desdemona, as in his expression of regret that he had ever learned of her supposed infidelity.

> What sense had I of her stol'n hours of lust?
> I saw't not, thought it not, it harm'd not me,

> I slept the next night well, was free and merry;
> I found not Cassio's kisses on her lips;
> He that is robb'd, not wanting what is stol'n,
> Let him not know't, and he's not robb'd at all.

> (III.iii.343–49)

> Часы, когда она принадлежала
> Другому, не заботили меня.
> Я их не видел и о них не ведал
> И в следующую за ними ночь
> Спал сладко с ней, спокоен был и весел.
> Я на губах у ней не находил
> Осадка кассиевых поцелуев.
> Тот не ограблен, кто не сознает,
> Что он ограблен.   (Р. 330)

(The hours when she belonged to another did not trouble me.
I did not see them or know about them, and in the night following them I slept sweetly with her, was peaceful and happy.
I did not find on her lips the aftertaste of Cassio's kisses. He is
not robbed, who does not realize that he has been robbed.)

Pasternak has replaced "her stol'n hours of lust" with
"chasy, kogda ona prinadlezhala / Drugomu" (the hours
when she belonged to another), and Pasternak's Othello
says not "I slept the next night well," but "spal sladko s
nei" (I slept sweetly with her). There is perhaps even less
to indicate that his longing for that which has been taken
from him is tainted, qualified.

Even a passage conveying the ferocity of Othello's desire
for proof is curiously changed in translation. Still uncon-
vinced of Desdemona's guilt, Othello warns Iago to present him with proof of her infidelity.

> I'll have some proof: her name, that was as fresh[6]
> As Dian's visage, is now begrim'd, and black

6. This is the only other point at which I find it necessary to depart
from the New Arden edition. Pasternak was apparently working with

As mine own face: if there be cords, or knives,
Poison, or fire, or suffocating streams,
I'll not endure it: would I were satisfied!   (III.iii.392–96)

> Я требую улик.
> Ее безукоризненное имя
> Луны белее было, а теперь
> Черно, как я, от твоего доноса.
> Я жажду ясности. На свете есть
> Ножи, костры, колодцы, петли, яды.
> Я не прощу. Но мне недостает
> Уверенности.   (P. 331)

(I demand evidence. Her irreproachable name was whiter than
the moon, but now is black as I from your denunciation. I
thirst for clarity. In the world there are knives, bonfires, wells,
nooses, poisons. I will not forgive. But I lack certainty.)

In translation the reference to the goddess of chastity (and
of the moon) is omitted; "her name, that was as fresh / As
Dian's visage" is replaced by "ee bezukoriznennoe imia /
Luny belee bylo" (her irreproachable name was whiter
than the moon), suggestive of purity in another way. And
in interpolating "ia zhazhdu iasnosti" (I thirst for clarity),
not to be found at all in the original text, Pasternak may
suggest not only the ferocity of Othello's desire for certainty of Desdemona's guilt, but also, almost paradoxi-
cally, his longing for the very element of light he once
associated with her.

If the dark vision of Desdemona which arouses distrust
and loathing in Othello is weakened in this translation,
Pasternak has remained close to the original text in suggesting the wonder with which Othello regards Desdemona, his identification of her with light and with life

---

an edition which used the second Quarto reading of the line "her name,
that was as fresh," rather than the first Quarto and Folio version "my
name, that was as fresh," to be found in Ridley's edition of the play.

itself; and indeed he has departed from the original text at some points to emphasize this. One of the more striking instances of this comes in his translation of the passage at the beginning of V.ii, where Othello approaches Desdemona's bed to carry out the murder:

It is the cause, it is the cause, my soul,
Let me not name it to you, you chaste stars:
It is the cause, yet I'll not shed her blood,
Nor scar that whiter skin of hers than snow,
And smooth, as monumental alabaster;
Yet she must die, else she'll betray more men.
Put out the light, and then put out the light:
If I quench thee, thou flaming minister,
I can again thy former light restore,
Should I repent me; but once put out thine,
Thou cunning pattern of excelling nature,
I know not where is that Promethean heat
That can thy light relume: when I have pluck'd the rose,
I cannot give it vital growth again,
It must needs wither; I'll smell it on the tree.   (V.ii.1–15)

Таков мой долг. Таков мой долг. Стыжусь
Назвать пред вами, девственные звезды,
Ее вину. Стереть ее с земли.
Я крови проливать ее не стану
И кожи не коснусь, белей чем снег
И глаже алебастра. И, однако,
Она умрет, чтоб больше не грешить.
Задую свет. Сперва свечу задую,
Потом ее. Когда я погашу
Светильник и об этом пожалею,
Не горе—можно вновь его зажечь,
Когда ж я угашу тебя, сиянье
Живого чуда, редкость без цены,
На свете не найдется Прометея,
Чтоб вновь тебя зажечь, как ты была.
Должна увянуть сорванная роза.
Как ты свежа, пока ты на кусте!   (P. 354)

(Such is my duty. Such is my duty. I am ashamed to name her
sin before you, chaste stars. To wipe her from the earth. I will
not shed her blood, nor touch her skin, whiter than snow and
smoother than alabaster. And yet she will die, so that she will
sin no more. I will blow out the light. First I will blow out the
candle, and then her. When I extinguish the lamp and regret it,
it is no misfortune—I can light it again. But when I extinguish
you, radiance of living wonder, rarity without price, no Pro-
metheus will be found on earth to light you again, as you were.
The plucked rose must wither. How fresh you are, while you are
on the bush!)

Instead of repeating "it is the cause" (in translation, "takov
moi dolg," such is my duty) a third time in the third line,
Pasternak has Othello anticipate Desdemona's annihilation at this point, interpolating into the original text
"steret' ee s zemli" (to wipe her from the earth). But even
as he contemplates the means for doing this—"Ia krovi
prolivat' ee ne stanu / I kozhi ne kosnus'" (I will not shed
her blood and will not touch her skin)—he returns to
images by which she is associated with purity and light:
"belei chem sneg / I glazhe alebastra" (whiter than snow
and smoother than alabaster). Pasternak does not make
the alabaster "monumental," and it might be recalled that
alabaster is translucent. Again Othello returns to the
thought of her annihilation, "And yet she will die," "I,
odnako, / Ona umret," with the translator softening "else
she'll betray more men" to "chtob bol'she ne greshit'" (so
that she will sin no more). And immediately he likens this
to the extinction of a light that cannot be "relumed." In
his translation, Pasternak makes a play upon various
words derived from "svet" (light)—"svecha" (candle),
"svetil'nik" (lamp). But most striking is his transformation
of Desdemona herself,

> but once put out thine,
> Thou cunning pattern of excelling nature,

into a source of living radiance:

> Когда ж я угашу тебя, сиянье
> Живого чуда, редкость без цены . . .

(But when I extinguish you, radiance of living wonder, rarity without price . . .)

The possibly negative connotations of "cunning" are gone. In language recalling that of Pasternak's own poetry, Othello here associates light not with purity but with the presence of life itself, and his anguish comes from the awareness of the imminence of its extinction.

The fear of inherent, incipient lust and depravity, rousing in Othello mistrust and loathing, does not come through very strongly in translation. But the pain caused by the threat of annihilation, the extinction of something infinitely precious, does; and one may be struck by the emphatic and repeated use of negative constructions in this translation, the allusions to absence, loss, extinction, annihilation, the coming of darkness. Almost immediately after the murder of Desdemona, Othello debates whether or not to let Emilia enter the room, and he is suddenly overwhelmed by the enormity of his loss:

> Yes, 'tis Emilia, by and by: she's dead:
> 'Tis like she comes to speak of Cassio's death;
> The noise was here; ha, no more moving,
> Still as the grave: shall she come in? were 't good?
> I think she stirs again; no, what's the best?
> If she come in, she'll sure speak to my wife.
> My wife, my wife, my wife; I ha' no wife;
> O, insupportable! O heavy hour!
> Methinks it should be now a huge eclipse
> Of sun and moon, and that the affrighted globe
> Should yawn at alteration.   (V.ii.92–102)

In translation "I ha' no wife" becomes "net bol'she u

menia zheny na svete" (I no longer have on earth a wife),
with "net" (no, there is no) dominating the construction
in a way not indicated in my English translation. Further,
Pasternak's Othello says not "Methinks it should be now
a huge eclipse / Of sun and moon," but speaks as if these
sources of light had actually disappeared: "Kak budto v
mire strashnoe zatmen'e, / Luny i solntsa net" (as if there
were a terrible eclipse in the world, there is no sun or
moon), and he adds "zemlia vo t'me" (the earth is in
darkness), not in the original text at all. Desdemona
herself, when first abused and "bewhor'd" by Othello,
responds to Emilia's query, "Good madam, what's the
matter with my lord?"

> *Desdemona*: With who?
> *Emilia*: Why, with my lord, madam.
> *Desdemona*: Who is thy lord?
> *Emilia*:   He that is yours, sweet lady.
> *Desdemona*: I ha' none, do not talk to me, Emilia,
>   I cannot weep, nor answer have I none,
>   But what should go by water: prithee, to-night
>   Lay on my bed our wedding sheets; remember,
>   And call thy husband hither.   (IV.ii.101–08)

Where there are five negatives in the original—"none,"
"do not," "cannot," "nor," "none"—there are seven in the
translation. For four lines in Desdemona's last speech,
every sentence, indeed every clause, begins with "net"
(there is not, there is no) or "ne" (no, not), emphasizing
the suggestion that at this moment Desdemona has nothing
at all left to her, that she is wholly bereft.

> Нет у меня на свете господина.
> Не спрашивай, Эмилия. Нет слов.
> Не в силах говорить, не в силах плакать.
> Нет слез, и нет ответа, кроме слез.
> Застелишь свадебными простынями
> Постель сегодня. Яго позови.   (P. 346)

(I have on earth no lord. Do not ask, Emilia. I have no words. I have no strength to speak, no strength to weep. I have no tears, and there is no answer, except tears. Spread the bed with my wedding sheets today. Call Iago.)

One of Iago's more powerful moments in the translation comes as he recognizes that Othello will never recover from the effect of the suspicions he has aroused:

> Look where he comes, not poppy, nor mandragora,
> Nor all the drowsy syrups of the world,
> Shall ever medicine thee to that sweet sleep
> Which thou owedst yesterday.   (III.iii.335–38)

> Вот он идет. Уже ему ни мак,
> Ни сонная трава, ни мандрагора,
> Ничто, ничто не восстановит сна,
> Которым спал он нынешнею ночью.   (Р. 330)

(Here he comes. For him now neither poppy, nor drowsy herbs, nor mandragora, nothing, nothing will restore the sleep, which he slept last night.)

To the original "not poppy, nor mandragora, / Nor all the drowsy syrups of the world," Pasternak's Iago adds that "nichto, nichto" (nothing, nothing) will restore to him the "sweet sleep" he once enjoyed.

In the translation as a whole, Pasternak does not alter the events of the drama, or the general framework of the play; many of the changes he introduces are subtle, and would probably escape notice without direct comparison of the texts. But the cumulative effect of these changes is drastic. He has omitted or weakened allusions and references to the elements in human nature which precipitate the tragic dénouement, leading to the destruction of both Othello and Desdemona. The most assured and articulate spokesman for a cynical and pessimistic view of humanity is deprived of much of his persuasiveness, vitality, and power. The assertion that man is drawn by his inherent sexual nature to perversion, unnaturalness, bestiality, and often his own ruin is markedly weakened. The means by which one man attains power over others, and then uses it to destroy them, becomes less credible, little more than a dramatic convention. The potential for cruelty and savagery, which can be aroused even in a man of apparent nobility and self-control, is obscured; the element of kinship between Othello and his tempter is lost. Pasternak weakens the portrayal of evil in man and the disgust and loathing which it evokes.

Yet Pasternak remains close to the original text in suggesting the wonder with which Othello regards Desdemona, his identification of her with light, and with life. His interpolation of "siian'e / Zhivogo chuda" (radiance of living wonder, miracle) into Othello's description of Desdemona recalls the language and the central themes of his own poetry. But in this work which, unlike his own, has little to say about rebirth or resurrection, the source of living radiance is subject to annihilation; and though Pasternak fails to communicate effectively the nature and the power of the forces that precipitate its destruction, he has recaptured faithfully the pain of loss, the suggestion of desolation, of a world plunged into darkness upon its extinction. With all its shortcomings, the translation retains much of the power of the original tragedy.

KING LEAR

Pasternak's translations of *King Lear*, first published in 1949, and *Macbeth*, published in 1951, contain fewer omissions and striking departures from the original text than are to be found in his earlier translations of Shakespeare's plays. As Pasternak's son Evgenii Borisovich has commented, in the more recent translations "the innovative caprice and the effort to express his own views with great force have weakened."[1] Criticism leveled at these earlier works and the requirement for extensive revision to bring them into line with the original had evidently discouraged him from taking liberties or exercising "that freedom, without which there is no approach to great things." In writing to Mikhail Morozov on September 30, 1947, about his new translation of *King Lear*,[2] Pasternak revealed none of the enthusiasm or self-confidence he had expressed regarding his first published translation of *Hamlet*. On the contrary, he was disparaging, comparing his own version unfavorably with "the splendid Lear of Druzhinin, which has entered so deeply into the Russian consciousness," or even that of Tat'iana Shchepkina-Kupernik, which he felt should be published by Detgiz rather than his own. There is no indication that he approached the new translation as an artistic or creative challenge, or as anything other than a routine, workmanlike task, a means of making a living. He seems to have abandoned with reluctance his earlier, freer method of translation, and admits here to having retreated from "that which seems and has reason to seem the Shakespearean element itself."

These later translations have aroused relatively little comment among Soviet critics, although Pasternak's *King Lear*, along with his *Othello*, was included in the recent Soviet edition of the complete works of Shakespeare. In

1. From a personal letter, dated October 29, 1973.

2. Published in "K perevodam shekspirovskikh dram" (On Translations of Shakespeare's Dramas), in *Masterstvo perevoda 1969* (Moscow: Sovetskii pisatel', 1970), pp. 361–63.

general, scholars and analysts of translation give far more
attention to Pasternak's celebrated, but highly controversial, *Hamlet*. But Pasternak's translation of *King Lear* is
not a lifeless copy and is neither uninspired nor uninterest-
ing. Henry Gifford recently singled it out among Pasternak's other translations of Shakespeare, commenting that
with Lear himself "language is carried to a pitch of intensity
not accessible to any one else in the play. The version by
Pasternak never fails Lear."[3] Technically the translation
is something of a *tour de force,* and Pasternak's handling
of songs, poems, and snatches of verse—particularly those
of the Fool and Poor Tom—will be examined in detail in
a later chapter. At this point, however, I am concerned
with another aspect of the work.

Even though, as Pasternak pointed out himself, the play
is set in the era of "pre-Christian barbarism," it may be
linked closely with the profoundly Christian strain in
Pasternak's own late work. The play has, of course, been
frequently regarded as having strongly Christian overtones, although some recent critics, such as William R.
Elton, have very persuasively argued against "the current-
ly widespread view that *Lear* is an optimistically Christian
drama," in which the protagonist is "regenerated," "redeemed," "saved," and a "cosmically derived plan . . .
somehow gives providential significance to the events of
the tragedy."[4] I do not wish to argue that Pasternak viewed
King Lear as an "optimistically Christian drama," or that
he portrayed the characters as being peculiarly or defini-
tively Christian rather than pagan or pre-Christian.[5] But

3. *Pasternak* (Cambridge: Cambridge University Press, 1977), p. 156.
4. Elton, *"King Lear" and the Gods* (San Marino, California: The
Huntington Library, 1968), p. 3.
5. Such diverse critics as Elton and Roland Mushat Frye (*Shakespeare*

Pasternak found more scope in this play than in any other
for the almost irrepressible expression of compassion
which sometimes crept into his other translations, even
where uncalled for by the original text. And evidence of
selfless concern for others is sustained, often strengthened
in Pasternak's handling of the text.

At the same time, Pasternak seems here to shy away less
from the portrayal of brute violence and evil. He does not
shrink from bringing out the egotism and savagery of Lear
himself, neither sentimentalizing the portrait of the old
man nor altogether mitigating his faults. It is far less difficult here than in Pasternak's *Othello* to grasp how and
why the play moves to a tragic conclusion, and the translator has done little to soften the ending of the play. If his
work has Christian overtones, they are not clearly dominant, or incompatible with tragedy. Indeed this translation, more than the others, recalls the closeness and tension
between tragic and Christian elements, most obviously
and dramatically illustrated in Pasternak's poem "Hamlet," and evident throughout much of his late work, particularly *Doctor Zhivago*.

In translating *Othello*, Pasternak had avoided references
to a potential monstrosity in man's nature; he is truer to
the text in translating *King Lear*. His version of

> If that the heavens do not their visible spirits
> Send quickly down to tame these vilde offences,
> It will come,
> Humanity must perforce prey on itself,
> Like monsters of the deep   (IV.ii.46–50)

---

and Christian Doctrine [Princeton: Princeton University Press, 1963])
point out that characteristics some readers of the play regard as distinc-
tively Christian were, in the view of religious thinkers of Shakespeare's
time, quite compatible with the beliefs and behavior of virtuous heathens.

differs markedly from the original only in that he does not
have Albany place his remaining hopes upon "the heavens."

> Нет, если не отмстится по заслугам
> Злодейство, доживем мы до того,
> Что люди станут пожирать друг друга,
> Как чудища морские.   (P. 404)

(No, if evildoing is not revenged according to its deserts, we will
live to see men begin to devour one another, like monsters of the
sea.)

The entire play centers around the breaking down of relationships between the closest of kin, particularly parent
and child, the assertion of self-will, the readiness to con-
sume or ruin any who do not serve its demands. And Pasternak deals more directly and effectively with this fundamental Shakespearean theme in *King Lear* than he did
perhaps anywhere else in his Shakespearean translations.
The recognition of cruelty and bestiality in man's nature is
seldom avoided or obscured in this work. Where the gods
themselves are seen as the sources of man's sufferings,
the translation is equally direct. Though slightly changed,
Gloucester's "As flies to wanton boys, are we to th' Gods; /
They kill us for their sport" (IV.i.36–37) is no less cruel in
translation: "Kak mukham deti v shutku, / Nam bogi
liubiat kryl'ia obryvat'" (p. 402) (As children do to flies
for a joke, the gods love to tear off our wings).

In his version of the opening scene, Pasternak mitigates
none of the savagery with which Lear rejects his youngest
daughter for failing to manifest complete love and unhesi-
tating obedience to him, introducing himself the first allusions to barbarians who devour their kin:

> Here I disclaim all my paternal care,
> Propinquity and property of blood,

And as a stranger to my heart and me
Hold thee from this for ever. The barbarous Scythian,
Or he that makes his generation messes
To gorge his appetite, shall to my bosom
Be as well neighbour'd, pitied, and reliev'd,
As thou my sometime daughter.   (I.i.113–20)

There has been some difference of opinion among critics as to whether the word "generation" means "offspring" or "parents." Pasternak, presumably following the interpretation of the editor of the text he used, clearly indicates that it is the former; and Lear is associated, however briefly, with savages who eat their young.

Клянусь, что всенародно отрекаюсь
От близости, отеческих забот
И кровного родства с тобой. Отныне
Ты мне навек чужая. Грубый скиф
Или дикарь, который пожирает
Свое потомство, будут мне милей,
Чем ты, былая дочь.   (P. 366)

(I swear that before all people I renounce propinquity, paternal care and blood relationship with you. Henceforth you are a stranger to me forever. The rude Scythian or savage who eats his offspring will be more dear to me than you, my former daughter.)

The curses he visits upon Goneril in I.iv may seem more deserved, but as A. C. Bradley has pointed out, at this early point in the play even they seem, at best, excessive and reveal that "the disposition from which his first error sprang is still unchanged."[6] These curses lose none of their virulence in Pasternak's translation of the long passage which begins

6. *Shakespearean Tragedy* (1904; rpt. London: Macmillan, 1964), p. 284.

> Hear, Nature, hear! dear Goddess, hear!
> Suspend thy purpose, if thou didst intend
> To make this creature fruitful!
> Into her womb convey sterility!
> Dry up in her the organs of increase,
> And from her derogate body never spring
> A babe to honour her! If she must teem,
> Create her child of spleen, that it may live
> And be a thwart disnatur'd torment to her! . . .
>
> (I.iv.284–92)

> Услышь меня, услышь меня, природа,
> И если создавала эту тварь
> Для чадородья, отмени решенье!
> Срази ее бесплодьем! Иссуши
> В ней навсегда способность к материнству!
> Пускай ее испорченная плоть
> Не принесет на радость ей ребенка.
> А если ей судьба иметь дитя,
> Пусть будет этот плод ей вечной мукой . . .   (P. 377)

(Hear me, hear me, nature, and if you were creating this creature for giving birth, annul your decision! Strike her with barrenness! Dry up in her forever the capacity for maternity! Let her tainted flesh not bring forth a child for her joy. And if it is her fate to have a child, let this fruit be her eternal torment . . .)

After Regan, too, has turned against him, Lear repeats his rejection of Goneril, but less vehemently:

> I prithee, daughter, do not make me mad:
> I will not trouble thee, my child; farewell.
> We'll no more meet, no more see one another.
>
> (II.iv.220–22)

Pasternak's Lear begins with the colloquial "dochka" (daughter), which may accentuate his gentleness here:

> Дочка, не своди
> Меня с ума. Я более не буду

> Мешать тебе. Прощай, мое дитя.
> Я больше никогда с тобой не встречусь.   (Р. 389)

(Daughter, do not drive me mad. I shall trouble you no more. Farewell, my child. I'll never meet with you again.)

But the tone rapidly changes, and the near impossibility of effecting the separation is apparent as he continues:

> But yet thou art my flesh, my blood, my daughter;
> Or rather a disease that's in my flesh,
> Which I must needs call mine.   (II.iv.223–25)

In translation this begins "no vse zh ty plot', ty krov', ty doch' moia" (but all the same you are my flesh, my blood, my daughter). In the Russian text, each of these words— "plot'" (flesh), "krov'" (blood), and "doch'" (daughter)— is feminine. The single "moia" (my), with its feminine ending, at the end of the line might apply to all of these words, and the line as a whole may suggest something of the intensity of Lear's possessiveness. Even Lear at this moment recognizes that the evil, the illness belongs to him:

> Or rather a disease that's in my flesh,
> Which I must needs call mine: thou art a boil,
> A plague-sore, or embossed carbuncle,
> In my corrupted blood.   (II.iv.224–27)

> Или, верней, болячка этой плоти
> И, стало быть, моя болезнь, нарыв,
> Да, опухоль с моею гнойной кровью.   (Р. 389)

(Or, rather, a sore in that flesh and, so, my disease, an abscess, yes, a swelling containing my infected blood.)

But more often he envisions himself as being afflicted with undeserved evils from without. When Goneril first turns against him, Lear is horrified and recognizes something essentially monstrous in her behavior:

> Ingratitude, thou marble-hearted fiend,
> More hideous, when thou show'st thee in a child,
> Than the sea-monster.   (I.iv.268–70)

And this, too, is translated directly:

> Неблагодарность с сердцем из кремня,
> Когда вселишься ты в дитя родное,
> Морских чудовищ ты тогда страшней!   (P. 376)

(Ingratitude, with a heart of flint, when you take root in one's own child you are then more terrible than sea monsters!)

Lear's response to what seems to him to be unprovoked and unmitigated evil seldom loses much in translation. He appeals to his second daughter, describing Goneril's cruelty toward him:

> O Regan! she hath tied
> Sharp-tooth'd unkindness, like a vulture, here.
>   (*Points to his heart.*)
> I can scarce speak to thee; thou'lt not believe
> With how deprav'd a quality—O Regan!
>
> (II.iv.135–38)

He is no more moderate or kindly disposed in translation.

> Она, как коршун, мне вонзила в грудь
> Жестокости своей дочерней когти.
>   (*Хватаясь за сердце.*)
> Не в силах говорить. Ты угадать
> Не можешь, сколько злости в ней, Регана!   (P. 387)

(Like a kite, she has thrust into my breast the claws of her filial cruelty. [*Clutching at his heart.*] I have no strength to speak. You cannot guess, how much malice there is in her, Regan!)

Although Pasternak has substituted the claw for the "sharp tooth" of the vulture, the image is still that of a bird of prey.

There is much in the play about division, dissension,
the destruction of ties between even the closest of kin.
Gloucester denies his relationship to his own son: "I never
got him" (II.i.78), "Ne moi on syn!" (p. 381) (He is not my
son). Lear rejects his youngest daughter, "So be my grave
my peace, as here I give / Her father's heart from her!"
(I.i.125–26), and Pasternak's translation may suggest the
breaking of a physical bond:

> Клянусь покоем будущим в могиле,
> Я разрываю связь с ней навсегда.   (Р. 366)

(I swear by my future peace in the grave, that I tear asunder the
bond with her forever.)

When he comes to Lear's aid during the storm on the
heath, Gloucester admits to Kent that he too has suffered
greatly:

> I'll tell thee, friend,
> I am almost mad myself. I had a son,
> Now outlaw'd from my blood; he sought my life,
> But lately, very late; I lov'd him, friend,
> No father his son dearer; true to tell thee,
> The grief hath craz'd my wits.   (III.iv.169–74)

Instead of saying that his son has been "outlaw'd from my
blood," Pasternak's Gloucester suggests that he has actually driven him away, "Ia ot nego otreksia i izgnal" (I
renounced and banished him); and in this context Pasternak's final line, "I vot toska ob etom / Mne ne daet pokoia"
(And now anguish about this gives me no peace), may
suggest a sense of guilt more than the original "the grief
hath craz'd my wits."

> Я тоже за себя
> Совсем не поручусь. Имел я сына.

> Я от него отрекся и изгнал.
> Он умышлял на жизнь мою недавно,
> Совсем на-днях. А я его любил,
> Как никого. И вот тоска об этом
> Мне не дает покоя...   (P. 396)

(I can't vouch for myself at all either. I had a son. I renounced and banished him. He plotted against my life recently, only a few days ago. But I loved him as no one else. And now anguish about this gives me no peace...)

The concomitant of such acts of estrangement is not only a sense of guilt or bitterness, but isolation and loneliness. Even when surrounded by others, the characters of the tragedy often seem to be alone in their suffering. Lear is accompanied on the heath by a handful of loyal followers who seek to aid him, though they can do little to help, and cannot ease his deepest anguish. The Gentleman who meets Kent on the heath tells of the struggle of the King, who is "contending with the fretful elements" (III.i. 4). In translation, Pasternak adds that he "srazhaetsia odin" (fights alone) with the raging elements. Asked who is with the King, the Gentleman replies, "None but the Fool, who labours to out-jest / His heart-strook injuries" (III.i.16–17). In translation, he begins "nikogo" (no one), and only then adds: "Odin lish' shut, / Staraiushchiisia shutkami razveiat' / Ego tosku" (Only the fool, trying to disperse his anguish with jokes) (p. 391), as if the Fool's presence were virtually irrelevant to Lear at this moment.

But there are times when the sharing of suffering does make a difference. Falsely accused by his brother Edmund, denounced by his father, outlawed, hunted, pursued, driven to assume the guise of a mad, naked beggar, Edgar nonetheless finds his own sorrows diminished when he witnesses the anguish of the maddened Lear:

> When we our betters see bearing our woes,
> We scarcely think our miseries our foes.
> Who alone suffers, suffers most i' th' mind,
> Leaving free things and happy shows behind;
> But then the mind much sufferance doth o'erskip,
> When grief hath mates, and bearing fellowship.
> How light and portable my pain seems now,
> When that which makes me bend makes the king bow;
> He childed as I father'd!   (III.vi.105–13)

There is some debate as to whether this passage, omitted in the Folio, is the work of Shakespeare or an interpolation by another writer; in either instance, the original is probably surpassed by the translation.

> Когда мы старших видим жертвой бедствий,[7]
> Бледнеет наше горе в их соседстве.
> Ужасно одиночество в беде,
> Когда кругом довольные везде,
> Но горе как рукой бывает снято
> В присутствии страдающего брата.
> Свои несчастья легче я терплю,
> Увидевши, как горько королю.
> Детьми обижен он, а я—отцом.   (P. 399)

(When we see our elders the victim of calamities, our grief grows pale in their company. Solitude in misfortune is terrible, when everywhere around are contented people. But grief is taken away as if by a hand in the presence of a suffering brother. I endure my misfortunes more lightly, having seen the misery of the king. He is offended by his children, and I by my father.)

The ambiguity and indeterminate meaning of the original are gone in Pasternak's straightforward, lucid translation. Instead of saying that when we observe "our betters . . . bearing our woes, / We scarcely think our miseries our

7. In the 1949 edition, this line is: "Pri vide blizhnikh v ikh godinu bedstvii" (Before the sight of neighbors in their time of misfortune).

foes"—an expression of uncertain meaning—Pasternak's Edgar remarks succinctly that "when we see our elders the victim of calamities," "bledneet nashe gore v ikh sosedstve" (our grief grows pale in their company). Exactly what is meant by the following line in the original, "Who alone suffers, suffers most i' th' mind," might be debated; but Pasternak's version is terse, clear, unambiguous: "Uzhasno odinochestvo v bede" (Solitude in misfortune is terrible). The central word here is "odinochestvo" (solitude, loneliness), far more conspicuous than the original "alone"; and throughout the passage Pasternak brings out the contrast between suffering borne in isolation, and that which is shared. His Edgar emphasizes simply and directly the effect of moving into the presence of suffering. Instead of stating rather vaguely that "who alone suffers" leaves "free things and happy shows behind," Pasternak's Edgar more pointedly suggests the intensification of suffering which occurs "kogda krugom dovol'nye vezde" (when all around are contented people). In translation, there is a direct and dramatic contrast between the man who is surrounded by contented (and presumably indifferent) people, and the one for whom "grief hath mates, and bearing fellowship," who finds himself "v prisutsvii stradaiushchego brata" (in the presence of a suffering brother). And Pasternak has here used a more powerful expression than "mates" and "fellowship" to suggest the equality of those who suffer.

When Edgar, disguised as Poor Tom, becomes the guide of his blinded father, Gloucester himself seems to feel pity for the naked beggar, at least a sense of justice that this poor man will profit from his misfortunes:

> Here, take this purse, thou whom the heav'ns' plagues
> Have humbled to all strokes: that I am wretched

> Makes thee the happier: Heavens, deal so still!
> Let the superfluous and lust-dieted man,
> That slaves your ordinance, that will not see
> Because he does not feel, feel your power quickly;
> So distribution should undo excess,
> And each man have enough.   (IV.i.64–71)

The translation is close, but there is one slight change
worth pointing out. The original "that I am wretched /
Makes thee the happier" could actually suggest that one
man may be pleased by the suffering of another. In translation, however, this becomes "svoei bedoi oslabliu ia
tvoiu" (by my misfortune I will lessen yours), which seems
more expressive of a desire or a determination to help, by
one's own suffering to ease that of another.

> Вот кошелек. Возьми его, бедняк.
> Ты стерт во прах небесною десницей.
> Своей бедой ослаблю я твою.
> Всегда б так было, боги! О, когда бы
> Пресытившийся и забывший стыд
> Проснулся и почуял вашу руку
> И поделился лишним! Всем тогда
> Хватило б поровну!—   (P. 403)

(Here is a purse. Take it, poor man. You are effaced into dust
by the right hand of the heavens. By my misfortune I will lessen
yours. Gods, if it were always thus! Oh, if the man who is
surfeited and has forgotten shame would wake up and feel your
hand and share his excess! There would be enough for all, in
equal portion!—)

It might be pointed out that Pasternak has added to the
final "and each man have enough" "porovnu" (equally, in
equal shares), further equalizing the conditions men should
enjoy.

Throughout his translation, Pasternak has retained expressions of pity and sympathy. A gentleman serving

Cordelia expresses his reaction to meeting the maddened Lear on the heath:

> A sight most pitiful in the meanest wretch,
> Past speaking of in a King!   (IV.vi.205–06)

Pasternak emphasizes that the viewer would be touched, moved to tears:

> В такой беде растрогал бы до слез
> Любой бедняк, несчастья ж государя
> Превыше слов.[8]   (P. 411)

(In such misfortune, any poor man would move you to tears, the misfortunes of a sovereign, though, are beyond words.)

In this play, however monstrous the actions of some, and despite the tendency toward division, dissension, and estrangement, there is always someone to bear witness to suffering, engaged in the effort to overcome it, and Pasternak excels in expressing this. In some instances the translation probably surpasses the original, as in the case of the speech of the King of France as he chooses Cordelia for his wife, though she has been cast off by Lear and deprived of her dowry:

> Fairest Cordelia, that art most rich, being poor;
> Most choice, forsaken; and most lov'd, despis'd!
> Thee and thy virtues here I seize upon:
> Be it lawful I take up what's cast away.
> Gods, gods! 'tis strange that from their cold'st neglect
> My love should kindle to inflam'd respect.
> Thy dowerless daughter, King, thrown to my chance,
> Is Queen of us, of ours, and our fair France:
> Not all the dukes of wat'rish Burgundy

8. In the 1949 edition, "S kem eto b ni sluchilos', bylo b strashno, / A kak uzhasno, esli s korelem!" (This would be terrible if it happened to anyone, but how horrible for a king!).

Can buy this unpriz'd precious maid of me.
Bid them farewell, Cordelia, though unkind:
Thou losest here, a better where to find.   (I.i.250–61)

Корделия, лишенная наследства,
Твое богатство—в бедности твоей.
Отверженная, я завладеваю
Тобой, мечта и драгоценный клад,
Как подбирают брошенные вещи.
О боги, боги, в этом униженье
Я лишь люблю ее неизреченней.
Приданого лишенная пристрастно,
Будь королевой Франции прекрасной.
Я этот перл бургундским господам
За многоводный край их не отдам.
Корделия, простись с двором суровым.
Ты лучший мир найдешь под новым кровом.[9]   (P. 368)

(Cordelia, deprived of your inheritance, your wealth is in your
poverty. Rejected one, I seize upon you, dream and precious
treasure, as men gather up things thrown away. O gods, gods,
in this abasement, I only love her the more inexpressibly. Deprived of your dowry through prejudice, be queen of fair

9. This is markedly different from the 1949 translation, in all but the
last four lines:

> Корделия-красавица, богачка
> В нужде и горе, славная моя
> В отверженности, я завладеваю
> Тобой, мечта и драгоценный клад,
> Хотя б как никому не нужной вещью.
> О боги, боги, в этом униженьи
> Я лишь люблю ее неизреченней
> И—бесприданницу и жертву гнева—
> Заставлю звать французской королевой.

(Cordelia-beauty, rich woman in need and misfortune, my glorious one
in rejection, I seize upon you, dream and precious treasure, although
you seem a thing no one needs. O gods, gods, in this abasement I only
love her the more inexpressibly and I will make her, a dowerless girl
and victim of wrath, be called the French queen.)

France. This pearl I will not give to the Burgundian lords for
their country abounding in waters. Cordelia, bid farewell to a
forbidding court. You will find a better world under a new roof.)

The series of paradoxes with which the original text
begins—"that art most rich, being poor; / Most choice,
forsaken; and most lov'd, despis'd"—is eliminated except
for the first, which is converted into the eloquently simple
"tvoe bogatstvo—v bednosti tvoei" (your wealth is in your
poverty). Pasternak's France also accentuates the "wealth"
she holds for him, though she comes without dowry or
blessing. Instead of being a "precious maid," whom he
will not let the Burgundians have, she is "etot perl" (this
pearl); and instead of speaking of "thee and thy virtues,"
he addresses her as "mechta i dragotsennyi klad" (a dream
and precious treasure). He emphasizes her worth by allud-
ing not only to material treasure, but to something wondrous and intangible, of the imagination. Pasternak has
also emphasized the source of her "poverty"; he has added
in the opening line that she is "lishennaia nasledstva"
(deprived of her inheritance) and speaks of her not as the
"dowerless daughter" of Lear, but as having been "pridanogo lishennaia" (deprived of her dowry). The participle
"lishennaia" (deprived) recalls the act of rejection, which
has just taken place, and it receives particular emphasis
because France uses it twice in addressing Cordelia. This
participle is complemented by two others—"otverzhen-
naia" (rejected) and "broshennye" (thrown away)—which
also refer to Cordelia's state as an outcast. These words
have equivalents in the original text—"forsaken," "cast
away"—but they are not so conspicuously placed. France
approaches Cordelia as one who has been cast off, rejected, and he is engaged in an effort to make restitution,

to restore her to "a better world." The crucial line in which
he offers to make her the queen of his own land is addressed in translation not to Lear ("Thy dowerless daughter, King, thrown to my chance . . .") but to Cordelia
herself:

> Приданого лишенная пристрастно,
> Будь королевой Франции прекрасной.

(Deprived of your dowry through prejudice, be queen of fair
France.)

In beginning "pridanogo lishennaia" (deprived of your
dowry), he would seem to be speaking of a condition of
impoverishment and denial which he seeks to overcome
and make amends for.

Even Lear, confronted by the misery of others during
the storm on the heath, begins to display a concern for
them, and realizes that more should be done to offset
their sufferings, as in the passage beginning "Poor naked
wretches, whereso'er you are" (III.iv.28ff). Some have
questioned whether the imperious, demanding, self-cen-
tered Lear has really changed very much by this time. And
Pasternak has not deprived him of his complexity and
the harsh arrogance or virulence in attacking those who
oppose him, which tend to make implausible a sudden
and complete change of heart on his part. This is not a
gentle, sentimental Lear. But in some respects he is transformed in translation. Pasternak's use of Russian colloquialisms, particularly diminutives and familiar or endearing terms of address, makes a homelier figure of Lear at
some points and brings him closer to the level of the
servants and common people he associates with. When
Goneril enters in I.iv, for example, to rebuke Lear for the

behavior of his followers, Lear greets her, "How now, daughter! what makes that frontlet on? You are too much of late i' th' frown" (I.iv.197–98), which may well sound like a rebuke. Pasternak begins with a diminutive form of address, "dochen'ka" (dear, or sweet daughter), which makes him sound gentler and more affectionate, perhaps even cajoling:

А, доченька! К чему эта хмурость? Последние дни ты все время дуешься. (Р. 375)

(Ah, my dear daughter! Why this gloom? The last few days you've been sulky all the time.)

Her abuse of him may seem even harsher by contrast with his mild approach. Such changes are not uncommon. After one of the Fool's mocking songs, Lear asks "Dost thou call me fool, boy?" (I.iv.154), which might seem a rather threatening question. In the translation, the use of an affectionate diminutive suggests a tone of gentle surprise: "Ty zovesh' menia durakom, golubchik?" (You call me a fool, my dear?) (p. 375). When Kent has proved his worth by knocking about the insolent Oswald, Lear addresses him as "my friendly knave" (I.iv.98), in translation "moi rabotnichek" (my dear workman). Familiar and endearing though the expressions he uses are, they may still seem condescending. And even such terms as "druzhishche," "drug," "druzhok," "brat," "bratets" (various forms of "friend," "brother")—freely substituted for "fellow," "my boy," "lad," and "sirrah" in Lear's address of Kent and the Fool—may also be used condescendingly, even contemptuously in Russian. In Pasternak's translation, Kent greets the detested Oswald, who claims not to have met him before, "Zato ia, brat, znaiu tebia" (But, then, brother, I know you) (p. 382). But their persistent use may suggest a sense of kinship and affection; and such terms are employed when Lear has begun to show concern for those who have accompanied him on the heath, in particular the Fool:

> Come on, my boy. How dost, my boy? Art cold?
> I am cold myself. Where is this straw, my fellow?
> The art of our necessities is strange,
> And can make vile things precious. Come, your hovel.
> Poor Fool and knave, I have one part in my heart
> That's sorry yet for thee.   (III.ii.68–73)

> Что, милый друг, с тобой? Озяб, бедняжка?
> Озяб и я.—Где, братец, твой шалаш?
> Алхимия нужды преображает
> Навес из веток в золотой шатер.
> Мой бедный шут, средь собственного горя
> Мне так же краем сердца жаль тебя.   (Pp. 392–93)

(How is it with you, dear friend? Do you feel cold, poor lad? I'm cold too.—Where is your hut, brother? The alchemy of need turns a shed made of twigs into a golden tent. My poor fool, amidst my own grief, at the edge of my heart I am also sorry for you.)

> In, boy; go first. You houseless poverty,—
> Nay, get thee in. I'll pray, and then I'll sleep.
>   (III.iv.26–27)

> Иди вперед, дружок. Ты нищ, без крова.
> Я помолюсь и тоже лягу спать.   (P. 394)

(Go ahead, friend. You are a pauper, without a roof. I will pray and then go to bed too.)

And there are other details which suggest a sense of kinship or identification between Lear and those who in some way serve him and accompany him on the heath.

On meeting Edgar in his guise as Poor Tom, Lear seeks to divest himself of everything that distinguishes him from this poor creature:

Unaccommodated man is no more but such a poor, bare, forked animal as thou art. Off, off, you lendings! Come; unbutton here. (III.iv.109–12)

Неприкрашенный человек и есть именно это бедное, голое двуногое животное, и больше ничего. Долой, долой с себя все лишнее! Ну-ка, отстегни мне вот тут. (P. 395)

(Unembellished man is just such a poor, naked two-legged animal, and nothing more. Off, off of me everything superfluous! Now then, unfasten me here.)

But Poor Tom is not the only character who might be taken to represent what man ultimately is, and Pasternak may have strengthened the case for another. The "noble Kent" takes the part of Lear's servant, a common man, but not such an abject, almost dehumanized wretch as Poor Tom. Exiled by Lear for taking Cordelia's part, Kent returns in disguise to serve his master, and Pasternak's translation of the scene of their first confrontation is almost literal, and yet strangely effective:

Lear: How now! what art thou?
Kent: A man, Sir.
Lear: What dost thou profess? What would'st thou with us?
Kent: I do profess to be no less than I seem; to serve him truly that will put me in trust; to love him that is honest; to converse with him that is wise, and says little; to fear judgement; to fight when I cannot choose; and to eat no fish.
Lear: What are thou?
Kent: A very honest-hearted fellow, and as poor as the King.

(I.iv.10–21)

Лир: Что тебе? Ты кто такой?
Кент: Человек.

Лир: Чем ты занимаешься? Что тебе от нас надо?

Кент: Вот мой род занятий: быть самим собой. В
   служить тому, кто мне доверится. Любить того, кто
   честен. Знаться с тем, кто рассудителен и мало говорит.
   Считаться с общим мнением. Драться, когда нет дру-
   гого выхода, и не есть рыбы.

Лир: А сам ты кто?

Кент: Подлинно честный малый, бедный, как король.

(P. 372)

(*Lear*: What do you want? Who are you?

Kent: A man.

Lear: What is your occupation? What do you need from us?

Kent: Here is my sort of work: to be my own self. To serve
   faithfully him that trusts me. To love him that is honest.
   To associate with him that is reasonable and says little. To
   give heed to the common opinion. To fight when there is
   no other way out, and to eat no fish.

Lear: But who are you yourself?

Kent: A truly honest fellow, poor as the king.)

Pasternak's translation of Kent's reply to Lear's first question, "A man, Sir," is close: "Chelovek." But the absence
of the article in Russian, and the elimination of the "sir,"
leave a single word which could be translated simply
"Man." And nothing in the lines which follow detracts
from the possible significance of this reply. Instead of "I do
profess to be no less than I seem," Pasternak's Kent asserts
as the first of his occupations, "byt' samim soboi" (to be
my own self, my very self), to be true to his own identity,
as well as to the man "that will put me in trust." And Lear's
continued probing—"What art thou?" "A sam ty kto?"
(But who are you yourself?)—brings forth an answer
which links the common serving man with the king.

A very honest-hearted fellow, and as poor as the King.

Подлинно честный малый, бедный, как король.

(A truly honest fellow, poor as the king.)

A comparable effect is created in the translation of the beginning of III.i, where Kent is searching for Lear during the storm on the heath:

> *Kent*: Who's there, besides foul weather?
> *Gentleman*: One minded like the weather, most unquietly.
> *Kent*: I know you. Where's the King?   (III.i.1–3)

> *Кент*: Эй, кто здесь, кроме бури?
> *Придворный*:   Человек,
>   Как буря, неспокойный.
> *Кент*:   Я вас знаю.
>   А где король?   (P. 391)

> (*Kent*: Hey, who's here, besides the storm?
> *Courtier*:   A man,
>   as restless as the storm.
> *Kent*:   I know you.
>   But where's the king?)

Here the irregular line division serves to isolate the answer: "Chelovek." The gentleman had appeared briefly in II.ii, but no other identification is offered for him, and Kent's immediate recognition of him may suggest, in the translation particularly, some sharing of identity.

At another point, Pasternak has further emphasized the close relationship between Kent and Lear. In II.ii, when the Duke of Cornwall threatens to call out the stocks to teach Kent a lesson for his rude behavior, he replies,

> Sir, I am too old to learn.
> Call not your stocks for me; I serve the King,
> On whose employment I was sent to you;

> You shall do small respect, show too bold malice
> Against the grace and person of my master,
> Stocking his messenger.   (II.ii.128–33)

In Pasternak's translation, Kent says not that such igno-
minious punishment would be an affront to "the grace and
person of my master," but that "ego gonets—dvoinik ego
osoby" (his messenger is the double of his person), virtually identifying himself with Lear.

If in his translation of the play Pasternak manages to
suggest the prevalence of something essentially monstrous
in human nature—an unremitting egotism, a readiness to
use, possess, destroy even the closest of kin—he also suggests the persistence of its opposite: the capacity for selfless
love, compassion, pity, sympathy with suffering, the
readiness to share it, the effort to alleviate it, an underlying
sense of kinship and fellow feeling. In his notes on *King
Lear*, Pasternak writes that

King Lear is as quiet a tragedy as *Romeo and Juliet*, and for the
same reason. In *Romeo and Juliet* the mutual love of a young man
and girl is in hiding and subject to persecution, while in *King Lear*
it is a daughter's love and in a broader sense love for one's neigh-
bor, love of truth. (III, 207)

In this respect, although Pasternak has made no attempt to
Christianize the play, it may accord with deeply Christian
elements in his own later writings. Some critics would
argue, as does Roy Battenhouse, that "the play is Christian
in its implicit world view," that in the grim final scene of
the tragedy,

as was true on Good Friday, no Easter vision has yet become
available to the sufferers of this moment's desolation. Nevertheless, amid the deep despair there can be (if pictured by an artist
of psychology like Shakespeare) occasional flickerings of a transcendent hope to punctuate the moment of darkness. For are not

the darkest hours just before dawn, and is not the Dark Night of the Soul the traditional preface to mystic vision?[10]

One might argue that some changes Pasternak has made in the final lines of the play mitigate the bleakness of the ending of the tragedy, at least slightly.

> The weight of this sad time we must obey;
> Speak what we feel, not what we ought to say.
> The oldest hath borne most: we that are young
> Shall never see so much, nor live so long.
>
> (V.iii.323–26)

> Какой тоской душа ни сражена,
> Быть стойким заставляют времена.
> Все вынес старый, тверд и несгибаем.
> Мы, юные, того не испытаем.[11]   (P. 424)

(Whatever anguish may overwhelm the soul, the times force one to be steadfast. The old man has borne all, firm and unbending. We, the young, will not experience that.)

In the original there may be something ominous about the final "nor live so long"; Pasternak has omitted it, and in his translation there is a stronger suggestion that the young will not have to undergo such suffering. The oldest have borne not "most," but "vse" (all); "staryi" (the old) is in the singular, perhaps referring simply to Lear himself.

10. *Shakespearean Tragedy, Its Art and Its Christian Premises* (Bloomington: Indiana University Press, 1969), p. 288.

11. In the 1949 translation:

> Какой тоской душа ни сражена,
> Быть твердым заставляют времена.
> Последуем примеру этой тени
> И в долголетьи и в долготерпеньи.

(Whatever anguish may overwhelm the soul, the times force one to be firm. Let us follow the example of this shade in long life and long-suffering.)

It might seem that by their sufferings, the old (or, more particularly, Lear) have relieved those that follow of the necessity of undergoing such things themselves. Instead of "we that are young / Shall never see so much," "togo ne ispytaem" (we will not experience that).

But this may seem, at best, a very slight counterpoise to the rest of the final scene, the general carnage and, above all, the suffering and deaths of Cordelia and of Lear, which cause the stricken observers to ask, " 'Is this the promis'd end?' / 'Or image of that horror?' 'Fall and cease' " (V.iii.263–64). In translation, the first question seems to be answered by the comments that follow: " 'Ne eto l' chas / Konchiny mira?' 'Ispolnen'e srokov.' / 'Konets vremen i prekrashchen'e dnei' " (p. 422) (Is this not the hour of the end of the world? The completion of the term. The end of time and cessation of days.) The "image of that horror" is omitted, but the sense of finality is only accentuated.

In even the most somber of Pasternak's own works, there is usually an anticipation of resurrection, of a renewal of life, and perhaps this is to be found somehow, at least by implication, in his translation of the final scene of *King Lear*. But even in *Doctor Zhivago*, despite the numerous direct and indirect allusions to the Resurrection, and the stubbornly affirmative outlook that finally emerges in the work, it is sometimes difficult to see beyond the enormity and at least apparent finality of suffering. In his *King Lear*, there is even less to modify the suggestion of its completeness, and of the finality of loss.

MACBETH

PASTERNAK's treatment of Shakespeare's *Macbeth* does not offer clear-cut support for the argument that he was unable to recognize or reproduce the darker, more pessimistic aspects of Shakespearean tragedy, evidence of the evil or demonic in man. His translation of the play, first published in 1951, provides a direct and obvious contradiction to his own comments on the Shakespearean original in his "Notes on Translations of Shakespeare's Tragedies," and it conveys some suggestion of the atmosphere of nightmarish horror that pervades the original. But even in this translation one may find unevenness and noticeable lapses, particularly in the portrayal of Macbeth as he first yields to the impulse to murder and later grows hardened to crime. Even here, Pasternak's ability to capture the dark vision of the original tragedy seems markedly and significantly limited. In portraying the aftermath of crime, its effect on the perpetrators, the criminals themselves, Pasternak seems less adept at recreating the guilt-ridden reenactment of Duncan's murder by the sleepwalking Lady Macbeth than in communicating the weariness of Lady Macbeth and her husband, their growing sense of the futility of an existence which has ceased to have any meaning for them.

In his "Notes" on *Macbeth*, Pasternak tends to stress such positive elements as can be found in the characters and to minimize some of their faults. Comparing Macbeth with Raskolnikov, Pasternak states that "murder is a desperate, dangerous business," requiring the ability "to consider everything carefully, to foresee all possibilities," and he asserts that Dostoevsky and Shakespeare have endowed their "heroes" with "a gift of foresight and imagination equal to their own. The capability for a timely clarification of details is the same for the authors and their heroes" (III, 210). He insists, further, that "Macbeth and Raskolnikov are not innately evil, not criminals from birth. They are turned into criminals by false mental constructs, by shaky, mistaken deductions." In writing of Lady Macbeth, he emphasizes her womanly qualities, describing her as a selfless and self-effacing wife.

As for Lady Macbeth. The traits of strong will and coldbloodedness are not the main ones in her character. It seems to me that more generally feminine characteristics predominate in her. This is the image of an active, persistent married woman, a woman who is the accomplice and support of her husband, not separating the interests of her husband from her own and taking his plans irrevocably on faith. She does not discuss them, does not subject them to analysis or appraisal. To reflect, to doubt, to make plans—this is the affair of her husband and his concern. (III, 210–11)

Yet all of these comments would seem to be contradicted, directly or indirectly, by passages from the play itself, even in Pasternak's translation. Pasternak's modest description of Lady Macbeth as passively accepting her husband's plans on faith would be difficult to reconcile with her instructions to her husband before Duncan's murder.

> He that's coming
> Must be provided for; and you shall put
> This night's great business into my dispatch;
> Which shall to all our nights and days to come
> Give solely sovereign sway and masterdom. . . .
> . . . Only look up clear;
> To alter favour ever is to fear.
> Leave all the rest to me.   (I.v.65–73)

In his translation Pasternak in no way mitigates the suggestion that Lady Macbeth has taken charge, that she is now making decisions and ordering her husband about.

> Придется позаботиться о госте.
> Ты мне самой подумать предоставь,
> Как сделать лучше нам ночное дело,
> Чтоб остальные ночи все и дни

Царили безраздельно мы одни. . . .
        . . . Но не робей,
Старайся быть как можно веселей
И предоставь все мне.   (Р. 432)

(The guest must be taken care of. You let me think out myself
how we should best do this night's business, so that all remaining
nights and days, we alone should hold full sway. . . . But don't
be timid. Try to be as cheerful as you can and leave everything
to me.)

Macbeth soon changes his mind and decides not to go
through with the murder of Duncan, and it is Lady Macbeth, of course, who persuades him to return to his original
plans.

                        What beast was't then,
That made you break this enterprise to me?
When you durst do it, then you were a man;
And, to be more than what you were, you would
Be so much more the man. Nor time, nor place,
Did then adhere, and yet you would make both:
They have made themselves, and that their fitness now
Does unmake you. I have given suck, and know
How tender 'tis to love the babe that milks me:
I would, while it was smiling in my face,
Have pluck'd my nipple from his boneless gums,
And dash'd the brains out, had I so sworn
As you have done to this.   (I.vii.47–59)

Так что за зверь в тот раз тебя заставил
Мне открывать намеренья свои?
Тогда ты мог, и ты был человеком.
Чем раньше вступишь ты на этот путь,
Тем больше будешь им. Хотя ни время,
Ни место не годились, ты в тот раз
Готов был их найти. Искомый случай
Представился, и вот ты отступил!
Кормила я и знаю, что за счастье

Держать в руках сосущее дитя.
Но если б я дала ,такое слово,
Как ты,—клянусь, я вырвала б сосок
Из мягких десен и нашла бы силы
Я, мать, ребенку череп размозжить!   (P. 433)

(So what sort of beast forced you at that time to reveal your
intentions to me? Then you were able and you were a man. The
sooner you enter upon this path, the more you will be one.
Although neither time nor place were fit, you were ready at that
time to find them. The chance you sought has presented itself,
and now you have backed down! I have nursed, and I know
what happiness it is to hold in my arms the sucking child. But if
I had given such a promise as you have, I swear I would tear
the nipple from its soft gums and find the strength, I, a mother,
to smash the child's skull!)

The translation is simple and relatively close, although one
might criticize the clumsiness of the first sentence, which
is longer in Russian; and such phrases as "ty byl chelove-
kom" (you were a man) and "tem bol'she budesh' im" (the
more you will be one), both employing words in the
instrumental case, lack the flavor of natural speech. Pasternak was perhaps most successful in handling the last
lines of the passage, beginning with "I have given suck."
This phrase becomes "kormila ia" (I have nursed, given
suck), which may actually seem a warmer expression in
Russian than in the original; and although the translator
left out "while it was smiling in my face," other phrases
referring to the baby find appropriate equivalents: "so-
sushchee ditia" (the sucking child) for "the babe that milks
me" and "miagkie desny" (soft gums) for "his boneless
gums." All the details which suggest an understanding of
the mother's tenderness for her child do not soften or hu-
manize Lady Macbeth but, on the contrary, make her resolution all the more terrible; and Pasternak has heightened

this effect by interpolating the emphatic "ia, mat'" (I, a mother) just before her final declaration of readiness "to smash the child's skull." The suggestion is of a ruthless determination. Nor has Pasternak noticeably weakened Lady Macbeth's invocation of the powers of darkness in an earlier scene:

> The raven himself is hoarse,
> That croaks the fatal entrance of Duncan
> Under my battlements. Come, you Spirits
> That tend on mortal thoughts, unsex me here,
> And fill me, from the crown to the toe, top-full
> Of direst cruelty! make thick my blood,
> Stop up th' access and passage to remorse;
> That no compunctious visitings of Nature
> Shake my fell purpose, nor keep peace between
> Th' effect and it! Come to my woman's breasts,
> And take my milk for gall, you murth'ring ministers,
> Wherever in your sightless substances
> You wait on Nature's mischief! Come, thick Night,
> And pall thee in the dunnest smoke of Hell,
> That my keen knife see not the wound it makes,
> Nor Heaven peep through the blanket of the dark,
> To cry, "Hold, hold!"   (I.v.38–54)

> С зубцов стены
> О роковом прибытии Дункана
> Охрипший ворон громко возвестил.
> Сюда, ко мне, злодейские наитья,
> В меня вселитесь, бесы, лухи тьмы!
> Пусть женщина умрет во мне. Пусть буду
> Я лютою жестокостью полна.
> Сгустите кровь мою и преградите
> Путь жалости, чтоб жизни голоса
> Не колебали страшного решенья
> И твердости его. Сюда, ко мне,
> Невидимые гении убийства,
> И вместо молока мне желчью грудь

Наполните. Оденься дымом ада,
Глухая ночь, чтоб нож не видел ран,
Которые он нанесет, и небо
Напомнить не могло: «Остановись!»   (P. 432)

(From the battlements, the hoarse raven has loudly heralded the fatal arrival of Duncan. Come here to me, evil inspirations, take hold in me, demons, spirits of darkness! Let the woman in me die. Let me be filled with fierce cruelty. Thicken my blood and block up the way of pity, that the voices of life will not shake my terrible resolution and its firmness. Come here, to me, unseen geniuses of murder, and in place of milk fill my breast with gall. Cover yourself with the smoke of hell, dead night, so that the knife would not see the wounds it inflicts, and heaven would not warn: "Don't do it!")

Pasternak emphasizes from the beginning that the "spirits that tend on mortal thoughts" are evil, demonic, substituting for this one phrase "zlodeiskie nait'ia, . . . besy, dukhi t'my" (evil inspirations, . . . demons, spirits of darkness). Despite his comment elsewhere that "more generally feminine characteristics predominate" in Lady Macbeth, the translator here has her ask, "Pust' zhenshchina umret vo mne" (Let the woman in me die), his version of "unsex me here." In translating "come to my woman's breasts, / And take my milk for gall, you murth'ring ministers," he has eliminated—possibly through a misreading—the suggestion that Lady Macbeth is actually offering to feed these "murth'ring ministers" at her breast; but she does still ask, in the Russian text, that her milk be replaced with gall, suggesting the perversion of her nurturing function to one of destruction. Throughout the passage, such phrases as "pust' budu / Ia liutoiu zhestokost'iu polna" (let me be filled with fierce cruelty), "sgustite krov' moiu" (thicken my blood), "strashnogo reshen'ia / I tverdosti ego" (my terrible resolution and its firmness), "nevidimye genii ubiistva" (unseen geniuses of murder) may seem expressive of the spirit and intent of the original passage, and their very sound may contribute to its power. Read aloud, the speech has an extraordinary effect. Although Pasternak minimized the "traits of a strong will and coldbloodedness" in discussing Lady Macbeth, he did not do so in this part of his translation.

Pasternak's assertion in his "Notes" that Macbeth is not "a villain by nature" may also seem to be contradicted by passages from his translation. While Hecate may not be considered the most authoritative spokesman in the play, she does tell the other witches at one point that

> Макбет—злодей
> Без ваших колдовских затей.
> Не из-за вас он впал в порок,
> А сам бездушен и жесток.　　　(P. 448)

(Macbeth is a villain without your witchcraft. He has fallen into vice not because of you, but [because] he is himself heartless and cruel.)

In the original passage, Hecate is not so direct in her assessment, describing Macbeth as a "wayward son," a more ambiguous term, and emphasizing his lack of loyalty to the witches:

> And, which is worse, all you have done
> Hath been but for a wayward son,
> Spiteful, and wrathful; who, as others do,
> Loves for his own ends, not for you.　　(III.v.10–13)

Perhaps more significant than this passage are others which indicate that promptings to evil are to be found not within Macbeth alone, but among mankind in general. On the night before the murder of Duncan, Banquo expresses fears about his own hidden desires, the dreams he will have if he sleeps.

> A heavy summons lies like lead upon me,
> And yet I would not sleep: merciful Powers!
> Restrain in me the cursed thoughts that nature
> Gives way to in repose!   (II.i.6–9)

> Сон, как свинец, мне веки тяжелит,
> А лечь я не решусь. Святые силы!
> Меня избавьте от проклятых дум,
> Нас искушающих в ночное время.   (P. 434)

(Sleep, like lead, weighs down my eyelids, but I do not dare to lie down. Holy powers! Spare me from the cursed thoughts that tempt us in the nighttime.)

Shakespeare's Banquo seems not to consider his disturbing thoughts peculiar to himself; Pasternak's Banquo speaks of the "cursed thoughts which tempt us," as if they afflicted mankind in general, not himself alone. Later, as Macbeth leaves to carry out the murder of Duncan, his surroundings seem to suit with his designs:

> Now o'er the one half-world
> Nature seems dead, and wicked dreams abuse
> The curtain'd sleep.   (II.i.49–51)

In Pasternak's translation, the dreams are not "wicked," but they "tempt those who sleep," as if they were not only evil, but attractive:

> Полмира спит, природа замерла,
> И сновиденья искушают спящих.   (P. 435)

(Half the world sleeps, nature has died away, and dreams tempt those who sleep.)

Here, too, the temptation to evil appears to be a general phenomenon, manifested in dreams, associated with darkness and night.

In his essay, Pasternak asserts that Macbeth is turned

into a criminal by false reasoning, and he emphasizes Macbeth's fatal reliance on the clear and logical impossibility that a forest could move or that an antagonist not born of woman could appear. In his comments on *King Lear* as well, Pasternak has associated logic and reason with evil: "Only [the criminals] are hypocritically eloquent and reasonable, and logic and reason serve as a pharisaical basis for their forgeries, cruelties, and murders" (III, 207). But in *Macbeth*, evil is in many instances associated with the irrational, with dreams and nightmares, the world of night itself.

Once the first murder has taken place, Macbeth is afflicted by nightmares, and the subsequent murders he undertakes are intended to free him from the dreams that haunt him.

> But let the frame of things disjoint, both the worlds suffer,
> Ere we will eat our meal in fear, and sleep
> In the affliction of these terrible dreams,
> That shake us nightly.   (III.ii.16–19)

The translation of the passage is direct:

> Но лучше пусть порвется связь вещей,
> Пусть оба мира, тот и этот, рухнут,
> Чем будем мы со страхом есть свой хлеб
> И спать под гнетом страшных сновидений.   (P. 443)

(But better let the bond of things burst, let both worlds, that one and this, crash down, than for us to eat our bread in fear and sleep under the oppression of terrible dreams.)

By the time Macbeth learns that Banquo has been killed, but his son Fleance has escaped, his entire life has taken on the aspect of nightmare.

> Then comes my fit again: I had else been perfect;
> Whole as the marble, founded as the rock,

As broad and general as the casing air:
But now, I am cabin'd, cribb'd, confin'd, bound in
To saucy doubts and fears.   (III.iv.20–24)

Тогда я болен вновь. Я полагал,
Что ожил, стал несокрушим, как мрамор,
Тверд, как скала, неудержим, как вихрь,
А я сбит с ног, прижат к земле и отдан
В добычу снам и страхам.   (P. 445)

(Then I am sick again. I thought that I had come to life, become
indestructible as marble, firm as a rock, unrestrainable as the
whirlwind, but I am knocked off my feet, pressed to the earth
and given over as a prey to dreams and fears.)

In translation, Macbeth is subject not "to saucy doubts and
fears" but "snam i strakham" (to dreams and fears); and
he is not "cabin'd, cribb'd, confin'd, bound in" by them,
but acted upon with violence ("ia sbit s nog, prizhat k
zemle," I am knocked off my feet, pressed to the earth),
and made their prey ("otdan v dobychu"), subject to forces
which do not belong to the rational at all.

It is repeatedly suggested that at night the forces of evil
come into their own, and Macbeth acquires an increasing
familiarity with them. As he anticipates the murder of
Banquo and his son Fleance, Macbeth tells his wife:

                    Light thickens; and the crow
        Makes wing to th' rooky wood;
        Good things of Day begin to droop and drowse,
        Whiles Night's black agents to their preys do rouse.
        Thou marvell'st at my words: but hold thee still;
        Things bad begun make strong themselves by ill.
                                              (III.ii.50–55)

                    Меркнет свет. Летит
        К лесной опушке ворон. На покое
        Все доброе, зашевелилось злое.

Но ты удивлена? Что мне сказать?
Кто начал злом, для прочности итога
Все снова призывает зло в подмогу.   (Р. 444)

(Light fades. The raven flies toward the edge of the wood.
Everything good is at rest, evil has begun to stir. But you are
amazed? What can I say? He who has begun by evil, for the
firmness of the result always calls evil to his aid again.)

The translation is fairly close, and Pasternak has brought
out clearly and emphatically Macbeth's reliance upon evil,
repeating the word "zlo" three times.

There are indications of the horror of the reign of terror
unleashed by Macbeth upon Scotland, which may have
had a special significance for a writer who had survived
the Stalinist purges. Rosse describes the country to Mal-
colm and Macduff on meeting them in England.

> Alas, poor country!
> Almost afraid to know itself. It cannot
> Be call'd our mother, but our grave; where nothing,
> But who knows nothing, is once seen to smile;
> Where sighs, and groans, and shrieks that rent the air
> Are made, not mark'd; where violent sorrow seems
> A modern ecstasy: the dead man's knell
> Is there scarce ask'd for who; and good men's lives
> Expire before the flowers in their caps,
> Dying or ere they sicken.   (IV.iii.164–73)

Страна неузнаваема. Она
Уже не мать нам, но могила наша.
Улыбку встретишь только у блажных.
К слезам привыкли, их не замечают.
К мельканью частых ужасов и бурь
Относятся, как к рядовым явленьям.
Весь день звонят по ком-то, но никто
Не любопытствует, кого хоронят.
Здоровяки хиреют на глазах

> Скорей, чем вянут их цветы на шляпах,
> И умирают, даже не болев.   (Р. 456)

(The country is unrecognizable. It is no longer a mother to us, but our grave. You meet with a smile only among simpletons. People have grown accustomed to tears and do not notice them. They regard glimpses of frequent horrors and tempests as a common occurrence. All day the bells ring for someone, but no one wonders who is being buried. Healthy men fall into decay before your eyes, more quickly than the flowers on their caps wither, and they die without even being sick.)

In translation, the passage is more laconic and subdued. Instead of speaking of Scotland as a land "where sighs, and groans, and shrieks that rent the air / Are made, not mark'd," Pasternak's Rosse says simply "k slezam privykli, ikh ne zamechaiut" (people are accustomed to tears, and do not notice them). Instead of continuing "where violent sorrow seems / A modern ecstasy," he emphasizes in the translation that loss and horror have become a commonplace, an everyday occurrence:

> К мельканью частых ужасов и бурь
> Относятся, как к рядовым явленьям.

(They regard glimpses of frequent horrors and tempests as a common occurrence.)

In translating "the dead man's knell / Is there scarce ask'd for who," Pasternak indicates that people have ceased even to wonder who has died.

> Весь день звонят по ком-то, но никто
> Не любопытствует, кого хоронят.

(All day the bells ring for someone, but no one wonders who is being buried.)

There is a suggestion of a numbness or dumb apathy
setting in among those who are subject to Macbeth's
bloody rule. A different effect is achieved in an earlier
passage. Shortly before Lady Macduff is murdered, Rosse
tells her:

> But cruel are the times, when we are traitors,
> And do not know ourselves; when we hold rumour
> From what we fear, yet know not what we fear,
> But float upon a wild and violent sea
> Each way, and move—   (IV.ii.18–22)

> Времена ужасны,
> Когда винят в измене и никто
> Не знает почему; когда боятся
> Ползущих слухов, не имея средств
> Опасность уяснить; когда безвестность
> Колышется кругом, как океан,
> И всех подбрасывает, как скорлупку.   (P. 452)

(The times are terrible, when accusations of treason are made
and no one knows why; when people fear creeping rumors,
without having means to clarify the danger; when obscurity
heaves all around, like the ocean, and tosses everyone up like
a shell.)

The obscurities of the original text are eliminated in the
translation. But Pasternak has introduced some ambiguities of his own. Shakespeare's Rosse repeatedly uses the
second person plural—"we," "ourselves"—presumably referring to those who suffer under the tyrant's rule: "when
we are traitors, . . . when we hold rumour . . ." In translation, Rosse uses the general third person: "Kogda viniat
. . . i nikto / Ne znaet pochemu; kogda boiatsia / . . .
kogda bezvestnosti / . . . vsekh podbrasyvaet . . ." (literally, when they accuse . . . and no one knows why;

when they fear . . . when obscurity tosses everyone up
. . .). The exact subject is never specified, and Rosse's
words could apply to the tyrant as well as his subjects. All
may be afflicted by uncertainties and undefined fears,
"creeping rumors" and "obscurity" ("bezvestnost'"; "bez
vesti" means literally "without news") and the threat of
treason. Fear and terror seem common to all, and even in
translation it appears that few, if any, are untouched by a
knowledge and a horror of evil.

Pasternak was not always successful, however, in de-
picting the hardening of Macbeth's criminal tendencies, his
growing acquaintance with and acceptance of evil, as
when, after the appearance of Banquo's ghost, Macbeth
tells his wife, "For mine own good, / All causes shall give
way: I am in blood / Stepp'd in so far, that, should I wade
no more, / Returning were as tedious as go o'er . . ." (III.
iv.134–37ff). There are many shortcomings especially in
Pasternak's handling of the central crime—the anticipation and, later, the tormented reenactment of the murder
of Duncan. Macbeth first consciously anticipates the murder of Duncan upon learning that the first two prophecies
of the witches have been fulfilled:

> This supernatural soliciting
> Cannot be ill; cannot be good:—
> If ill, why hath it given me earnest of success,
> Commencing in a truth? I am Thane of Cawdor:
> If good, why do I yield to that suggestion
> Whose horrid image doth unfix my hair,
> And make my seated heart knock at my ribs,
> Against the use of nature? Present fears
> Are less than horrible imaginings.
> My thought, whose murther yet is but fantastical,
> Shakes so my single state of man,

That function is smother'd in surmise,
And nothing is, but what is not.   (I.iii.130–42)

Те сверхъестественные поощренья
Не могут быть ни к худу, ни к добру.
Они не к худу: в этих предсказаньях
Скрывалась правда. Я кавдорский тан.
Они не могут быть к добру: иначе
Я б разве мог внушеньям уступать,
Которых ужас волосы мне дыбит
И заставляет сердце в ребра бить?
Воображаемые страхи хуже
Действительных. Я весь оледенел
При допущенье этого убийства,
И жизнь передо мной заслонена
Плодом воображенья, небылицей.   (Р. 430)

(These supernatural encouragements can be neither good nor bad.
They are not bad: in these prophecies was hidden a truth. I am
Thane of Cawdor. They cannot be good: otherwise could I really
have yielded to suggestions, of which the horror makes my hair
rise up and forces my heart to beat against my ribs? Imagined
terrors are worse than actual ones. I've become numb with cold
at the very thought of this murder, and life before me is hidden
by the fruit of the imagination, fantasies.)

Shakespeare's Macbeth begins, "This supernatural soliciting / Cannot be ill; cannot be good," rejecting first one
possibility, then the other; and he seems to be left with
nothing definite to hold on to, no means of making judgment. He continues by questioning, "If ill, why hath it
given me . . . / If good, why do I yield . . . ," as if nothing
were certain or definite. In translation, the opening lines
are changed only slightly, but nonetheless made to seem
more matter-of-fact, as if Macbeth were possessed of cer-
tainties and still in control of the situation.

Те сверхъестественные поощренья
Не могут быть ни к худу, ни к добру.

(These supernatural encouragements can be neither bad nor good.)

Pasternak's Macbeth goes on to state as a fact, "Oni ne k khudu . . . / Oni ne mogut byt' k dobru . . . (They are not bad . . . They cannot be good . . .). The contradiction is still there, but not the uncertainty, the questioning, the unsettling inability to grasp or judge anything, which may contribute to "the impression of 'a phantasma, or a hideous dream,' "[1] in this passage, and which leaves Macbeth susceptible to

> that suggestion
> Whose horrid image doth unfix my hair,
> And make my seated heart knock at my ribs,
> Against the use of nature.

These lines, too, are changed in translation. Shakespeare's Macbeth speaks of the "horrid image" that "doth unfix my hair," presumably picturing the murdered Duncan (another "strange image of death"). In translation, Macbeth refers more indirectly and colorlessly to "vnushen'iam . . . / Kotorykh uzhas volosy mne dybit" (suggestions, of which the horror raises my hair on end). And while this "zastavliaet serdtse v rebra bit' " (forces my heart to beat against my ribs), he does not add "against the use of nature"; in translation, the comment may imply mere nervousness, not the response to something "strange," unnatural. Shakespeare's Macbeth goes on to add, "Pres-

---

1. L. C. Knights, "How Many Children Had Lady Macbeth?" in *Explorations* (1947; rpt. New York: New York University Press, 1964), p. 35. Knights quotes from *Julius Caesar* (II.i.65) in describing this passage from *Macbeth*.

ent fears / Are less than horrible imaginings," which may suggest that he sees beyond present fears to imagined horrors yet to be realized. The worst is yet to come. Pasternak has reversed the meaning of this, translating it "voobrazhaemye strakhi khuzhe / Deistvitel'nykh" (imagined terrors are worse than real ones); these may seem the words of a man trying to get hold of himself, reminding himself that things seem worse than they actually are, or will be. He is not so completely given over to horror. On the whole Pasternak has distorted or eliminated those details which serve to suggest the uncanniness and horror with which Macbeth regards the murder of Duncan, toward which he seems now to be inevitably drawn.

Pasternak is not much more successful in capturing the hallucinatory effect of a passage which comes very shortly before the murder.

> Is this a dagger, which I see before me,
> The handle toward my hand? Come, let me clutch thee:—
> I have thee not, and yet I see thee still.
> Art thou not, fatal vision, sensible
> To feeling, as to sight? or art thou but
> A dagger of the mind, a false creation,
> Proceeding from the heat-oppressed brain?
> I see thee yet, in form as palpable
> As this which now I draw.
> Thou marshall'st me the way that I was going;
> And such an instrument I was to use.—
> Mine eyes are made the fools o' th' other senses,
> Or else worth all the rest: I see thee still;
> And on thy blade, and dudgeon, gouts of blood,
> Which was not so before.—There's no such thing.
> It is the bloody business which informs
> Thus to mine eyes.—   (II.i.33–49)

> Откуда ты, кинжал,
> Возникший в воздухе передо мною?

Ты рукояткой обращен ко мне,
Чтоб легче было ухватить. Хватаю—
И нет тебя. Рука пуста. И все ж
Глазами не перестаю я видеть
Тебя, хотя не ощутил рукой.
Так, стало быть, ты—бред, кинжал сознанья
И воспаленным мозгом порожден?
Но нет, вот ты, ничем не отличимый
От вынутого мною из ножон.
Ты мой дорожный знак, напоминанье,
Куда итти и что мне захватить.
Так близоруко ль я обманут, или,
Наоборот, так вижу далеко,
Но ты маячишь снова пред глазами,
В крови, которой не было пред тем,
Обман, которого не существует,
Как бы собой наглядно воплотив
Кровавый шаг, который я задумал.—   (P. 435)

(Where do you come from, dagger, that have appeared in the
air before me? You are turned with your handle toward me, the
more easily to be grasped. I grasp—and you are not there. My
hand is empty. And yet I do not cease to see you with my eyes,
although I have not felt you with my hand. So, it follows that
you are a delirium, a dagger of the consciousness and engendered
by the fevered brain? But no, there you are, in no way distin-
guishable from the one I have drawn from its sheath. You are my
road marker, a reminder of where to go, and what I am to take
along. Am I thus nearsightedly deceived, or, on the contrary, do
I see so far, but you loom before my eyes again, covered in blood,
which was not there before, a deception which does not exist, as
if it visually embodied the bloody step which I planned.—)

Shakespeare's Macbeth asks, "Is this a dagger, which I see
before me, / The handle toward my hand?" as if not certain of the reality of any of this. Pasternak's Macbeth asks
instead "Otkuda ty, kinzhal . . . ," Where do you come
from, dagger . . .), not questioning the existence of the

dagger itself; and he goes on to state that "ty rukoiatkoi obrashchen ko mne" (you are turned with your handle toward me) and to explain why this is so: "chtob legche bylo ukhvatit'" (the more easily to be grasped). The vision may seem hallucinatory anyway—the opening lines are probably the best in the translation of the passage—but a certain matter-of-fact quality has entered into Macbeth's speech. As with the earlier "cannot be ill; cannot be good," Macbeth's "I have thee not, and yet I see thee still" implies a contradiction that would make any ascertainment of what is real impossible. And he keeps questioning,

> Art thou not, fatal vision, sensible
> To feeling, as to sight? or art thou but
> A dagger of the mind, a false creation,
> Proceeding from the heat-oppressed brain?

Pasternak's Macbeth instead makes statements:

> И все ж
> Глазами не перестаю я видеть
> Тебя, хотя не ощутил рукой.
> Так, стало быть, ты—бред, кинжал сознанья
> И воспаленным мозгом порожден?

(And yet I do not cease to see you with my eyes, although I have not felt you with my hand. So, it follows that you are a delirium, a dagger of the consciousness and engendered by the fevered brain?)

The latter sentence is technically a question, but this would become apparent only on reaching the question mark at the end. Until then it might seem that Macbeth had figured everything out and was simply summing up the situation. In the original text, he continues, "I see thee yet, in form as palpable / As this which now I draw." This is clearly fixed as the moment when he draws the dagger he will use to murder Duncan. And with "thou marshall'st me the way that I was going," he seems actually to be led toward the enactment of the murder; the dagger serves as something more potent than a "dorozhnyi znak" (road marker) or "napominan'e" (reminder), the terms used in the translation. And in the original text there is a curious suggestion of detachment toward what he had earlier determined to do, as if he were not engaged in such actions at this moment—an effect which would be lost if he said "am going," "am to use":

> Thou marshall'st me the way that I was going;
> And such an instrument I was to use.—

Here, too, the translation is more straightforward, matter-of-fact, and Macbeth no longer seems out of control, or even out of touch with present events:

> напоминанье,
> Куда итти и что мне захватить.

(a reminder of where to go and what I must seize).

Shakespeare's Macbeth continues,

> I see thee still;
> And on thy blade, and dudgeon, gouts of blood,
> Which was not so before.—

—the sign of the crime's execution—and this is followed by "There's no such thing," as if the dagger had disappeared, or Macbeth had managed somehow to deny its existence, refusing still to confront the results of the murder. The translator runs these two sentences together, and the latter no longer represents a separate step in Macbeth's imaginative enactment of the crime:

> Но ты маячишь снова пред глазами,
> В крови, которой не было пред тем,
> Обман, которого не существует,
> Как бы собой наглядно воплотив
> Кровавый шаг, который я задумал.—

(But you loom before my eyes again, covered in blood, which was not there before, a deception which does not exist, as if it visually embodied the bloody step which I planned.—)

The translator has scarcely captured the suggestion that Macbeth is caught up in a state resembling a waking nightmare, given over to hallucinations, envisioning things he fears to look upon, yet is drawn to bring to realization. Pasternak's translation of the scene in which the murder actually takes place is, in short, competent but uninspired.

Similar shortcomings of his version of Lady Macbeth's sleepwalking scene, her tortured recollection of the crime, are apparent on examining even a few lines from it.

Out, damned spot! out, I say!—One; two: why, then 'tis time to do't.—Hell is murky.—Fie, my Lord, fie! a soldier, and afeard? —What need we fear who knows it, when none can call our power to accompt?—Yet who would have thought the old man to have had so much blood in him? (V.i.34–39)

Ах ты, проклятое пятно! Ну когда же ты сойдешь? Раз, два... Ну что же ты? Пора за работу. Ада испугался? Фу, фу, солдат, а такой трус! Кого бояться? После того как это будет сделано, кто осмелится нас спрашивать? Но кто бы мог думать, что в старике окажется столько крови! (P. 458)

(Ah you, cursed spot! When will you ever come out? One, two... Well what are you doing? It's time to get to work. Are you afraid of hell? Fie, fie, a soldier, and such a coward! Who is there to fear? After this has been done, who will dare to question us? But who could have thought that there would be so much blood in the old man!)

The commanding "Out, damned spot! out, I say!" is expanded to the more familiar and colloquial "Akh ty, prokliatoe piatno! Nu kogda zhe ty soidesh?" (Ah you, cursed spot! When will you ever come out?). And other changes follow. Shakespeare's Lady Macbeth continues, "One; two: why, then 'tis time to do't," as if she had heard a clock, and was roused again to commit the murder. Pasternak has her already berating her husband at this point, and she rapidly begins to sound like a nagging housewife: "Raz, dva... Nu chto zhe ty? Pora za rabotu" (One, two... Well what are you doing? It's time to get to work). Shakespeare's Lady Macbeth continues, "Hell is murky," which may reveal something about her own fearful state of mind, her need always to have a light beside her. Pasternak translates this, "Ada ispugalsia?" (Are you afraid of hell?), and it becomes part of her scornful mockery of her husband. The translation of "fie, my Lord, fie! a soldier, and afeard?" may seem fairly direct: "Fu, fu, soldat, a takoi trus!" (Fie, fie, a soldier, and such a coward!). But Shakespeare's Lady Macbeth had at least addressed her husband with the respectful "my Lord," and though she asked if he were "afeard," she never directly called him a coward. By the time Pasternak's character reaches "Kogo boiat'sia? Posle togo kak eto budet sdelano, kto osmelitsia nas sprashivat'?" (Who is there to fear? After this has been done, who will dare to question us?), she sounds as if she were pointing out the obvious to a fool. And when she then exclaims, "No kto by mog dumat', chto v starike okazhetsia stol'ko krovi!" (But who could have thought that there would be so much blood in the old man!), there is little to suggest the nightmarish quality of guilt, which Lady Macbeth can no longer hold back, even as she relives her assurance to her husband that they will not be called to account for the murder.

The original passages are extremely subtle and complex, and the translator's difficulty in capturing their effect and implications may be readily understood. But the problems were perhaps not wholly technical. The translation may in these places reflect the interpretative slant revealed in Pasternak's notes on the play. To quote at greater length from Pasternak's comparison of the play with Dostoevsky's *Crime and Punishment*:

Macbeth and Raskolnikov are not inherent villains, not criminals from birth. They are made criminals by false mental constructs, by shaky, mistaken deductions.

In one instance, the prophecy of the witches serves as the stimulus, the starting point, kindling in the man an entire conflagration of ambition. In the other, it is the nihilistic assumption, carried too far, that if there is no God, then everything is permitted, and that means that even the committing of murder is in no way distinguished from any other human deed or action. (III, 210)

Pasternak's assertion that Macbeth is led astray by false reasoning (especially in the case of the witches' assurances about his being safe from any man born of woman, or invincible until Birnam Wood come to Dunsinane) is not in itself ill taken and has been brought up by other critics; and of course, suspicion of reason, logic, pure intellect is very conspicuous in Dostoevsky's work. But when Macbeth first responds to the witches' prophecies ("This supernatural soliciting . . ."), there seems to be a virtual breakdown in his ability to reason effectively (even falsely), to deduce or determine anything with certainty; he seems a man going out of control, "yielding" to an impulse that horrifies him, not persuaded to act by rational argument. As he moves toward the murder itself ("Is this a dagger . . ."), he lacks even the illusion of reasoned control over himself or his own actions, which Pasternak implies he maintains in stating that he must "think over and consider all possibilities" before the crime, and that like Raskolnikov he possesses "the gift of foresight" and "a capacity for a timely clarification of details." In the original play, there is an unsettling ambiguity, indefiniteness, and uncertainty which appear to render Macbeth helpless to grasp, much less control, the situation. And this has virtually disappeared in the more matter-of-fact translations of the passages cited above.

Even Pasternak's reference to the idea that leads Raskolnikov into crime needs some qualification. He speaks of it as "the nihilistic assumption, carried too far, that if there is no God, then everything is permitted, and that means that even the committing of murder is in no way distinguished from any other human deed or action." Pasternak leaves out the crucial fact that Raskolnikov assumes everything is permitted only to the extraordinary man, the superman, the Napoleon, who has the daring to overstep the laws and moral restraints binding on ordinary men, and who can perpetrate even murders with no twinge of conscience or reason for regret. Indeed, by the murder he commits Raskolnikov intends to demonstrate that *he* is such a man. It is an effort to prove or assert himself at the expense of another human being, a phenomenon not unfamiliar in other Dostoevskian protagonists. However sharply Raskolnikov's immediate ambitions and scope may differ from Macbeth's, his ultimate motive may be somewhat akin to that which A. P. Rossiter attributes to Macbeth:

the passionate will-to-self-assertion, to unlimited self-hood, and especially the impulsion to force the world (and everything in it) to *my* pattern, in *my* time, and with my own hand. . . . A similar force is in *Richard III*; but there it is more intellectual, more conscious: in *Macbeth* the springs of action are deeper, more mysterious and more alarming, because they seem so utterly beyond intelligent control, and so involved in the whole human scheme of things.[2]

Some of the major weaknesses, then, of this translation of *Macbeth* lie in Pasternak's handling of the central crime of the murder of Duncan, viewed with horror by its perpetrators, before and long after it has taken place. Despite the skill with which Pasternak captures the atmosphere of horror and nightmare permeating much of the play, and the forcefulness of his Lady Macbeth in many crucial scenes, he seems to have fallen short of confronting or dealing effectively with something in Macbeth himself which is irrational, a source of destruction, ultimately evil.

However, if Pasternak was not successful in suggesting the source of the crime or in portraying the development of Macbeth's criminality, he did much better in conveying other effects of the crime on the criminals themselves: their sense of alienation, of estrangement from life itself, the weariness with which they regard an existence that has grown senseless, devoid of meaning or comfort. In a number of places Pasternak seems to equate what pertains to the good, the natural, natural feelings—all of which Macbeth and Lady Macbeth have renounced or been divorced from—with "zhizn'," life. Instead of asking "that no compunctious visitings of Nature / Shake my fell purpose" (I.

2. *Angel with Horns*, ed. Graham Storey (New York: Theatre Art Books, 1961), p. 218.

v.45–46), his Lady Macbeth asks "chtob zhizni golosa / Ne
kolebali strashnogo reshen'ia" (p. 432) (that the voices of
life not shake my terrible resolution). She later tells her
husband, "You lack the season of all natures, sleep" (III.
iv.140). In translation, "Ty malo spish', a son—spasen'e
zhizni" (p. 447) (You sleep little, and sleep is the salvation
of life). On learning of the murder of his wife and children,
Macduff cannot immediately master his grief:

> I cannot but remember such things were,
> That were most precious to me.   (IV.iii.222–23)

In Pasternak's translation:

> И не могу забыть того, что жизни
> Давало смысл.   (Р. 457)

(And I cannot forget what gave meaning to life.)

For Macbeth, by the end of the play, life is empty of
worth, and there is nothing terrible about its loss. Leaving
for his final battle, he acknowledges,

> I 'gin to be aweary of the sun,
> And wish th' estate o' th' world were now undone.
>
>   (V.v.49–50)

In Pasternak's version:

> Я жить устал, я жизнью этой сыт
> И зол на то, что свет еще стоит.   (Р. 463)

(I have grown tired of living, I am sated with this life and angry
that the world still stands.)

His most famous, and most extended, expression of the
futility and senselessness of life comes shortly before, when
he learns of his wife's death:

To-morrow, and to-morrow, and to-morrow,
Creeps in this petty pace from day to day,
To the last syllable of recorded time;
And all our yesterdays have lighted fools
The way to dusty death. Out, out, brief candle!
Life's but a walking shadow; a poor player,
That struts and frets his hour upon the stage,
And then is heard no more: it is a tale
Told by an idiot, full of sound and fury,
Signifying nothing.   (V.v.19–28)

Мы дни за днями шепчем: «завтра, завтра».
Так тихими шагами жизнь ползет
К последней недописанной странице.
Оказывается, что все «вчера»
Нам сзади освещали путь к могиле.
Конец, конец, огарок догорел!
Жизнь—только тень, она—актер на сцене.
Сыграл свой час, побегал, пошумел—
И был таков. Жизнь—сказка в пересказе
Глупца. Она полна трескучих слов
И ничего не значит.   (P. 462)

(Day after day we whisper: "Tomorrow, tomorrow." So life creeps by with quiet steps to the last, still uncompleted page. It turns out that all "yesterdays" have lighted us, from behind, the path to the grave. The end, the end, the candle has burned out! Life is only a shadow, it is an actor on the stage. He has played his part for an hour, run about, made some noise—and that's the last of him. Life is a tale in the retelling of a fool. It is full of bombastic words, and means nothing.)

Some of the bitterness seems to be gone from his speech. Macbeth says not that our yesterdays have "lighted fools" the way to "dusty death," but that they have lighted us, "nam," the way to the grave, "put' v mogilu." Life is not a "poor player," but simply "akter na stsene" (an actor on a stage). In the translation, Macbeth does not call for an end to everything ("Out, out, brief candle!"), but simply announces that life has drawn to a close: "Konets, konets, ogarok dogorel!" (The end, the end, the candle has burned out!). But the translation is not without effectiveness. Although the bitterness of the original has been mitigated, Pasternak's Macbeth still emphasizes that life is a meaningless process, leading only to death. His version of the opening line, "To-morrow, and to-morrow, and to-morrow," lacks the weighty sonority of the original and suggests not so much the inexorable passing of time, as the persistent hope with which men anticipate the morrow: "My dni za dniami shepchim: 'zavtra, zavtra'" (Day after day we whisper: "Tomorrow, tomorrow"). But opposed to this hope is the inevitable movement toward a final conclusion, an end which has been all but reached:

> Так тихими шагами жизнь ползет
> К последней недописанной странице.

(So life creeps by with quiet steps to the last, still uncompleted page.)

In translating

> And all our yesterdays have lighted fools
> The way to dusty death

> все «вчера»
> Нам сзади освещали путь к могиле

(all "yesterdays" have lighted us, from behind, the way to the grave)

he suggests a physical perspective—emphasized by the directional "szadi" (from behind)—with, as its end, "mogilu" (the grave).

In "konets, konets, ogarok dogorel!" (the end, the end, the candle has burned out!) he uses the verb "dogoret'" (to burn down, to burn out), the perfective form of "goret'" (to burn), indicating that a process has been completed, something completely consumed. And in the following lines, he traces a progressive disintegration.

> Life's but . . . a poor player,
> That struts and frets his hour upon the stage,
> And then is heard no more.
>
> Жизнь . . . актер на сцене.
> Сыграл свой час, побегал, пошумел—
> И был таков.

(Life . . . is an actor on the stage. He has played his part for an hour, run about, made some noise—and that's the last of him.)

He passes from a complex, controlled action ("sygral," played, performed, acted) to undirected movement ("pobegal," ran about), to the making of meaningless sound ("poshumel," made some noise), and finally to a dismissal of what had come before ("i byl takov," and that's the end of him, all that is heard of him). Only Pasternak's translation of "it is a tale / Told by an idiot," "zhizn'—skazka v pereskaze / Gluptsa" (life is a tale in the retelling of a fool) may undercut the suggestion of finality, since there is no assurance that this retelling will be the last (or, for that matter, that better ones may not follow); but at this moment, a prolongation or repetition of life is not necessarily to be desired. "Zhizn' . . . polna treskuchikh slov / I nichego ne znachit" (Life is full of bombastic words and means nothing). Pasternak has made it clear that for Macbeth it has become a progress toward death, without sense or meaning.

In his first autobiography, *Safe Conduct*, Pasternak wrote,

In the world there are death and prevision. The unknown is dear to us, and what is known in advance is frightening, and every passion is a blind leap aside from the onrolling inevitable. Live species would have nowhere to exist and repeat themselves, if passion had nowhere to leap from that common road along which rolls the common time which is the time of the gradual disintegration of the universe.[3]

In studies of Pasternak's work, stress is often laid on the theme of rebirth, renewal, the ability of "live species . . . to exist and repeat themselves," and on the expression of sheer joy in living. Victor Erlich, for instance, writes of Pasternak's early poetry:

This joy of existence is primordial, and is so fundamental an aspect of Pasternak's *Weltgefühl* as to be literally irrepressible, undaunted. Asserting itself time and again, as T. S. Eliot would phrase it, "in excess of facts as they appear," the Pasternakian ecstasy fills his more buoyant poems to the brim (in "Our Storm" the poet asks almost helplessly: "What shall I do with my joy?"), and proves nearly impervious to disappointment and defeat.[4]

But in his translation of *Macbeth*, Pasternak emphasizes the very opposite, a sense of the emptiness and futility of a life reduced to the movement of "the common time which is the time of the gradual disintegration of the universe," senseless and devoid of worth.

3. *Sochineniia*, II, 266. I use here Beatrice Scott's translation of *Safe Conduct* (1947; rpt. New York: Signet Books, 1959), p. 84, with slight changes.

4. *The Double Image* (Baltimore: The Johns Hopkins Press, 1964), p. 139. Olga R. Hughes has traced expressions of a joy in existence, asserting itself even in the face of hardship and personal tragedy, in Pasternak's letters as well as his literary works. See *The Poetic World of Boris Pasternak* (Princeton: Princeton University Press, 1974), pp. 153–67.

In Pasternak's translation of *Macbeth* there remains something of the atmosphere of nightmare and horror which pervades the original work, and he has managed to suggest the commonness of promptings to evil and the power and ruthlessness of Lady Macbeth's own determination early in the play to make her husband king. Pasternak seems less able, however, to communicate the horror which the murder of Duncan evokes in her long after it has been committed and "cannot be undone," or in Macbeth as he is drawn earlier toward its enactment. Indeed, in his comments on the play, Pasternak denies directly and firmly that Macbeth and Lady Macbeth are innately evil or criminal. But the weariness, the sense of futility and distaste for life itself which follow the deed find expression in the translation—the very antithesis of the attitude toward life usually expressed in Pasternak's own writings. Whatever its cause (or even if its cause is unrecognizable), such negation apparently held for him a central and tragic significance.

CONCLUSION

PASTERNAK's translations of Shakespeare's tragedies reveal a highly sensitive, though sometimes personal and idiosyncratic, interpretation of the original works. He appears to have reacted against the implications of certain images, turns of phrase, and textual details, and where he was called upon to express attitudes that he did not share or even approve of, he did not always succeed in communicating them unchanged. As an imaginative artist, he seems to have faced problems in recreating the malignant genius of Shakespeare's Iago, whose peculiar artistry was so fundamentally opposed to his own, and in his portrayal of the character Pasternak divests him of much of his power. His bowdlerization of the texts—not an extraordinary matter in itself for Russian translators[1]—reflects a reticence characteristic of his own work, though it may have resulted in some measure from his lack of sympathy with the misogynistic attitude underlying many of the passages he modifies. Pasternak criticizes Hamlet, highly idealized in his interpretation, only for his "pitiless" treatment of Ophelia. And many of the sexual allusions which Pasternak omits or changes in his translation occur originally as part of a direct and bitter attack against women (Hamlet in his diatribes against Ophelia and his mother) or an expression of disillusionment and disgust with the baseness and bestiality of their nature (Iago and Othello discussing Desdemona, Lear railing against women, as well as Hamlet speaking of Ophelia and Gertrude). Pasternak's own work reveals an attitude toward women which set him at odds with Shakespearean characters he otherwise admired, and it is hardly surprising that in his translation of *Othello* an expression of sympathy and concern for Desdemona repeatedly tempers Othello's harsh judgment of her.

1. Major Russian translators of the nineteenth century, among those most admired by Pasternak, had often omitted or modified bawdy passages and direct sexual allusions in Shakespeare. (See, for example, the comments on Kroneberg and Druzhinin in *Shekspir i russkaia kul'tura* [Moscow-Leningrad: Nauka, 1965], pp. 385, 480–81.) More literal translations of the Soviet period may have resulted not from greater openness and freedom in dealing with such matters, but from stricter demands for textual accuracy. Certainly Soviet editors have been known to be prudish on occasion in their handling even of classical texts and works of established authors (though, as pointed out in the Appendix, Pasternak himself seems to have sought the changes made in his *Hamlet*). And Soviet critics who complain of other changes Pasternak made in the Shakespearean texts rarely mention his modification of bawdy passages.

In general, throughout the tragedies Pasternak mitigates the dark, pessimistic strain of the original works, making evil seem less inexorable, not so completely beyond man's ability to contain, control, or overcome. He modifies Hamlet's sense of the inevitability of contamination and corruption, and Iago's certainty of the underlying bestiality and monstrosity of man's (and more particularly woman's) nature and his ability to provoke men to act in accordance with his assumptions. Even in Pasternak's translation of *Macbeth*, in which the realm of nightmare, irrational fears, the sense of guilt, and the potential for evil are often brought out most effectively, Pasternak fails to suggest Macbeth's terrifying loss of control as he first begins to yield to the impulse to murder Duncan and later proceeds to the act itself. Pasternak's argument that Macbeth is turned into a criminal by false reasoning may actually serve to gloss over and prevent any recognition of something irrational and essentially destructive within Macbeth himself, which ultimately escapes his power to restrain or direct. Further, if in his translation of *King Lear* Pasternak has been far more faithful to the original text in portraying the savagery, violence, and ruthless egotism of many of the central characters, he has been able to emphasize in this work, as in no other, something which persistently opposes these evils: a fundamental sense of kinship, a capacity for love and mutual concern that survive and run counter to the egotism, brutality, isolation, and estrangement that often seem to predominate in the tragedy.

Pasternak tends to accentuate what is most positive and affirmative in the works, the more admirable aspects of Shakespeare's characters. The essential nobility of Othello or Hamlet is not called into question in his analyses, the purity of Ophelia or Desdemona is not so directly impugned by the protagonists of the plays in his translations. There are markedly Christian overtones to Pasternak's interpretations. He retains, even strengthens, many indications of a capacity for compassion and self-sacrifice which run deep in human nature. In his poem and "Notes" on *Hamlet*, Pasternak makes free use of Biblical language and religious terminology, clearly relating Hamlet's actions to the sacrifice of Christ. In his early essay on *Othello*, he refers to the death of Desdemona as a "sacrificial immolation." Yet this does not confer an easy optimism on Shakespeare's works. The Christian elements which emerge in Pasternak's translations and comments on the plays are those closest to the realm of tragedy—the scene in the Garden of Gethsemane, the necessity for suffering and self-sacrifice, the Passion rather than the Resurrection. One may, of course, assume the coming of the Resurrection from the very sequence of events that leads to a Good Friday or to the dark night of the soul. Certainly, in Pasternak's own writings, no theme is more powerful or persistent than that of rebirth or resurrection, often occasioned and demonstrated by the act of creation itself, the very resurgence of creative power. But in these tragedies, such a possibility may seem uncertain at best, prefigured only obscurely or indirectly. And Pasternak remains close to the original works in indicating that life itself or that which gave it meaning may be destroyed or lost, and man left to confront the finality of suffering and death, the failure of the most intensely compassionate efforts to prevent anguish or catastrophe, the pain of bereavement, the reduction of existence to a meaningless and inescapable progress toward annihilation.

II. Pasternak's Realism

PASTERNAK SAW in Shakespeare not only "the father and teacher of realism"; he also acknowledged his influence on the German Romantics and considered him "the fore-runner of the future symbolism of Goethe in *Faust*" and of "the late, inspired theater of Ibsen and Chekhov."[1] But he was clearly drawn himself toward the realistic aspect of Shakespeare's work, and throughout his notes on trans-lating Shakespeare he emphasizes above all the realism of Shakespeare, who

will always be the favorite of generations that are historically mature and have endured much. Numerous ordeals teach one to value the voice of facts, real knowledge, the grave and pithy art of realism. (III, 192)

As Olga R. Hughes points out, Pasternak's concept of "realism" is idiosyncratic, coinciding neither with tradi-tional nineteenth-century views nor with more recent Soviet dictates concerning "socialist realism"; and, while Pasternak did not engage in polemics on the subject, the very frequency with which he returned to it in his writings may indicate a desire to establish "the divergence of his 'realism' from the accepted interpretation of the term."[2]

1. "Notes on Translations of Shakespeare's Tragedies," *Sochineniia*, III, 208–09.
2. *The Poetic World of Boris Pasternak* (Princeton: Princeton University Press, 1974), pp. 62 and 68.

In his "Notes," however, Pasternak never attempts to define what he means by realism, and in fact his comments
on it sometimes seem contradictory and may raise basic
questions concerning his meaning. He was quite consistent
in one respect: in his criticism of allegorical and literary
conventions, rhetoric and any linguistic usage which he
found unnatural and false to life. But his writings reveal
some ambiguity as to whether "realism" implies a sober
objectivity on the part of the artist or admits of subjective involvement and prejudice. And his insistence that
"realistic" art is to be focussed on the details of common,
everyday life—"byt"—does not appear to preclude the attraction to idealism or a preoccupation with the fantastic
and extraordinary. These concerns and apparent contradictions must be examined as a preliminary to further
consideration of the translations themselves and a more
direct examination of Pasternak's "realism" as a translator.

Shakespeare is criticized several times by Pasternak for
his failure to free himself completely from unrealistic literary and dramatic conventions. Pasternak saw on occasion in Shakespeare's plays the lingering influence of the
"moral allegories of the Middle Ages," a display of "the
formalism of outmoded scholasticism," and "an overly
blind faith in the power of logic and the supposition that
moral abstractions exist in reality" (III, 199–200).

> The portrayal of characters with believably distributed chiaro-
> scuro alternates with generalized images of virtue or vice. An
> artificiality appears in the disposition of actions and events,
> which begin to follow the dubious order of clever deductions,
> like syllogisms in a reasoned argument. (III, 119)

In the "Notes" Pasternak also mentions that the highly
figurative language of Shakespeare's poetry occasionally
exceeds the limits of the believable:

The streams of his blank verse are highly metaphorical, sometimes without need, and then in detriment to credibility. (III, 194)

He insists that the language of both original artist and translator should be unaffected and true to life:

As much as the original author, the translator should avoid a vocabulary that is not natural to his own use, and the literary affectation which is involved in stylization. Like the original, the translation should create an impression of life and not of verbiage. (III, 193–94)

In general he found that Shakespeare had succeeded in doing this. As early as 1923, Pasternak had alluded to the naturalness of the language of Shakespeare's tragedies. In the poem "To Briusov" he asks whether Briusov had not taught his followers

> Ломиться в двери пошлых аксиом,
> Где лгут слова и красноречье храмлет?..
> О! Весь Шекспир, быть может, только в том,
> Что запросто болтает с тенью Гамлет.   (I, 237)

(To force open the doors of trivial axioms, where words tell lies and rhetoric limps. O! All Shakespeare may lie just in the fact that Hamlet chats in a simple manner with a shadow.)

This attitude was probably responsible for one of the most widely discussed and highly controversial aspects of Pasternak's translations of Shakespeare: his use of simple, idiomatic, colloquial Russian. Indeed, a consideration of Pasternak's "realism" as a translator might well begin with an examination of his use of colloquial Russian, and his efforts to convey the impression of "life and not of verbiage."[3]

3. Critics have frequently pointed out the prosiness, the colloquial idiom, of Pasternak's own verse. Marina Tsvetaeva, for instance, wrote

Another aspect of Pasternak's use of the term "realism" is more contradictory: the complicated matter of whether or not "realism" implies "objectivity" and detachment on the part of the artist. In writing about *Antony and Cleopatra*, Pasternak insisted that the Roman plays were Shakespeare's most realistic works, that his very distance from the subject allowed him to be more objective than he was in writing his English chronicle plays.

A portion of the events which Shakespeare described in his chronicle plays continued in the events of the life surrounding him, and Shakespeare could not treat them with sober impartiality.

In this respect, notwithstanding the internal realism with which the creation of Shakespeare was imbued, we would search in vain for objectivity in works in the categories of the kind listed above [including the chronicle plays]. It is to be found in his Roman dramas. (III, 201)

Yet in discussing *Henry IV* and the events in the author's life which Pasternak felt provided Shakespeare material for the tavern scenes in that play, Pasternak speaks of "the birth of his realism," asserting that "his realism saw the light not in the solitude of a work room, but in the morning, in an untidy room of an inn, a room charged with everyday life [byt] as if with gunpowder" (III, 207). Here

---

that "Pasternak's prosaic quality, apart from being his native clear-sightedness, is the divine rebuff of Life to aestheticism: the ax to the snuffbox." See "Svetovoi liven'" (The Luminous Downpour) in *Proza* (New York: Chekhov Publishing House, 1953), p. 363. Nikolai Aseev found that Pasternak's poetry displayed "the principle of expression through intonation, the amazing ability to construct a line of verse in accordance with the most ready-to-hand, most colloquial speech." See "Melodika ili intonatsiia?" (Melody or Intonation?), in *Dnevnik pisatelia* (Diary of a Writer) (Leningrad: Priboi, 1929), p. 139; the translation of this passage is from Donald Davie, ed., *Pasternak* (London: Macmillan, 1969), p. 76.

Pasternak emphasizes not distance and sober objectivity as the basis for realism, but immediacy and a personal grappling with life, with the events which were to become the subject of Shakespeare's "realistic" dramas. There is a repeated implication in these "Notes" of a tension, a struggle on the part of the artist, an effort at asserting his own power, not simply remaining a passive observer or recorder of facts. Abandoning the unnatural conventions of previous writers, Shakespeare

realized how much he would gain if, from the conventional distance, he went up to life on his own feet, and not on stilts, and contending with it in endurance, forced it to lower its eyes first before the stubbornness of his unblinking gaze. (III, 206)

The very definition of art given in *Safe Conduct*—"focussed on a reality which feeling has displaced, art is a record of that displacement"—implies that "reality" is affected, "displaced," by the artist. Pasternak evidently did not take as his ideal or artistic goal a completely objective detachment on the part of the poet or dramatist or translator. Even in discussing Shakespeare as the "ideal and summit" of "realism," Pasternak identifies two apparently contradictory traits in him:

No one has attained such accuracy in his knowledge about man, no one has been so self-willed in expounding it. At first glance, these are contradictory characteristics. But they are bound by a direct dependence. In the first place, there is the miracle of objectivity. There are his well-known characters—a gallery of types, ages and temperaments with their distinctive actions and particular ways of speaking. And it does not disturb Shakespeare that their conversations are interlaced with the outpourings of his own genius. (III, 192)

Pasternak seems at times to relate "realism" to objectivity, detached and accurate observation. Yet "realism" appears to him to be compatible with the "outpourings of [the author's] own genius," something "self-willed" ("svoe-vol'no"), coming from within the artist himself, in tension with the reality which lies outside of him.

Pasternak's reference to Shakespeare's "objectivity" in the Roman dramas is clearly related to his emphasis on the study of the ordinary details of everyday life as the basis for realistic art.

Julius Caesar and particularly *Antony and Cleopatra* were written not from love for art, not for the sake of poetry. These are the fruits of the study of unadorned everyday life [povsednev-nosti]. Its study comprises the highest passion of each artist. This study led to the "Physiological Novel" of the nineteenth century and comprised the still more unarguable charm of Chekhov, Flaubert and Lev Tolstoy. (III, 201)

The association between realism and the artist's immersion in "byt" (common everyday life, the routine of life) emerges as well in the comments on *Henry IV* already cited, Pasternak's reference to the emergence of Shakespeare's "realism" in "a room charged with 'byt.'" But Pasternak was not consistent in this respect either. In describing Shakespeare only a few lines earlier as a "somber youth, striding rapidly into the future in seven-league boots," Pasternak introduces elements of legend or fairy tale, and suggests that this extraordinary individual is free of the ordinary limitations of time. In his "Notes" on *Antony and Cleopatra*, only a few lines after he had emphasized Shakespeare's study of "unadorned everyday life," Pasternak appears to contradict himself by commenting that

Antony and Cleopatra is the romance of a rake and a seductress. Shakespeare describes their dissipation in the tones of mystery, as befits a real bacchanalia in the ancient sense. (III, 202)

And in writing on love in *Romeo and Juliet* Pasternak speaks of the language of love as something other than an everyday commonplace:

The very highest that art can dream of is to overhear [love's] own voice, its always new and unprecedented language. (III, 198)

His early poem "Shakespeare" (1919) demonstrates the tension between the author's commitment to the base, common, everyday world and the pull toward something higher. In this poem Shakespeare himself is depicted as a rather Falstaffian figure ("obriuzgshii," grown paunchy, fat and flabby), who appears amidst the dismal gloom of a London snowfall, calls for shaving materials in a tavern, and responds boisterously to the display of wit of his companion as he shaves himself. At this point the sonnet he had written the previous night speaks to him, rebuking him for his low habits and companions; obviously the sonnet finds himself out of place in the tavern in which he was written. He addresses his author as his father, and there is a curious reversal of the positions of Shakespeare's Prince Hal and King Henry IV, who rebukes his profligate son for frequenting the taverns.

> Простите, отец мой, за мой скептицизм
> Сыновний, но, сэр, но, милорд, мы—в трактире.
> Что мне в вашем круге? Что ваши птенцы
> Пред плещущей чернью? Мне хочется шири!
>
> Прочтите вот этому. Сэр, почему ж?
> Во имя всех гильдий и биллей! Пять ярдов—
> И вы с ним в бильярдной, и там—не пойму,
> Чем вам не успех популярность в бильярдной?

(I, 62)

(Pardon me, my father, for my filial scepticism, but sir, but my lord, we're in a tavern. What am I to do in your circle? Why are your fledglings before an applauding rabble? I want wider expanses! Here, read to this one. Sir, what is this? In the name of all guilds and bills! Five yards—and you're in a billiard room with him, and there—will I ever understand why popularity in a billiard room doesn't mean success to you?)

But the rebuke is decisively rejected.

> —Ему?! Ты сбесился?—И кличет слугу,
> И, нервно играя малаговой веткой,
> Считает: полпинты, французский рагу—
> И в дверь, запустив в привиденье салфеткой.

(To him?! Have you gone mad?—And he calls to the servant, and, nervously playing with a Malaga stem, counts up: half a pint, French ragout—and he's through the door, after flinging a napkin at the apparition.)

The sonnet reveals an obvious distaste for the tavern atmosphere, and a disapproving amazement at finding this the grounds for the work of the imaginative artist; and yet the author refuses to abandon it, and he may be guided not solely by self-indulgence. The elemental vitality which makes creative work possible may be inescapably associated with aspects of life which might appear crude, gross, even sordid. But the argument of the sonnet suggests that Shakespeare's poetry itself has an independent vitality and tends to draw its author to a higher, more idealistic level of existence, above the element he lives in. (The tension may reflect Prince Hal's own ambivalent attitude toward Falstaff and his tavern world.) The personification of the sonnet in Pasternak's poem may be explained as a means of objectifying an actual conflict within the artist, but this device is whimsical, even fantastic. Despite his insistence on the importance of realism and the study of everyday life, Pasternak's writings often express the pull of idealistic tendencies, a fascination with the artist of extraordinary creative abilities, and with phenomena which are "unprecedented," and which may be described in terms of the fantastic or legendary, or even "in the tones of mystery."

This tension may be evident even in Pasternak's translations, and in examining his *Henry IV, parts 1 and 2* and *Antony and Cleopatra* in particular, I shall consider how the peculiarities of Pasternak's views on "realism" are reflected in the translations and how they may alter the plays, revealing both disparities between Pasternak's approach and that of the original author, and discrepancies in Pasternak's own work between a highly concrete and earthy "realism" and an awareness of a transcendent and apparently nonmaterial "reality." But this matter may be best approached by first considering Pasternak's general use of idiomatic Russian in his effort to create an impression of reality, of life itself.

Some critics have found that despite Pasternak's insistence on natural, lifelike speech, his language at some points in the translations is difficult to pronounce or to understand, syntactically awkward, or obviously influenced by phrases from earlier Russian translations that had entered the language and become commonplaces.[4] There were instances in which Pasternak's own goals and ideals as a translator were not realized. But even where he came closer to succeeding, the very use of colloquial Russian provoked condemnation and an indignant response

4. See, for example, M. Alekseev, *"Gamlet* Borisa Pasternaka" (Boris Pasternak's *Hamlet), Iskusstvo i zhizn'*, No. 8 (1940), pp. 14–16; M. M. Morozov, *"Gamlet* v perevode Borisa Pasternaka" (*Hamlet* in the Translation of Boris Pasternak), *Teatr*, No. 2 (1941), p. 146; and Iu. Gavruk, "Nuzhen li novyi perevod *Gamleta* na russkii iazyk?" (Is a New Translation of *Hamlet* Needed in Russian?), in *Masterstvo perevoda 1966* (Moscow: Sovetskii pisatel', 1968), pp. 130–31.

from some readers. One reviewer of his translation of
Hamlet criticized the "emphatic vulgarity of his vocabulary" and asserted that

all the characters of the tragedy—kings, princes, courtiers, grave-
diggers, and even the ghost himself—try to outdo one another in
an especially recherché selection of expressions which are not
current in the literary language, and are uncommon or primitive
in their coarseness.[5]

But Pasternak was frequently praised by others for the
vividness and naturalness of his characters, and for his
ability to individualize and make distinctive their different
voices and modes of speech. This undoubtedly resulted
from the use of commonly recognizable, colloquial Russian, not a stilted, archaic, or "literary" language, and
helps to explain the widespread use of Pasternak's translations in Russian dramatic productions, their acceptance
"as a kind of 'official' Shakespearean text by all our [So-
viet] theatres."[6]

In a review of Pasternak's *Hamlet* in 1940 N. Vil'iam-
Vil'mont remarked that

the language of various characters is remarkably individualized.
These are brilliant linguistic characteristics. The genius of Shake-
spearean humor has found here its most successful reincarnation.
We have never read a Polonius who speaks Russian so comically.
It is as if he were already played by an excellent comic actor.[7]

Mikhail Morozov commented further in a review written
in 1941:

5. Alekseev, "*Gamlet* Borisa Pasternaka," p. 15. See also L. Reztsov,
"Prints datskii v novom osveshchenii" (The Danish Prince in a New
Light), *Literaturnoe obozrenie*, No. 20 (1940), pp. 52–55.

6. Olga Akhmanova and Velta Zadornova, "The Present State of
Shakespeare Translation in the USSR (Russian Translations of Shakespeare)," *Shakespeare Translation*, No. 2 (1975), p. 40.

7. "*Gamlet* v perevode Borisa Pasternaka" (*Hamlet* in the Translation
of Boris Pasternak), *Internatsional'naia literatura*, Nos. 7–8 (1940), p. 290.

Within each play [of Shakespeare] the speech of the characters is individualized. As early as the eighteenth century the poet Alexander Pope remarked that in Shakespeare we would always recognize the person speaking, even if there were no indication in the text. This individualization of speech, as it seems to us, was virtually missing in all earlier translations of *Hamlet*. The comment of Pope is hardly applicable to them. But in the translation of Pasternak, without doubt, the contours of individualization have taken shape.[8]

He contrasts the homely speech of Pasternak's Polonius, who says to Ophelia after her encounter with Hamlet in III.i:

> Ну что, дочурка?
> Не повторяй, что Гамлет говорил.
> Слыхали сами

(Well, daughter? Don't repeat what Hamlet said. We heard it ourselves)

with the speech of Claudius, "a grave, rough . . . man, laughing when he is with other people, and gloomy when he is alone by himself":

> Грехом моим воняет до небес.
> На нем печать древнейшего проклятья:
> Убийство брата. Жаждою горю,
> Всем сердцем рвусь,—и не могу молиться.
> Вина тяжеле тяжести души.

(My sin stinks to heaven. On it is the mark of the most ancient curse: a brother's murder. I burn with thirst, I strive with all my heart,—and I cannot pray. My sin is heavier than the weight of [my] soul.)

Pasternak's insistence on using language which was natural

8. "*Gamlet* v perevode Borisa Pasternaka," p. 145. See also L. Lozinskaia, "Novyi perevod *Romeo i Dzhul'etty*" (A New Translation of *Romeo and Juliet*), *Ogonek*, No. 46 (1942), p. 13.

to himself, his effort to recapture the effect of life itself, was surely responsible for this success in characterization, the vividness of individual portraits in his translations—as well as for the modernization, vulgarization, and russification so frequently condemned in them. Whether or not one reacts favorably to Pasternak's use of colloquial, idiomatic speech in his translations of Shakespeare, however, the fact remains that in many instances style, tone, and personal characteristics of the speakers have been altered, and some of the translator's tendencies are marked and recurrent. His use of idiomatic Russian has led on occasion to a russification of the original text and characters, though this is often subtle, not particularly obtrusive, and sometimes even curiously effective. Furthermore, although Pasternak was quite capable of reproducing the lofty, elegant, or formal speech of empresses, kings, and noblemen, the predominant tendency toward the use of simple, colloquial Russian in these translations sometimes served to democratize the characters in the plays, bringing them closer to the level of the common people. Finally, the rhetorical or fanciful use of language by characters on various social levels frequently gave way to a simpler form of speech, more direct and down to earth. The extravagance and elaborateness of romantic poetry, explosions of wit and ebullient, high-spirited, imaginative transformations of fact and unpleasant reality, the suggestion even of the possibility of personal transformation or transcendence, are all tempered, altered in some way by the translator and his insistently "realistic" approach to the drama of Shakespeare. Such changes may be traced throughout these translations, and most of the plays will be considered here, at least in passing. But, particularly in dealing with the last of these tendencies, I will focus primarily on Pasternak's translations of Shakespeare's early romantic tragedy

Romeo and Juliet, on *Henry IV*, *parts 1 and 2* (especially the sections involving Falstaff and his companions), and on the late tragedy *Antony and Cleopatra*.

A literary work inevitably undergoes a certain degree of russification simply on being translated into Russian, and in the view of many, this should be minimized. Such critics as K. I. Chukovsky have insisted that while normal Russian syntax should be employed in translations into Russian, peculiarly Russian expressions and forms of speech, such as diminutives, should be avoided.[9] Pasternak placed no such restraints upon himself, and there has been some criticism of the "russizms" in his Shakespearean translations. This is perhaps least distressing in his handling of Shakespeare's commoners. He translates the speech of Juliet's Nurse, for instance, as she approaches Romeo to ask about his plans for marrying her mistress, still agitated by the bawdy sallies of Mercutio:

Now, afore God, I am so vexed that every part about me quivers. Scurvy knave!—Pray you, sir, a word; and as I told you, my young lady bade me inquire you out; what she bade me say, I will keep to myself: but first let me tell ye, if ye should lead her into a fool's paradise, as they say, it were a very gross kind of behaviour, as they say; for the gentlewoman is young, and therefore, if you should deal double with her, truly it were an ill thing to be offered to any gentlewoman, and very weak dealing. (II.iv.145–53)

Боже правый, я до сих пор не могу притти в себя, и всю меня так и трясет! Подлый хвастун!.. Ах, сэр, ведь я-то пришла совсем по другому делу. Моя барышня, как говорится, просила меня узнать. Что она просила, это, конечно, моя тайна, но если вы, сударь, собираетесь ее одурачить,

9. *Iskusstvo perevoda* (The Art of Translation) (Moscow–Leningrad: Akademiia, 1936), p. 82.

это я уж просто слов не найду, как нехорошо. Потому что
моя барышня совсем еще молоденькая, и если вы ее обма-
нете, хорошие люди так не поступают. И вам так не годится, ей-богу не годится. (P. 52)

(Just God, I still can't come to my senses and I'm shaking all
over! The foul braggart!.. Ah, sir, well now I came about something completely different. My young mistress, as they say, asked
me to find out. What she asked is, of course, my secret, but if
you, sir, are going to make a fool of her, that's I simply can't
find the words to say how bad. Because my mistress is still very
young, and if you deceive her, good people don't act that way.
And you shouldn't, really you shouldn't.)

Pasternak has found fairly close, but distinctly Russian
equivalents for some expressions: "afore God," "Bozhe
pravyi" (just God); "scurvy knave," "podlyi khvastun"
(foul braggart); "my young lady," "moia baryshnia" (my
young lady, my young mistress; literally, the "barin's," or
lord's daughter); "truly," "ei-bogu" (really, truly). He has
the Nurse use the diminutive form in referring to her mistress as being "still young," "eshche moloden'kaia." And
while the English "sir" appears in near transliterated form
at one point, "ser," the Nurse elsewhere uses the rather
old-fashioned Russian "sudar'" instead. All this serves to
russify the text somewhat, but this is perhaps less important than the fact that the character retains vitality and a
distinct individuality. Certainly she is no earthier in translation than in the original, and she does display the
"contours of individualization" which Morozov noticed in
Pasternak's handling of Shakespeare's characters. Pasternak has not only substituted Russian expressions for the
original English ones, but has utilized the resources of his
own language to reproduce unexpected syntactic disrup-
tions and incoherencies in the Nurse's speech, which create
a rather comical effect, and are revelatory of the nature of

the workings of her mind. In the original text, for instance, the Nurse's first words to Romeo are "and as I told you, my young lady bade me inquire you out," which may seem something of a non sequitur, since according to the text she had told him no such thing before (a problem which some stage directors solve by having the Nurse whispering to Romeo earlier in the scene). Pasternak handles this somewhat muddled line in a different way. He has the Nurse insert a completely pointless "kak govoritsia" (as it is said, as they say) into the middle of her "moia baryshnia . . . prosila menia uznat'" (my young lady . . . asked me to find out), and then he leaves the "uznat'" (to find out) without an object, as if the Nurse had suddenly decided not to let Romeo know what she was supposed to find out. This is borne out as she continues, "Chto ona prosila, eto, konechno, moia taina" (What she asked is, of course, my secret). (In the original, she says, "what she bade me say, I will keep to myself," which would rather effectively defeat her purpose as a messenger.) But then she immediately reveals the drift of Juliet's intent by saying, "but first let me tell ye, if ye should lead her into a fool's paradise . . ." "no esli vy, sudar', sobiraetes' ee odurachit' . . ." (but if you, sir, are going to make a fool of her . . .).

The warning which follows, "it were a very gross kind of behaviour, as they say," takes on a remarkable vehemence in the Russian translation: "eto ia uzh prosto slov ne naidu, kak nekhorosho" (that's I simply can't find the words to say how bad). Everything between "eto" and "kak nekhorosho" serves to emphasize just how bad the Nurse thinks such behavior would be, but this might not be understood at once, and the immediate effect of the interpolation might be disconcerting and disruptive of any remaining vestige of logical continuity. The illogicality of the statement may be further heightened by the fact that

the Nurse builds up so vehemently to the final word of
condemnation and disapproval for any dishonorable action on Romeo's part, and when it arrives, it is the mildest
of pejorative terms: "nekhorosho" (bad, not good). The
Nurse goes on to warn Romeo "and therefore, if you
should deal double with her," "i esli vy ee obmanete" (and
if you deceive her); but she ends with a rather mild and
generalized condemnation of such behavior: "truly it were
an ill thing to be offered to any gentlewoman, and very
weak dealing," "khoroshie liudi tak ne postupaiut" (good
people don't act that way).

Although the Nurse appears vigorous in warning Romeo
against taking advantage of her young mistress, she always
ends up (particularly in the translation) with a relatively
mild and quite general criticism of such behavior. It seems,
perhaps, that she feels obliged to condemn the possibility
of seduction, but cannot bring herself to criticize it very
strongly in the end. The bias of her attitude is obvious.
Although Pasternak has made free use of his own language
in recreating Juliet's Nurse, he remains fundamentally
faithful to the portrait drawn by the original author.

In some instances, characters are more markedly
changed, as in the translation of IV.vi of *King Lear*, where
Edgar adopts a new disguise and a rustic dialect in defending his blind father from Goneril's servant Oswald. In the
original he is blunt, straightforward, and plainspoken,
obviously independent and refusing to be pushed around
by anyone.

Good gentleman, go your gait, and let poor volk pass. And
'chud ha' bin zwagger'd out of my life, 'twould not ha' bin zo
long as 'tis by a vortnight. Nay, come not near th' old man; keep
out, che vor' ye, or ise try whither your costard or my ballow be
the harder. Chill be plain with you. (IV.vi.238–44)

["And 'chud" (if I could); "che vor' ye" (I warrant you); "costard" (head); "ballow" (cudgel); "chill" (I will)]

Pasternak has not attempted to introduce an equivalent Russian dialect in translating this, but he has made use of such popular expressions as "putem-dorozhen'koi" (by the wayside; literally, by the path—by the little road); "podo-bru-pozdorovu" (in good time, while you're still whole); etc.

Проходи, господин хороший, путем-дороженькой и не свя-зывайся с простым народом. И не поминай мне, сделай милость, про смерть, а то как бы вправду я не помер со страху. А от старичка подальше, подалыше от старичка, а то двину я тебя по башке дубиной, посмотрю, что крепче. Уходи, голубчик, подобру-поздорову. (Р. 412)

(Pass by the wayside, good gentleman, and don't get mixed up with simple folk. And do me the favor not to remind me about death, or else I might really die of fright. And stay a little farther from the old man, a little farther from the old man, or else I'll hit your noggin with my cudgel and see which is harder. Go along, my dear, while the going is good.)

The very character of the speaker is subtly transformed. He is still outspokenly determined to protect Gloucester from his assailant, but there is a touch of ironic familiarity and even protectiveness in his manner of dealing with his antagonist. He employs the familiar "ty," "tebia" (thou) in addressing Oswald, even calling him "golubchik" (my dear), and the use of diminutives softens the edge of his statements. Where Shakespeare's Edgar gives the very straightforward, unqualified command, "Nay, come not near th' old man," Pasternak's character uses the more modest and softened warning, "podal'she ot starichka" (a little farther from the old man). Where the original Edgar

says, "And 'chud ha' bin zwagger'd out of my life, 'twould
not ha' bin zo long as 'tis by a vortnight," an assertion of
independence and of a refusal to be pushed around by
anyone, Pasternak's Edgar responds to Oswald's threat to
kill him with, "I ne pominai mne, sdelai milost', pro smert',
a to kak by vpravdu ia ne pomer so strakhu" (And be good
enough not to remind me about death, or else I might
really die of fright). He adopts a pose of such exaggerated
timidity that his irony is obvious, but he never loses the
appearance of politeness, throwing a "sdelai milost'" (be
so good) into the middle of his statement. Both ironic
politeness and the pose of timidity are foreign to the bluff
honesty of Shakespeare's character, and the difference is
borne out again in the final lines of the speech. After
threatening to strike Oswald with his club if he comes near
Gloucester, Shakespeare's Edgar ends, "Chill be plain with
you," again bluff, honest, straightforward. Pasternak's
Edgar states at this point, "Ukhodi, golubchik, podobru-
pozdorovu" (Go along, my dear, while the going is good).
The affectionate familiarity of "golubchik" (my dear) is
certainly peculiar to the Russian text; and the expression
"podobru-pozdorovu" (while the going is good, in good
time) represents both a reiteration of a threat, and an expression of concern for Oswald's safety, perhaps not
wholly ironic. Pasternak has transformed the bluff, independent English peasant portrayed by Edgar into a more
crafty and soft-spoken Russian counterpart, whose very
display of concern for his betters provides him a service-
able means for dealing with them.

In general, Pasternak was adept and imaginative in dealing with Shakespeare's commoners, often comic characters
—the clown who brings Cleopatra the asps, Justice Shal-
low in *2 Henry IV*, etc. The problems and discrepancies

produced by Pasternak's use of Russian colloquialisms
are more noticeable in the case of characters belonging
to the aristocracy or upper classes. Although he was by
no means incapable of bringing out their dignity or nobility of speech, they could be brought jarringly down
to earth by the appearance of an unexpected or inappropriate colloquialism. It does not add to the dignity of
Othello, or of Desdemona, for example, to have Desdemona's original response to Othello's tales of youthful
hardship and suffering, "She swore i' faith 'twas strange,
'twas passing strange" (I.iii.160), changed to " 'Net,'—
akhala ona,—'kakaia zhizn'!' " ("No," she gasped, "What a
life!"); or to have Othello exclaim, as he spies on Cassio,
"Skazhi pozhaluista, uzhe smeetsia" (What do you know,
he's already laughing), rather than "Look how he laughs
already!" (IV.i.109). Numerous other examples could be
given, and a few more will be cited at a later point; but
the use of idioms and colloquial expressions, even where
they have markedly altered the tone of the original text,
is not always clumsy, awkward, obtrusive, or trivial. Pasternak's Polonius was received well by the two critics cited
earlier. Morozov also quotes, as another felicitous example
of his natural and lifelike speech, Polonius' instructions
to his servant Reynaldo as he leaves to obtain news of
Laertes in Paris:

> You shall do marvellous wisely, good Reynaldo,
> Before you visit him, to make inquiry
> Of his behaviour. (II.i.3–5)

> Да было б хорошо
> До вашего свидания, голубчик,
> Разнюхать там, как он себя ведет. (P. 250)

(And it would be good, my dear, for you to smell out how he's
behaving, before you meet him.)

As Morozov points out, "razniukhat'" (to smell out) is
not only natural and effective in context, but highly appropriate to the speech of this old man, who spends so much
time "whispering and eavesdropping" on others. But it
should be noted that this rather earthy and homely phrase
replaces "to make inquiry," which is more appropriate to
the language of a diplomat or statesman; and the Russian
"golubchik" (my dear) is less formal, more affectionately
familiar than "good Reynaldo." Many such changes may
be found in Polonius' speech in translation. His warning
to Ophelia to avoid Hamlet's advances in the future retains,
in the original, some reminders of the language of a
statesman:

> From this time
> Be somewhat scanter of your maiden presence.
> Set your entreatments at a higher rate
> Than a command to parley.   (I.iii.120–23)

The translation is much simpler, and the final piece of
advice sounds like a homely and typically Russian folk
saying:

> Будь поскупей на будущее время.
> Пускай твоей беседой лорожат.
> Не торопись навстречу, только кликнут.[10]   (Р. 245)

(Be a little stingier in the future. Let them value your conversation. Don't rush out to meet everyone as soon as they call.)

Pasternak has made of Polonius a somewhat homelier
figure, displaying a trace of peasant shrewdness, rather
than the reflection or reminder of statesmanlike astuteness.

---

10. In the 1940 edition, the last two lines are "Puskai tvoei besedoi
dorozhat / Povyshe, chem radush'em po prikazu" (Let them value your
conversation more highly than commanded cordiality).

Still it may not seem odd or inappropriate to hear this old privy councillor addressing his daughter familiarly as "dochurka" or his servant as "golubchik." It may produce more of a surprise when Pasternak's King Lear does much the same, particularly in speaking to Kent (disguised as a serving man), Edgar (disguised as Poor Tom), and the Fool, calling them "golubchik," "druzhok," "bratets," etc. (my dear, friend, brother). But even this may seem natural in context and justifiable according to a certain interpretation of the play, as indicated in the preceding chapter on *King Lear*. Yu. D. Levin has pointed out very different implications in Druzhinin's famous translation of *King Lear*, first published in 1856, and highly esteemed by Pasternak. "Throughout the entire tragedy the translator has almost imperceptibly heightened the arrogance of Lear."[11] Druzhinin openly states his own admiration of Kent's unwavering loyalty to his monarch, and "in the translation the loyalty of Kent to his king and master is slightly but at the same time consistently accentuated."[12] Kent is addressed by his appreciative master as "chestnyi rab" (honest serf, slave). Druzhinin has accentuated the imperiousness of Lear, his position as king; Pasternak has brought out Lear's familiarity with his servants, his relationship, identification, and sense of kinship with the common man.

A comparable phenomenon has been noted in Pasternak's translation of Goethe's *Faust*. E. Etkind has pointed out that in Faust's monologue in the scene "Vor dem Tor," where Faust describes the coming of spring and the crowds flocking into the countryside, Pasternak has introduced

11. *Shekspir i russkaia kul'tura* (Shakespeare and Russian Culture), ed. M. P. Alekseev (Moscow–Leningrad: Nauka, 1965), p. 482.
12. Ibid., p. 483.

some homely expressions, occasionally from Russian peasant dialect, and "Faust is no longer a bookish scholar, he
acquires the features of a muzhik."[13] "Before us is such a
peasant-like Faust, belonging to the common people,—
does he have anything in common with Goethe's bookish
sage, tormented by a thirst for knowledge?"[14]

Pasternak's use of simple, idiomatic Russian affects not
only class, tending to bring the nobility and intelligentsia
down to the level of the common people; it also serves to
deflate high-flown rhetoric, leading to simplification of
precious or elaborate metaphors. The style of some scenes
from *Romeo and Juliet* is particularly changed. Although
he found much to criticize in Pasternak's translation of the
play, Mikhail Morozov praised it as being on the whole a
remarkable achievement, and he singled out Pasternak's
handling of the balcony scene, "where a genuinely lofty
poetic quality is combined with winning simplicity."[15]
More recently, however, V. Levik, himself an outstanding
translator of Shakespeare and other Western European
poets, has pointed out that this scene has been much
altered by Pasternak. The dialogue is more natural, lifelike, and suited to modern tastes. In Levik's opinion, a
more literal translation would be more declamatory, but
marked by a greater "turbulence of images" and an in-
creased "pictorial force."[16] Images and usages typical of
the late Renaissance would not be lost. Levik points out

13. *Poeziia i perevod* (Poetry and Translation) (Moscow–Leningrad:
Sovetskii pisatel', 1963), p. 207.

14. Ibid., p. 208.

15. "K perevodam shekspirovskikh dram" (On Translations of Shakespeare's Dramas), in *Masterstvo perevoda 1969* (Moscow: Sovetskii
pisatel', 1970), p. 351.

16. "Nuzhny li novye perevody Shekspira?" (Are New Translations
of Shakespeare Necessary?), in *Masterstvo perevoda 1966* (Moscow:
Sovetskii pisatel', 1968), p. 99.

that Pasternak completely altered one image by omitting
the last two lines of one of Romeo's speeches:

> She speaks.—
> O, speak again, bright angel! for thou art
> As glorious to this night, being o'er my head,
> As is a winged messenger of heaven
> Unto the white-upturned wondering eyes
> Of mortals, that fall back to gaze on him,
> When he bestrides the lazy-pacing clouds
> And sails upon the bosom of the air.   (II.ii.25–32)

> Проговорила что-то. Светлый ангел,
> Во мраке над моею головой
> Ты реешь, как крылатый вестник неба
> Вверху, на недоступной высоте,
> Над изумленною толпой народа,
> Которая следит за ним с земли.[17]   (P. 45)

(She uttered something. Bright angel, in the darkness over my
head you hover, like a winged messenger of heaven, above, at
an inaccessible height, over the astonished crowd of people,
who follow after him from the earth.)

It might be pointed out, however, that this is still a highly
idealized portrait of Juliet, and the translation has its own
striking features. Pasternak has kept, even accentuated,
the allusion to the appearance of a figure of light (Juliet) in

17. The passage is considerably different in the 1944 edition (Moscow:
GIKhL).

> Проговорила что-то. Светлый ангел,
> Во мраке на балконе надо мной
> Ты реешь, как крылатый вестник неба
> Над головами пораженных толп,
> Которые рассматривают снизу,
> Как он над ними по небу плывет.   (P. 42)

(She uttered something. Bright angel, in the darkness on the balcony
above me you hover, like a winged messenger of heaven above the
heads of the startled crowds who watch from below, as he floats through
the heaven above them.)

the midst of darkness. The "bright angel" who is "as glorious to this night . . ." becomes "svetlyi angel, / Vo mrake nad moeiu golovoi" (bright angel, in the darkness above my head). And Pasternak has emphasized the perspective of the viewer, watching this wondrous being from the ground below: "o'er my head" becomes "nad moeiu golovoi" (over my head); "unto the white-upturned wondering eyes / Of mortals" is replaced by "nad izumlennoiu tolpoi naroda" (above the astonished crowd of people); and Pasternak has introduced an entirely new expression, describing the "messenger of heaven" as being "vverkhu, na nedostupnoi vysote" (above, at an inaccessible height). Some specific pictorial detail has been lost, and yet there is a striking visual effect which comes from the elemental (and symbolic) contrast between light and darkness, and a dramatic visual perspective, which emphasizes Romeo's sense of awe and wonder on Juliet's first appearance. Elsewhere in the scene, however, Pasternak showed a tendency not only to simplify language, but to bring his lovers more firmly down to earth. He has curbed elaborate courtliness, the use of euphuisms, sustained artifice, the tendency to call things by something other than their common names. Shakespeare's Juliet exclaims, on learning that Romeo has overheard her declaration of love for him:

> Thou know'st the mask of night is on my face,
> Else would a maiden blush bepaint my cheek
> For that which thou hast heard me speak to-night.
>
> (II.ii.85–87)

The image of "the mask of night" suggests a degree of artificiality, the playing of a part, as well as introducing a sophisticated allusion to the masked ball at which they had just met. In translation, Juliet says simply,

Мое лицо спасает темнота   (P. 46)

(The darkness saves my face).

And instead of maintaining a further suggestion of artifice by speaking of a blush "painting" her cheek, she states merely,

А то б я, знаешь, со стыда сгорела,
Что ты узнал так много обо мне.

(Or else, you know, I would burn with shame, because you have learned so much about me.)

The inclusion of "znaesh'" (you know) further suggests an unpretentious confiding in her listener. As she continues, the patterned elegance of the original,

Fain would I dwell on form, fain, fain deny
What I have spoke; but farewell compliment!

gives way to the straightforward simplicity of:

Хотела б я восстановить приличье,
Да поздно, притворяться ни к чему.

(I would like to restore decorum, but it's too late, there's no use pretending.)

At this point, Shakespeare's Juliet asks very simply, "Dost thou love me?" and it becomes clear that she is concerned herself about the possibility of deception and misleading appearances, and that she wishes to know the reality they may be hiding:

I know thou wilt say 'Ay,'
And I will take thy word; yet, if thou swear'st,
Thou mayst prove false; at lovers' perjuries,

They say, Jove laughs. O gentle Romeo,
If thou dost love, pronounce it faithfully.

Ты любишь ли меня? Я знаю, верю,
Что скажешь «да». Но ты не торопись.
Ведь ты обманешь. Говорят, Юпитер
Пренебрегает клятвами любви.
Не лги, Ромео. Это ведь не шутка.

(Do you really love me? I know, I believe, that you will say
"yes." But don't hurry. Why, you will deceive me. They say
that Jupiter scorns the vows of love. Don't lie, Romeo. Why,
this is not a joke.)

The natural simplicity of Pasternak's Juliet here may make
the classical allusion to Jove, scorning vows of love, seem
almost out of place. (In the original 1943 edition, Juliet
used a more commonplace colloquial phrase: "Ne stavit ni
vo chto liubovnykh kliatv," Doesn't think lovers' vows
are worth anything.) And the appearance of such homely
expressions as "Ne lgi, Romeo. Eto ved' ne shutka" (Don't
lie, Romeo. Why, this is not a joke) may only intensify
the suggestion of her vulnerability and add to the poignancy of her efforts to break through the possible façade
of deceiving appearances. Similar touches might be noted
throughout the rest of the speech. Juliet becomes simpler,
less sophisticated, an ordinary young girl who has just
fallen in love for the first time. The purist or the admirer
of the elaborate poetry of the original might disapprove of
Pasternak's handling of the scene, but others have found
Pasternak's unpretentious young Juliet persuasive and
quite touching. Morozov asserted in a later essay,

Perhaps there is less brilliance in the speeches of the lovers (the
sonnet of the Renaissance is generally foreign to Pasternak),
and less Shakespearean, raging, all consuming passion in their

feelings, but on the other hand the tenderness of these feelings is somehow manifested very deeply.[18]

The frank practicality of Pasternak's Juliet is particularly noticeable in another passage. Shakespeare's Juliet tells Romeo shortly before her final departure:

> Three words, dear Romeo, and good night, indeed.
> If that thy bent of love be honourable,
> Thy purpose marriage, send me word to-morrow,
> By one that I'll procure to come to thee,
> Where and what time thou wilt perform the rite,
> And all my fortunes at thy foot I'll lay
> And follow thee my lord throughout the world.
>
> (II.ii.142–48)

This is quite frank and direct, but still Juliet expresses herself in courtly terms, speaking of "thy bent of love," honor, the rite of marriage. In translation, there is no reference to love or honor, but simply to the decision to marry:

> Если ты, Ромео,
> Решил на мне жениться не шутя   (P. 47)

(If you, Romeo, have decided in earnest to marry me)

with the "ne shutia" (in earnest, not joking, not in jest) adding a colloquial touch. Further, Pasternak reduces Juliet's request to know "where and what time thou wilt perform the rite" to simple, businesslike terms:

> Дай завтра знать, когда и где венчанье.

(Let me know tomorrow when and where the wedding will be.)

18. From "Shekspir v perevodakh B. Pasternaka" (Shakespeare in the Translation of B. Pasternak), *Literaturnaia gazeta*, Aug. 7, 1943.

Her promise to send someone to him the next day to receive his answer is expressed in language that would be appropriate to the working out of a business decision:

> С утра к тебе придет мой человек
> Узнать на этот счет твое решенье.

(My man will come to you in the morning to find out your decision on that account.)

The promise of Shakespeare's Juliet to lay "all my fortunes at thy foot" suggests her surrendering herself and her future to her husband. Pasternak's translation picks up the connotation primarily of property or belongings:

> Я все добро сложу к твоим ногам

(I will lay all my possessions at your feet).

There is an overt practicality here which marks the death of romantic illusion.

Pasternak's modification of the "highly metaphorical" style of Shakespeare in this scene does not merely rob the language of extraneous decoration; it sometimes changes its meaning. In the same scene, Romeo explains to Juliet how he managed to climb over the high walls surrounding the Capulets' garden:

> With love's light wings did I o'er-perch these walls,
> For stony limits cannot hold love out:
> And what love can do, that dares love attempt;
> Therefore thy kinsmen are no let to me.   (II.ii.66–69)

> Меня перенесла сюда любовь,
> Ее не останавливают стены.
> В нужде она решается на все,
> И потому—что мне твои родные!   (P. 46)

(Love transported me here; walls cannot stop it. In need, it resolves on anything, and therefore—what are your kinsmen to me!)

After the allusion to flight in his opening statement ("With
love's light wings did I o'er-perch these walls"), Romeo's
assertion that "what love can do, that dares love attempt"
seems to infer an extraordinary power, beyond normal
human limitations. In the translation, however, Pasternak
eliminates the metaphorical reference to flight in the first
line, mentioning only the force of love itself ("menia pere-
nesla siuda liubov'," love transported me here), and he
introduces in the third line the word "nuzhda" (need,
necessity), which has no place in the original speech.
Shakespeare's Romeo has entirely denied the constraints of
necessity; Pasternak's Romeo speaks of encountering and
overcoming them: "V nuzhde ona [liubov'] reshaetsia na
vse" (In need, [love] resolves on anything). His final statement may thus carry more of a connotation of sheer determination, "I potomu—chto mne tvoi rodnye!" (And
therefore—what are your kinsmen to me!), than the original, "Therefore thy kinsmen are no let to me." The extravagant connotations of the entire speech have been
toned down.

Pasternak has by no means eliminated all evidence of
Romeo's extravagance and ebullient confidence, or of the
wondrous, dreamlike quality of the encounter:

> O blessed, blessed night! I am afeard,
> Being in night, all this is but a dream,
> Too flattering-sweet to be substantial.
>
> (II.ii.139–41)

> Святая ночь, саятая ночь! А вдруг
> Все это сон? Так непомерно счастье,
> Так сказочно и чудно это все!   (P. 47)

(Holy night, holy night! But then, what if all this is a dream? My happiness is so excessive, everything is so fantastic and wondrous!)

But even here the language of Pasternak's Romeo is more commonplace, with colloquial turns of speech making an appearance ("A vdrug / Vse eto son?" But then, what if all this is a dream?), and he is brought closer to the everyday world.

More apt material for a "study of unadorned everyday life" would seem to be available in the tavern scenes of *Henry IV, parts 1 and 2*, which center on the figure of Falstaff and involve thieves, tapsters, prostitutes, and carriers, as well as an erring young prince who scandalizes his father by the base company he keeps. The tendency to use earthy, colloquial language would seem quite appropriate in these scenes from the play, which apparently held a particular importance for Pasternak.[19] But even the

19. There is considerable evidence that Pasternak had a deep and abiding interest in Falstaff. In a letter to the editor of Detgiz in 1942, Pasternak defended the fact that, despite the liberties he took in his translation of *Romeo and Juliet*, he called it a translation and not a "peredelka," a reworked version of the play: "When, for example, I make of the two-part *Henry IV* a one-part *Falstaff*, that will be a reworking" (*Masterstvo perevoda 1969* [Moscow: Sovetskii pisatel', 1970], p. 358). In editing the letter, Pasternak's son commented that "in 1956–57, Pasternak realized this intention. The manuscript of a shortened, one-part version of *Henry IV* in 4 acts and 14 scenes is preserved in the archives of Boris Pasternak" (ibid.). Before his translation of *Henry IV* actually appeared in its complete version in 1948, a number of scenes from it were published in 1946 in *Zvezda* (Nos. 2–3, pp. 118–44), all centering on Falstaff, most of them set in the taverns or streets of London: from *part 1*, I.ii, II.ii, II.iv, III.iii; from *part 2*, I.ii, II.i, V.iii, V.v. Further, Pasternak seems to have identified Falstaff, more directly than any other character from the plays, with the historical Shakespeare himself. In his notes on *Henry IV*, he says almost nothing about the play, but focuses rather on the figure of its author, newly immersed in the turbulent low life of London, in company with "actors, writers and

grossly corpulent Falstaff, a frequenter of the taverns and obviously devoted to fleshly indulgence, is brought more unrelentingly down to earth in the translation of Pasternak. In the original work, Falstaff himself continually uses his extraordinary imaginative resources to evade or transform any facts of reality which may be unpleasant, unflattering, or incriminating to him. And his high-spirited and unfailingly ingenious efforts to further his own interests give the character much of his appeal.

Shakespeare's Falstaff refuses, for instance, to acquiesce to the claims of time. He is introduced in the second scene of *1 Henry IV* by Hal's explosive response to his request to know the time of day.

What a devil hast thou to do with the time of the day? Unless hours were cups of sack, and minutes capons, and clocks the tongues of bawds, and dials the signs of leaping-houses, and the blessed sun himself a fair hot wench in flame-coloured taffeta, I see no reason why thou shouldst be so superfluous to demand the time of the day. (I.ii.6–12)

In this passage the elements of time (hours, minutes, clocks, dials, the blessed sun) are transformed into the instruments of Falstaff's pleasure (cups of sack, capons, tongues of bawds, signs of leaping-houses, a fair hot wench), since time, as marked by ordinary men, is simply irrelevant to him. (There is a common analogy between the sun and the king, and the passage also implies Falstaff's disavowal of order and the royal head of state.)

---

their patrons, who went from tavern to tavern, bullied strangers, and continually risking their necks, made fun of everything in the world. . . . Perhaps a fat old glutton like Falstaff really did belong to this circle of youth. Or perhaps this was a later remembrance of that time, embodied in the form of fiction" (III, 206–07). In Pasternak's poem "Shakespeare" there are Falstaffian touches in the portrait of Shakespeare, who is "obriuzgshii" (grown paunchy, fat and flabby) and at home in the tavern.

When the Chief Justice attempts to force him to recognize in himself the signs of age, Falstaff retorts:

My lord, I was born about three of the clock in the afternoon, with a white head, and something a round belly. For my voice, I have lost it with hallooing, and singing of anthems. To approve my youth further, I will not: the truth is, I am only old in judgment and understanding; and he that will caper with me for a thousand marks, let him lend me the money, and have at him! (*2 Henry IV*, I.ii.186–93)

Here he transforms the marks of old age into the signs of youth and piety.

Falstaff also uses his wit to avoid the claims of debt and justice. Throughout *2 Henry IV* he is pitted against the Chief Justice, who attempts again and again to bring him to admit his debts and misdeeds and make restitution for them. But by his play of wit he evades any admission of the charges the Justice attempts to bring against him; and through his powers of manipulation, he manages not only to avoid repaying Mistress Quickly but to borrow more money from her as well.

He opposes, too, the attempts of his companions to force him to acknowledge the base characteristics they recognize in him: cowardice, meanness, depravity, and an incorrigible tendency to lie. Falstaff is indeed so much the creature of his own imagination, so quick-witted and ready to reshape events to suit his own purposes, that it is difficult to determine where falsehood ends and truth begins in assessing his character; to decide what the realities of his character are, how much he believes what he says, how much truth there may be in his statements. Much speculation has centered in particular upon the incident of the men in buckram. This famous display of imaginative exaggeration comes in the second act of *1 Henry IV*, after

Falstaff and his companions have been robbed of the spoils
of a holdup by Prince Hal and Poins, disguised as another
crew of robbers. In his description of the event afterwards
to the Prince, Falstaff not only blows up the proportions
of the encounter to those of a gigantic conflict, but allows
them to grow in exaggeration as he tells the story—as the
number of men in buckram suits who attacked him in-
creases from two to four to seven to nine to eleven. When
Hal attempts to call him to account for the untruth of his
extravagant inventions by pointing out their inconsisten-
cies and general impossibility, Falstaff escapes with a display of righteous indignation:

What, upon compulsion? 'Zounds, and I were at the strappado,
or all the racks in the world, I would not tell you on compulsion.
Give you a reason on compulsion? If reasons were as plentiful
as blackberries, I would give no man a reason upon compulsion,
I. (II.iv.231–36)

And when the Prince reveals that Falstaff's attackers were
only himself and Poins, and that the entire story of Falstaff's valiant battle is an invention, Falstaff saves himself
from admitting this by another piece of imaginative
reasoning:

By the Lord, I knew ye as well as he that made ye. Why, hear
you, my masters, was it for me to kill the heir-apparent? Should
I turn upon the true prince? Why, thou knowest I am as valiant
as Hercules: but beware instinct—the lion will not touch the true
prince; instinct is a great matter. I was now a coward on instinct.
(II.iv.263–69)

The obvious explanation of this would be that his story
represents an attempt to transform a flagrant display of
cowardice into an act of superhuman heroism—an extravagant fiction which the Prince can never quite manage to

disprove. But many critics would take exception to such an interpretation.

Maurice Morgann, who devotes his essay on Falstaff to proving that the fat knight was not a coward, asserts that Falstaff could not have meant his wildly exaggerated statements to be taken seriously, that he is here "making his lyes too extravagant for practised imposition,"[20] and could not be making an attempt to hide any display of cowardice. J. Dover Wilson credits Falstaff with even greater subtlety of wit, presenting the theory that Falstaff actually recognized the Prince and Poins as his assailants from the beginning, and that the original two men in buckram in Falstaff's description were meant to represent them, his progressive exaggeration of the number being part of a joke on Hal.[21]

The willingness to accept Falstaff's statements as conscious design, if not as absolute truth, and to view his character as being above the level of the basest possible interpretation, the readiness to take him, at least in part, at his word, point to an attractiveness which is to some degree the product of the play of the imagination. Shakespeare's Falstaff, then, is continually using his wit and power of imagination to stave off the claims of time, truth, debt, justice, and possibly the reality of his own nature, and only with the Prince's rejection of him on acceding to the throne, at the end of *2 Henry IV*, do Falstaff's resources fail him. Pasternak's own reading of passages from II.iv and III.iii of *1 Henry IV* in 1947—recorded at the time and recently released on a Melodiya record—reflect the zest

20. *Essay on the Dramatic Character of Sir John Falstaff*, ed. W. A. Gill (1777; rpt. London: Henry Frowde, 1912), p. 143.

21. *The Fortunes of Falstaff* (Cambridge: Cambridge University Press, 1944), pp. 48–56.

with which he approached the character of Falstaff, the immense vitality and humor which he found in Falstaff and his companions.[22] Yet the text of his translation may seem in itself somewhat heavy-handed, lacking the lightness of touch, the play of wit and imaginative extravagance of the original. Details which relate Falstaff to the physical rather than to the imaginative realm are strengthened, subtly but persistently. Pasternak often maintains the vitality of the characters, as when the Prince interrupts Falstaff's increasingly exaggerated account of the battle with the men in buckram:

Prince: I'll be no longer guilty of this sin. This sanguine coward, this bed-presser, this horse-back-breaker, this huge hill of flesh,—

Falstaff: 'Sblood, you starveling, you eel-skin, you dried neat's-tongue, you bull's-pizzle, you stock-fish—O for breath to utter what is like thee!—you tailor's-yard, you sheath, you bow-case, you vile standing tuck!   (II.iv.237–44)

["stock-fish" (dried cod); "standing tuck" (stiff upended rapier)]

Принц: Ну, долго я тебя принуждать не стану. Слушайте, господа. Этот полнокровный трус, этот сокрушитель конских хребтов и кроватей, эта непомерная гора мяса...

Фальстаф: Эй, полегче ты, заморыш, рыбья кожа, кишка коровья, телячий язык! У человека нехватит голоса перебрать все то, на что ты похож худобой. Молчал бы лучше, портновский аршин, колчан без стрел, сточившийся клинок! (*Переводит дыхание.*)[23]   (P. 100)

22. "Vil'iam Shekspir v perevodakh S. Marshaka i B. Pasternaka: chitaiut avtory perevodov" (William Shakespeare in the Translations of S. Marshak and B. Pasternak: The Authors of the Translations Read) (Moscow: Melodiya, 1976), side 2, M40-38965-66.

23. In the version of the translation published in *Zvezda* (Nos. 2–3) in 1946, the phrasing is slightly clumsier. The phrase "etot sokrushitel'

> (*Prince*: Well, I won't compel you any longer. Listen, gentle-
> men. This full-blooded coward, this crusher of horses' spines
> and beds, this enormous hill of meat...
> *Falstaff*: Hey, take it easy, you, starveling, fish skin, cow's gut,
> calf's tongue! A man doesn't have enough voice to name
> everything that you resemble in thinness. You had better
> be quiet, tailor's yardstick, quiver without arrows, ground-
> off blade! [*He catches his breath.*])

But changes occur even here. Some of the lightness and
swiftness of movement of the language disappears when it
is translated into polysyllabic Russian, though the stream
of insults retains a rhythm of its own and could be read
with great energy and vigor. And certain aspects of the
original play on words are simply lost. In Shakespeare's
play, the two characters are not simply directing undiffer-
entiated streams of abuse at one another. With imaginative
exuberance, they exaggerate one another's characteristics
of physical immensity and of thinness to impossible extremes as a means of insult. Each of the Prince's epithets
emphasizes Falstaff's weight and immensity; the last one,
"this huge hill of flesh," takes him beyond the limits of
human size altogether. Falstaff's epithets, on the other
hand, exaggerate Hal's leanness; all represent things thin,
dried up. As A. R. Humphries notes, "the idea of elongated

konskikh khrebtov i krovatei" (that crusher of horses' backs and beds)
is longer and more unwieldy: "etot sokrushitel' konskikh khrebtov i
prodavlivatel' krovatei" (that crusher of horses' backs and breaker of
beds). Two phrases in Falstaff's speech are slightly changed as well. The
earlier (1946) "chelovecheskogo dykhaniia nekhvatit . . ." (human breath
will not suffice . . .) becomes more conversational: "U cheloveka nekhvatit golosa . . ." (A man won't have voice enough . . .). And the translation for "you vile standing tuck," which was "oruzheinaia stoika"
(support for weapons) in the 1946 edition, appears as "stochivshiisia
klinok" (ground-off blade) in the later ones. All passages cited in this
study are the same in the 1948 edition of the translation as in the 1953 one.

shrivelled dryness is brought out in all these metaphors."[24]
Pasternak's insertion of a direct reference to Hal's thinness
in the translation ("na chto ty pokhozh khudoboi . . . ,"
that you resemble in thinness) may represent an attempt to
compensate for the weakness of his lines in otherwise
bringing out the very conception of thinness. In particular,
Pasternak has marred the consistency of Falstaff's indication of thinness and desiccation by introducing such terms
as "kishka korov'ia" (cow's gut) and "teliachii iazyk" (calf's
tongue); the latter obviously replaces the "dried neat's-
tongue" of the original, but loses the connotation of something shriveled up. It could be argued that in leaving out
the "bull's-pizzle" and generally weakening "the idea of
elongated shrivelled dryness," brought out in the original
metaphors, Pasternak avoided a sexual insult implicit in
the original speech. And yet in a sense the translation is
earthier, introducing an element of crude organic physicality, unresolved into the original patterning. It might be
noted, too, that the Russian word "miaso" (meat), employed in the translation of "this huge hill of flesh," does
not have the abstract and figurative uses of the English
"flesh." Falstaff is kept more to the level of a solidly
physical entity here.

Such changes are typical of Pasternak's translation.
Earlier in the same scene, Shakespeare's Prince summons
Falstaff with the exclamation, "call in Ribs, call in Tallow"
(II.iv.109). In Pasternak's translation this is expanded to
the unwieldy phrase, "Siuda ego, etu otbivnuiu kotletu,
siuda ego, zhirnyi kom sala" (Bring him here, that meat
chop, bring him here, that greasy lump of fat). The lightness is gone from the phrasing; the epithets by which

24. From Humphries' notes to the Arden edition of *1 Henry IV* (1960),
p. 61.

Pasternak's Falstaff is named are so physically explicit that little opportunity is left for the playful ambiguities of the original phrase. "Ribs" could obviously refer to a piece of meat, but the word could also ironically refer to thinness. (At other points Hal does refer jokingly to Falstaff's leanness, as in line 322 of the same scene: "Here comes lean Jack, here comes bare-bone.") "Tallow" refers to drippings of fat from cooked meat, but the image is not so explicitly defined as "zhirnyi kom sala" (greasy lump of fat). A bit of untransformed physical reality has been brought into the translation.

Even more striking changes occur in Pasternak's translation of Hal's speech in the same scene as he acts the part of the King, condemning Falstaff to his son.

Why dost thou converse with that trunk of humours, that bolting-hutch of beastliness, that swollen parcel of dropsies, that huge bombard of sack, that stuffed cloak-bag of guts, that roasted Manningtree ox with the pudding in his belly, that reverend vice, that grey iniquity, that father ruffian, that vanity in years? Wherein is he good, but to taste sack and drink it? wherein neat and cleanly, but to carve a capon and eat it? wherein cunning, but in craft? wherein crafty, but in villainy? wherein villainous, but in all things? wherein worthy, but in nothing? (II.iv.442–53)

Зачем ты знаешься с этим чурбаном? Этот человек—целая кладовая всякого свинства, это вздутие от водянки и чудовищный бурдюк с хересом, это целиком зажаренный ярмарочный бык с кашей. Чем он одарен, кроме уменья пробовать херес? Чему научился, кроме разрезывания и пржирания каплунов? Чем он проявил себя, кроме обмана и подлости? Какие у него достоинства? Никаких. Какие недостатки? Все решительно.[25] (P. 104)

25. The phrasing of the 1946 edition is slightly different. The Prince there says "eto tselaia kladovaia . . ." (that is a whole storeroom . . .) instead of "etot chelovek—tselaia kladovaia . . ." (that man is a whole storeroom . . .), as in the later edition. In the 1946 edition, he continues

(Why do you associate with that blockhead? That man is a whole storeroom of every sort of swinishness, he is a dropsical swelling and a monstrous wineskin full of sack, he is a bull with kasha, roasted whole at the fair. In what is he gifted, except the ability to taste sack? What has he learned, except the cutting and devouring of capons? In what has he shown his worth, except deceit and baseness? What virtues does he have? None. What are his defects? Absolutely all.)

In the original, there had been simply a stream of descriptive epithets suggesting an explosive and uncontained force, as the supposed King vented his spleen against the corrupter of his son: "Why dost thou converse with that trunk of humours, that bolting-hutch of beastliness, that swollen parcel of dropsies . . ." Hal's terms of abuse explode the limits of reality, even when he refers to real, physical objects. He takes the low characteristics and gross physical realities of Falstaff ("humours," "beastliness," "dropsies," "guts") out of normal contexts, placing them not in a real body, but in such unexpected containers as a "trunk," "bolting-hutch," "parcel," "cloak-bag." This kind of abstraction is not only comically absurd, but serves to give exaggerated emphasis to Falstaff's gross, physical corpulence and, at the same time, to take this characteristic out of the realm of normal reality altogether. He focuses on the real in such a way as to make it unreal, on the physical in such a way as to make it an abstract epitome of physicality.

"eto chudovishchnyi burdiuk s kheresom, eto tselikom . . ." (he is a monstrous wineskin of sack, he is a [bull roasted] whole . . .), which is later incorporated into a single phrase: "eto chudovishchnyi burdiuk s kheresom i tselikom . . ." (he is a monstrous wineskin of sack and a [bull roasted] whole . . .). One other phrase is changed. Instead of "chem on proiavil sebia" (in what has he shown his worth), the Prince asks in the earlier edition, "chem on vydvinulsia" (how has he distinguished himself).

The containers grow larger and more crammed as the passage progresses: "swollen," "huge," "stuffed." On reaching this point, Hal expresses Falstaff's immensity in terms of that which was consumed to cause that immensity: "that roasted Manningtree ox with the pudding in his belly." After this he moves into the realm of the prototypes of the old morality plays, ironically giving to the vices the characteristics of venerability: "that reverend vice, that grey iniquity, that father ruffian, that vanity in years." These are epithets which may be seen as indicative of Falstaff's role throughout the play as a figure of Vice, of Riot and Misrule, which the Prince must eventually cast out, as the Vice is cast out in a morality play. Pasternak has completely omitted these latter allegorical references. Of the former epithets, he has retained only one which suggests the comic abstraction of the original passage: "that bolting-hutch of beastliness" becomes "tselaia kladovaia vsiakogo svinstva" (a whole storeroom of every sort of swinishness). Even here he has lost the alliteration and the rhythmical parallelism with following phrases, which conveyed a sense of play in language in the original. "That swollen parcel of dropsies" is made into a clinically realistic term: "vzdutie ot vodianki" (dropsical swelling). And the two remaining epithets he retains are more or less plausible physical references: "chudovishchnyi burdiuk s kheresom" (monstrous wineskin full of sack) and "tselikom zazharennyi iarmarochnyi byk s kashei" (a bull with kasha, roasted whole at the fair). He holds the description of Falstaff made by Hal much closer to a level of physical realism and fails to recapture the exuberant imaginative play which exploded the representation of Falstaff into something out of context and out of proportion with normal reality.

Even changes in verbal mood and sentence form may suggest a slightly more "realistic" approach to the characters. In *1 Henry IV*, after Hal and Poins have played a game with Francis the drawer, to demonstrate the limitation of his vocabulary practically to the words, "Anon, anon," the Prince muses, "That ever this fellow should have fewer words than a parrot, and yet the son of a woman! His industry is up-stairs and down-stairs, his eloquence the parcel of a reckoning . . ." (II.iv.96–99). Instead of the subjunctive "That ever this fellow should have . . ." Pasternak places the main clause of the first sentence in the indicative. Francis is brought directly into the realm of reality; the note of speculative wonder on which the original speech opened is lost, and Hal's contemplation of his shortcomings may seem somewhat more sarcastic: "I podumat', chto etot mal'chishka, u kotorogo men'she slov, chem u popugaia, rozhden zhenshchinoi!" (p. 98) (And to think that this fellow who has fewer words than a parrot was born of a woman!). Whether or not Pasternak meant to heighten the Prince's underlying criticism of Falstaff and his companions, his translation sometimes has that effect, and the less admirable traits of Falstaff himself emerge more clearly. Shortly after his extravagant defense of his actions at Gadshill, Falstaff parries accusations of cowardice by asserting that his instinct would not allow him to harm the crown prince, even when he did not recognize him as such; and the play on the word "instinct" is maintained throughout the scene. At one point, Falstaff asks about Hal's own fears in his dangerous situation as the crown prince:

> But tell me, Hal, art not thou horrible afeard? Thou being heir apparent, could the world pick thee out three such

enemies again, as that fiend Douglas, that spirit Percy, and
that devil Glendower? Art thou not horribly afraid? Doth
not thy blood thrill at it?

Prince: Not a whit, i'faith, I lack some of thy instinct.

(II.iv.361–67)

Но воображаю, Гарри, как в глубине души ты пере-
пуган! Ты прав, трудно подыскать более страшную
угрозу на твоем пути к престолу, чем этот чорт Дуглас,
этот оборотень Перси и этот дьявол Глендаур. Тебя,
конечно, это повергает в содроганье, не правда ли? И
у тебя заледенела кровь?

Принц: Честное слово, нисколько. Очевидно, мне недостает
твоего инстинкта.[26]   (Р. 102)

(But I can imagine, Harry, how frightened you are in the
depths of your soul! You are right, it would be hard to find
a more terrible threat on your path to the throne, than that
devil Douglas, that werewolf Percy, and that demon Glendower. Of course, this makes you shudder, doesn't it? And
hasn't your blood turned to ice?

Prince: On my word of honor, not at all. Apparently, I lack
your instinct.)

In referring to this passage, one critic asserted that Falstaff's
questions are inspired by "curiosity, not cowardice," that
"the kind of soldier who *likes* fighting, who actually seeks
out champions to strive with, puzzles him."[27] Shakespeare's Falstaff indeed manages to convey a certain sense
of awe and wonder in considering the Prince's enemies,
which does much to mitigate the suggestion of sheer
cowardice in fearing them. His entire speech is expressed

26. There is one slight change in phrasing in the later version of this
passage. In the 1946 edition, Falstaff says, "Ty, konechno, v sodroganii"
(Of course, you are shuddering), which is altered to "Tebia, konechno,
eto povergaet v sodrogan'e" (Of course, this makes you shudder).

27. J. Dover Wilson, *The Fortunes of Falstaff*, p. 87.

in questions, suggesting that he is probing into something he does not really know about. Pasternak's Falstaff, on the other hand, expresses himself in indicative statements, saying with certainty "ty prav" (you are right) and "konechno" (of course). Only the last two sentences are questions, and the first of these is made so only by the "ne pravda li" (is that not so) which ends it. Falstaff is actually describing Hal's fear to him, the opening sentence suggesting this to be something Falstaff understands well himself: "No voobrazhaiu, Garri, kak v glubine dushi ty perepugan" (But I can imagine, Harry, how frightened you are in the depths of your soul). When the latter denies being afraid, there is a remaining implication that the fear described is Falstaff's own, and may even be something he is trying to foist off on the Prince. The reality of his cowardice is brought out more strongly, and he may appear more contemptible.

One of the most striking changes in the text of Pasternak's translation occurs in *2 Henry IV*, after Falstaff has been commanded by the Chief Justice to make restitution for past debts to Mistress Quickly. In response to this attempt to force upon him the lessons of courtesy, Falstaff begins to ask the Justice's man Gower to dinner with him, very politely but very insistently, at the very moment when the two wish to leave. The Chief Justice finally asks in exasperation:

Chief Justice: What foolish master taught you these manners, Sir John?

Falstaff: Master Gower, if they become me not, he was a fool that taught them me. This is the right fencing grace, my lord; tap for tap, and so part fair.

Chief Justice: Now the Lord lighten thee, thou art a great fool.
(II.i.185–90)

Верховный судья: Что за дурацкие повадки! Где вы им
     научились, сэр Джон?
Фальстаф: Так эти повадки не нравятся вам, мистер Гауэр?
     Действительно, только дурак мог научить меня им.
     (*Со смехом оборачиваясь к судье.*) Я их перенял у
     вас, ваша милость. Как аукнется, так и откликнется.
Верховный судья: Наставь вас господь. Вы невыносимы!
                                                          (P. 144)

(*Chief Justice*: What idiotic manners! Where did you learn
     them, Sir John?
Falstaff: So you don't like these manners, Mister Gower? Really
     only an idiot could have taught them to me. [*Turning to the
     judge with a laugh.*] I learned them from you, your grace.
     The echo responds to the call.
Chief Justice: May God edify you. You are unbearable.)

Both characters are changed in the translation. The Chief
Justice takes on a tone of greater harshness; he begins
with a pejorative exclamation, "Chto za duratskie povadki!" (What idiotic manners!) rather than the relatively
polite question of the original Justice, "What foolish
master taught you these manners, Sir John?" Correspond-
ingly, Falstaff is made more mockingly impudent toward
his opponent. His first response is the question, "Tak eti
povadki ne nraviatsia vam, mister Gauer?" (So you don't
like these manners, Mister Gower?), which is not to be
found in the original text and may seem openly sarcastic.
The original Falstaff had continued to address Gower,
turning back upon the Justice his own accusations: "Master
Gower, if they become me not, he was a fool that taught
them me." Pasternak, however, inserts the startling stage
direction, "so smekhom oborachivaias' k sud'e" (turning
to the judge with a laugh). This might represent an attempt to show the character's good humor, but it may well
come across instead as an indication of direct mockery on

Falstaff's part, out of keeping with the light, playful thrusts of the original character. Pasternak's Falstaff, who has turned directly to the Justice, states specifically that he learned these annoying tricks from the Justice himself: "Ia ikh perenial u vas, vasha milost'" (I learned them from you, your grace). What was left as playful insinuation in the original becomes an uncompromisingly direct accusation.

The original Falstaff emphasizes the fact that he is playing a game with the Justice: "This is the right fencing grace, my lord; tap for tap, and so part fair." This line is left out of the translation altogether. The original Justice replies in kind, with a pun: "Now the Lord lighten thee, thou art a great fool." His word "lighten" could mean either "enlighten" or "make lighter"; his reference to Falstaff as "a great fool" could be a comment either on the greatness of his folly, or the greatness of size of this fool. The latter part of the reply of Pasternak's Justice might be taken as a pun on Falstaff's weight:

Наставь вас господь. Вы невыносимы!

(May God edify you. You are unbearable!)

But if so, it is a clumsy one, and the effect of the statement is more strictly pejorative than the original.

On the whole, Pasternak's treatment of Falstaff in his translation of *Henry IV, parts 1 and 2* brings out such unflattering characteristics as his meanness, cowardice, and sarcasm. And Pasternak has bound the character more closely to the physical elements of his milieu, depriving him of much of the imaginative spontaneity which gives appeal to the original figure. Pasternak seems more interested in the unadorned and sometimes unflattering "realities" of Falstaff's nature, than in his playful capacity to evade or transform them and, for a time at least, to escape their consequences.

If Falstaff represents the epitome of fleshly indulgence, Hotspur represents his opposite, the extravagant idealist, willing to venture anything for the sake of honor. Each pits the force of imagination and desire against actuality: Falstaff denies the realities of his nature and the exigencies of life itself; Hotspur attempts to give reality to something not grounded in fact and ultimately impossible to realize. Pasternak fails to recapture in his representation of Hotspur, as in his treatment of Falstaff, this display of imaginative agility, and Hotspur, too, emerges as a duller and less admirable figure in the translation of the play. Curiously enough, the effect achieved by injecting elements of physical realism into the speech of Falstaff is paralleled by attenuating or removing concrete elements which serve to give the appearance of validity to Hotspur's assertions.

In the first act of *1 Henry IV*, for example, Hotspur makes his famous assertion of commitment to honor:

> By heaven, methinks it were an easy leap
> To pluck bright honour from the pale-fac'd moon,
> Or dive into the bottom of the deep,
> Where fathom-line could never touch the ground,
> And pluck up drowned honour by the locks,
> So he that doth redeem her thence might wear
> Without corrival all her dignities:
> But out upon this half-fac'd fellowship!   (I.iii.199–206)

> Поверите ли, для стяжанья славы
> Я, кажется, взобрался б на луну
> И, не колеблясь, бросился б в пучину,
> Которой дна никто не достигал,
> Но только б быть единственным и первым.
> Я в жизни равенства не признаю.   (Р. 88)

(Will you believe that to gain glory I would climb up, so it seems, onto the moon, and without hesitating would throw myself into the deep, whose bottom no one has ever reached? But just to be first and foremost. I do not recognize equality in life.)

J. Dover Wilson comments on these lines, referring particularly to the phrase, "So he that doth redeem her thence might wear / Without corrival all her dignities":

The glory to be shared with others is not worth having. In a word, the honour of which he dreams is personal renown and nothing else; a conception which, for all its implications of bravery in battle and contempt for danger and death, is a purely selfish one.[28]

Pasternak's translation echoes such an interpretation. The very use of the word "slava" as a translation for "honour" in his text is suggestive of this, as it carries the meaning of "glory" or "renown," but no indication of adherence to a code of principles. (The Russian word "chest'," employed by Birukova in her translation,[29] is closer to the English word in this respect.)

Hotspur's ambition is made to seem empty through the changing or omitting of details which serve in the original to suggest the objective reality of honor. The original verbs indicate that honor is actually grasped and taken by force: "To pluck bright honour from the pale-fac'd moon," "And pluck up drowned honour by the locks." The phrase "dlia stiazhan'ia slavy" (for the gaining of glory), on the other hand, is an idiomatic one which indicates obtaining or getting honor, but not necessarily seizing it physically. In

28. Ibid., p. 70.
29. In the fourth volume of William Shakespeare, *Polnoe sobranie sochinenii v vos'mi tomakh* (Complete Works in Eight Volumes), ed. A. Anikst and A. Smirnov (Moscow: Iskusstvo, 1957–60).

translation, "honour" is no longer envisioned as being "bright," and the personification of "drowned honour" is left out altogether. Without the suggestion that "honour" is lying there to be seized, Hotspur's assertion of readiness to throw himself onto the moon or into the deep loses much of its point, and may seem merely ostentatious boasting.

In summing up his declaration by saying, "So he that doth redeem her thence might wear / Without corrival all her dignities," the original Hotspur reveals an undisguised ambition to be above anyone else. But the feminine personification of honor is maintained, and there is still a suggestion that "her dignities" are the reward for idealistically chivalric behavior. Pasternak's translation of these lines indicates only Hotspur's desire to be the first, to be on top, losing the original emphasis on the importance of the action of "redeeming" honor: "No tol'ko byt' edinstvennym i pervym" (But just to be first and foremost). The final statement of the original Hotspur indicates his unwillingness to compromise in his relationship with King Henry: "But out upon this half-fac'd fellowship!" There is at least a possible implication of principle behind his statement. That of Pasternak's Hotspur indicates simply a blatant desire to be above everyone else: "Ia v zhizni ravenstva ne priznaiu" (I do not recognize equality in life).

The ambition of Hotspur is ultimately shown to be a futile one. His cause is lost at the battle of Shrewsbury, he himself is slain by Prince Hal, and as a crowning irony, credit for his death is claimed by Sir John Falstaff, whose view of honor is the opposite of his own: "What is honour? A word. What is in that word honour? What is honour? Air. A trim reckoning!" (V.i.134–35). But Pasternak does not even give the magnificence and figurative substantia-

tion to Hotspur's presentation of his ideal, which could
cause one critic to write,

Logically we might feel that Hotspur's 'honour' was to be condemned; imaginatively, we shall attend rather to the striking
imagery by which . . . 'honour' is associated with an infinite
splendour of purpose.[30]

In his translation, Hotspur is presented as a more arrogant-
ly and emptily ambitious young man, lacking any real
purpose or goal; and whatever splendor or pathos he
possessed in the original work is largely lost. In this speech
and elsewhere, Pasternak fails to reproduce the brilliant
verbal fabrications through which the original character
gives substance to ideals which cannot be realized in actuality and events which are to some extent the product
of his own imagination.

Pasternak may not have intended to provide a disapproving portrayal of Hotspur or Falstaff—certainly he had
deep sympathies with the latter. But he achieved a relatively sober and unflattering effect by making them both
more "realistic," by not recapturing some of the imaginative play of the original language, and by curbing the
characters' ebullient power to defy, deny, transform, or
postulate their own reality. A certain heavy-handedness
and an emphasis on a base and often crude physical reality
may be evident as well in some passages from Pasternak's
Antony and Cleopatra. His translation of this play is no
less persistently and, on occasion, awkwardly "realistic"
than his other translations of Shakespeare, and it seems at
times as relentlessly earthbound. To cite a single example,
as Cleopatra and her attendants hoist the dying Antony up

30. G. Wilson Knight, *The Imperial Theme* (1931; rpt. London:
Methuen, 1954), p. 4.

into the monument where they have taken refuge, Cleopatra says,

> Here's sport indeed! How heavy weighs my lord!
> Our strength is all gone into heaviness,
> That makes the weight. Had I great Juno's power,
> The strong-wing'd Mercury should fetch thee up,
> And set thee by Jove's side. Yet come a little,
> Wishers were ever fools, O, come, come, come.
>   (IV.xv.32–37)

> Поднять тебя не шутка.
> Какой ты грузный! Вероятно, скорбь
> Былую силу превратила в тяжесть.
> О, если б власть Юноны, я б тебя
> Перенесла с Меркурием на крыльях
> К столу Юпитера. А ну еще.
> А ну еще. Всегда безумьем было
> Желать недостижимого. А ну,
> Еще чуть-чуть.   (Р. 521)

(It's no joke to raise you. How heavy you are! Probably, grief
has turned your former strength into weight. O, if I had the
power of Juno, I would bear you with Mercury on wings to the
table of Jupiter. Once more now. Once more now. It was always
madness to wish for the unattainable. Once more, just a little
further.)

In translation, the half-joking quality of the opening lines
("Here's sport indeed . . .") is lost, and Cleopatra seems
to be more seriously preoccupied with Antony's physical
weight ("It's no joke to raise you!"). Further, Pasternak has
substituted for "Yet come a little" the reiterated "A nu
esche. / A nu eshche" (Once more now. Once more now),
which obviously applies to the heaving up of the heavy
body, emphasizing the physical effort needed to raise it
up. In this context, Cleopatra's thought of flying with
Antony to the gods, of escaping the earthbound condition

of men, may seem even more futile: "It was always madness to wish for the unattainable."

But Pasternak's translation of this play may reflect the inconsistency in his "Notes" between the emphasis on the study of common, everyday reality as the very basis for art, and his attraction to the extraordinary and miraculous. The tendency to make imagery more concrete and earthy is not in evidence, for example, in Pasternak's translation of Enobarbus' description of Cleopatra in her barge on the Nile:

> The barge she sat in, like a burnish'd throne
> Burn'd on the water: the poop was beaten gold;
> Purple the sails, and so perfumed that
> The winds were love-sick with them; the oars were silver,
> Which to the tune of flutes kept stroke, and made
> The water which they beat to follow faster,
> As amorous of their strokes. For her own person,
> It beggar'd all description: she did lie
> In her pavilion—cloth of gold, of tissue—
> O'er-picturing that Venus where we see
> The fancy outwork nature. On each side her,
> Stood pretty dimpled boys, like smiling Cupids,
> With divers-colour'd fans, whose wind did seem
> To glow the delicate cheeks which they did cool,
> And what they undid did. (II.ii.191–205)

> Ее баркас горел в воде, как жар.
> Корма была из золота, а парус
> Из пурпура. Там ароматы жгли.
> И ветер замирал от восхищенья.
> Под звуки флейт приподнимались в лад
> Серебряные весла, и теченье
> Вдогонку музыке шумело вслед.
> Ее самой словами не опишешь.
> Она лежала в золотом шатре
> Стройней Венеры, а ведь и богиня
> Не подлинность, а сказка и мечта.

По сторонам у ней, как купидоны,
Стояли, с ямочками на щеках,
Смеющиеся дети с веерами,
От веянья которых пламенел
Ее румянец.   (P. 482–83)

(Her boat gleamed in the water, like embers. The poop was of
gold, and the sail of purple. There incense was being burned. And
the wind died away from rapture. To the sound of flutes, the
silver oars were raised in harmony, and the current came noisily
after in pursuit of the music. You cannot describe her own person
in words. She lay in a golden tent, more shapely than Venus, but
even the goddess is not the actuality, but tale and dream. By her
side, like cupids, there stood, with dimples in their cheeks, smiling children with fans, whose blowing enflamed her glowing
color.)

Pasternak here tends to make the imagery even less sub-
stantially concrete than that of Shakespeare. He removes
from the first sentence the simile "like a burnish'd throne,"
eliminating the play on "burn'd" and "burnish'd," and has
Enobarbus say instead that Cleopatra's barge gleamed
(literally "burned," "gorel") in the water "kak zhar" (like
embers, heat). There is no reference to a concrete object,
as in the original, but simply to a meeting of the elements
of fire and water.

Where Shakespeare describes the poop as being of
"beaten gold," clearly a material substance, Pasternak
refers simply to "zoloto" (gold): "Korma byla iz zolota"
(The poop was of gold). This could refer strictly to a color,
especially since the following phrase, parallel in its construction, does refer to a color: "a parus / Iz purpura" (and
the sail of purple). Pasternak's image is defined visually in
terms of contrasting areas of color, without further indication of concrete substance. (Cf. Donskoi's translation:
"Plamenela / Iz kovanogo zolota korma. / A purpurnye
byli parusa," The poop of beaten gold blazed, and the sails

were purple. The "gold" remains a definite substance, the "purple," an adjective serving to describe the sails.[31])

The most remarkable manifestation of this tendency of the translator comes in the description of Cleopatra herself, where the queen is suggested to resemble something beyond even the works of the imagination. Shakespeare writes that "she did lie / In her pavilion . . . / O'er-picturing that Venus where we see / The fancy outwork nature." He refers to her as a work of art herself, surpassing ("o'er-picturing") a painting or statue of a goddess, in which fancy has improved upon natural reality. Pasternak, however, manages to suggest a remarkable transformation. He first compares Cleopatra not to a picture but to the reality, the goddess herself:

> Она лежала в золотом шатре
> Стройней Венеры.

(She lay in a golden tent, more shapely than Venus.)

He then removes the goddess from the terms of comparison, "a ved' i boginia / Ne podlinnost'" (but even the goddess is not the actuality), and substitutes something from the realm of the imagination: "a skazka i mechta" (but tale and dream). Cleopatra is compared ultimately to something which can only be conceived of, existing beyond the realm of divinity itself.

If Pasternak's de-substantiation of the figure of Cleopatra here appears to contradict the tendency manifested in his treatment of Falstaff, it is perhaps because he accepted as a reality the potential, implied here, for a grandeur and beauty in a human being that surpasses anything the imagination can create or visualize.

31. Shakespeare, *Polnoe sobranie sochinenii*, VII, 241.

On turning away from the figure of Cleopatra herself, Pasternak reverts to the practice of making the original text more concretely specific, shortening the description of Cleopatra's waiting women and removing many of the details indicating their extreme delicacy and fairylike appearance. Instead of "a seeming mermaid steers," he writes "odna vela barkas" (one guided the boat); instead of "the silken tackle / Swell with the touches of those flower-soft hands," simply "v rukakh drugoi / Tak i snovali shelkovye snasti" (in the hands of another scurried the silken tackle). The tendency toward concrete realism reasserts itself, when he moves from the description of this figure who has surpassed the bounds of common reality.

Pasternak's affirmation that the ultimate grandeur of both Antony and Cleopatra is based on reality and not on subjective illusion comes out in his handling of some of the final passages of the play. Cleopatra's magnificent description of Antony, as he appeared to her after his death (V.ii. 76–100), opens with a slight but significant change in the translation. Shakespeare's Cleopatra begins, "I dreamt there was an Emperor Antony." The phrasing and use of the indefinite article indicate that this is not necessarily the Antony she had known, but a creature of new identity, resembling him. Pasternak's "Mne snilos', byl Antonii gosudar'" (I dreamed that Antony was emperor) indicates, on the contrary, that this is the same Antony, who has taken on a new title and grandeur. Pasternak's phrasing makes it less possible to consider him a creation of the imagination. (Cf. Donskoi's translation: "Mne snilos'—zhil kogda-to imperator / Po imeni Antonii," I dreamed there once lived an emperor by the name of Antony.[32])

32. Ibid., VII, 241.

Shakespeare undercuts the reality of the image Cleopatra has developed, as she asks Dolabella, "Think you there was, or might be such a man / As this I dreamt of?" and is answered, "Gentle madam, no." She immediately defends herself: "You lie up to the hearing of the gods," but this assertion is strongly compromised as she continues: "But if there be, or ever were one such, / It's past the size of dreaming." She maintains only the possibility of the reality of such a being, surpassing even the bounds of the imagination:

> nature wants stuff
> To vie strange forms with fancy, yet to imagine
> An Antony were nature's piece, 'gainst fancy,
> Condemning shadows quite.   (V.ii.97–100)

Pasternak takes all compromise and uncertainty from Cleopatra's statements. Instead of the subjunctive, "But if there be, or ever were, one such," she asserts emphatically, "On zhil, on zhil!" (He lived, he lived!).[33] In stating that his life has simply passed without leaving a trace, she alludes to the realm of insubstantial dreams: "No zhizn' ego sred' nas / Mel'knula bez sleda, kak snoviden'e" (But his life among us flashed by without a trace, like a dream). But her assertion that nature's creation of Antony surpassed the creations of the imagination is not in the subjunctive, as in the original, indicating a speculative possibility, but an indicative assertion of fact:

> Природе нехватает вещества,
> Чтобы с мечтой соперничать. Однако,

33. In the earliest edition of the translation (1944), this and the following line have a very different meaning: "No esli dazhe on i predstavim / To vse ravno, kak son, nedosiagaem" (But even if he can be imagined, he is all the same as unattainable as a dream).

> Придумавши Антония, она
> Воображенье перещеголяла.   (P. 525)

(Nature lacks substance to vie with dreams. But having invented
Antony, she surpassed the imagination.)

This is an affirmation of the ultimate possibility for
grandeur in a human being, which both characters approach by the end of the play, after fluctuating throughout
between the extremes of capriciousness and steadfastness,
self-indulgence and dedication, and earthiness and lofti-
ness of expression.

The most powerful affirmation in the play comes with
Cleopatra's final speech, expressing again the sense of
transition to some higher form of being, and the ultimate
triumph over death itself.

> Give me my robe, put on my crown, I have
> Immortal longings in me. Now no more
> The juice of Egypt's grape shall moist this lip.
> Yare, yare, good Iras; quick: methinks I hear
> Antony call. I see him rouse himself
> To praise my noble act. I hear him mock
> The luck of Caesar, which the gods give men
> To excuse their after wrath. Husband, I come:
> Now to that name, my courage prove my title!
> I am fire, and air; my other elements
> I give to baser life. So, have you done?
> Come then, and take the last warmth of my lips.
> Farewell, kind Charmian, Iras, long farewell.
>   (V.ii.279–91)

> Подай мне мантию, надень венец.
> Я вся объята жаждою бессмертья.
> Ах, больше этих губ не освежит
> Букет египетского винограда.
> Скорей, скорее, Ира! Мне пора.

Я чувствую, меня зовет Антоний.
Он просыпается, чтоб похвалить
Меня за доблесть. Он смеется. Боги,—
Он говорит,—шлют Цезарю успех,
Чтобы отнять его потом в возмездье.
Иду к тебе, супруг мой. Зваться так
Дает мне право беззаветность шага.
Я воздух и огонь. Другое все
Я оставляю праху. Вы готовы?
Вот губ моих последнее тепло.
Пора прощаться, Ира, Хармиана.   (P. 529)

(Give me my robe, put on my crown. My whole being is seized
by a thirst for immortality. Ah, the bouquet of the Egyptian grape
will no longer refresh these lips. Hurry, hurry, Iras! It is time. I
feel that Antony is calling me. He awakens to praise me for my
valor. He laughs. "The gods," he says, "send Caesar success, in
order to take it away later in revenge." I come to you, my husband. The selflessness of the step gives me the right to be called
thus. I am air and fire. All else I leave to the dust. Are you
ready? Here is the last warmth of my lips. It is time to bid farewell, Iras, Charmian.)

Cleopatra assumes the identity of a queen as she prepares
to die, putting aside sensual pleasures ("the juice of Egypt's
grape") for fulfillment of the more exalted side of her
nature ("I have / Immortal longings in me"). The suggestion of actual transmutation appears in her statement: "I
am fire, and air; my other elements / I give to baser life."
And the vision of Antony, awaiting her in another life,
provides the strongest affirmation of her scorn for this life
and for the power of death. In the original, Antony is
presented always through the senses of Cleopatra: "methinks I hear / Antony call. I see him rouse himself / . . .
I hear him mock . . ." In the translation he takes on a more
independent existence: "On prosypaetsia . . . On smeetsia

. . . On govorit . . ." (He awakens . . . He laughs . . . He says . . .). The possibility of subjective illusion on Cleopatra's part is lessened, the suggestion of the reality of the Antony she envisions intensified. A subtle change in the nature of Cleopatra's attitude, too, is to be seen in the substitution of "bezzavetnost' shaga" (the selflessness of the step) for "courage," as the quality which gives her the right now to look to Antony as her husband.

Although Pasternak often tends to bring Shakespeare's nobler, more refined, or exuberantly imaginative characters down to the level of common, unadorned everyday life, his translations do suggest as well his responsiveness to the possibility of transcendence and the realization of an ultimate potential in man for beauty, nobility, and self-sacrifice. In his translation of *Antony and Cleopatra* he has brought out that which ultimately makes the death of Cleopatra triumphant rather than tragic.

In conclusion, then, Pasternak's persistent "realism" affected his translations of Shakespeare's plays in a number of ways. His insistence that the translator use language natural to himself, that he attempt to convey "the impression of life" itself, is reflected in his own use of colloquial, idiomatic Russian, which helped him to individualize Shakespeare's characters and make them more natural and lifelike than had been common in Russian translations of the plays, but which also resulted in some marked distortions of the text. Characters tend to be russified and are occasionally brought jarringly down to earth. The speech of noblemen and aristocrats is often interlaced with expressions used by commoners. Intricate, elaborate, highly metaphorical poetry is simplified; euphuisms and other evidence of artifice, rhetorical or nonnatural forms of speech, are eliminated. Pasternak altered more than figures of speech and wordplay, however. He toned down in his translations elements which would make it possible to relate Falstaff, Hotspur, even Romeo, to the "over-reachers" of English Renaissance drama—their extravagant defiance of necessity, of ordinary human limitations, the exhilarating, though often short-lived, sense of being able to change, control, or reorder the world, reality itself, in order to gratify the needs and wishes of individual desire. Pasternak's "realistic" approach serves to alter the very tone and spirit of the original works; characters are made more mundane, though they often remain lifelike, energetic, or poignant. In his own essays and poetry, Pasternak envisioned Shakespeare as finding his inspiration as an artist in the stuff of common reality, the life of Elizabethan London, and this is reflected in his translations. Yet he sometimes managed to suggest, particularly in his translation of *Antony and Cleopatra*, the reality of the transcendent as well, an actual capacity for transformation in man, the possibility for realizing something extraordinary, a reality surpassing even the workings and the products of the imagination. If he often presented Shakespeare's characters as being bound to base matter and earthly necessity, he also suggests the possibility for their transmutation into something incorporeal, not subject to death or the passage of time.

III. The Style of the Translator

PASTERNAK's handling of verbal detail and formal structure in his translations of Shakespeare has already received attention in the first two sections of this study. Indeed any consideration of Pasternak's interpretation of the original works requires examination of details of style and linguistic usage which markedly alter, or sustain, the tone and meaning of individual passages. In addition to the obvious and much discussed matter of Pasternak's use of colloquial, idiomatic Russian, there has been reference so far to Pasternak's handling of Shakespeare's imagery, the simplification of the original language, the omission of classical references, the use of verbal and negative constructions, the effect of minor alterations in phrasing, or of changes in the tense or mood of verbs, the transformation of questions into declarative statements, and so forth. Such factors are often relatively unimportant taken by themselves, but they acquire significance when they recur and reappear as part of a broader pattern. Indeed, the very possibility of regarding translations as significant interpretations depends on their possessing a certain coherence and integrity, an internal structure of their own, patterns of recurrent verbal usage, images, allusions, and peculiarities of speech, which make it possible to regard deviations from the original text as other than chance aberrations.

In the two chapters of this final section, which will be devoted specifically to matters of form and style, I will not

attempt to summarize and synthesize all that has gone
before. My concern will be rather to explore two matters
which are crucial to the success and effectiveness of the
translations, but have so far been considered only in passing: first, Pasternak's handling of prosody, verse structure,
and patterns in sound; second, his response to the inescapable necessity of simplifying the complexities of the Shakespearean text, and his development of a clear and simple
poetic style which is far different from that of his own
chaotic, complex, turbulent, and elusive early verse. Pasternak's use of rhythm and sound is subtle, diverse, and
often remarkably expressive, one of the fundamental
strengths of his work as a poet-translator. And the classically simple, at times almost Pushkinian, style he employed allowed him to make a virtue of necessity, often
communicating with clarity and force some essential
aspects of the Shakespearean text, when he could not hope
to include all the details of the original. His handling of
placement, movement, or development in time and space
is particularly important and may indeed be crucial to the
effectiveness of his "classical" style as a translator.

PROSODY AND VERSE STRUCTURE

In his "Notes on Translations of Shakespeare's Tragedies,"
Boris Pasternak repeatedly emphasizes the expressive
power of sound, rhythm, musicality in verse—the sound
of the speech of different characters in *Hamlet*, the rhythm
of dialogue, the softness or musicality of entire scenes in
Romeo and Juliet and *King Lear*. At the same time he
shows no interest in examining the structure of the verse
or attempting to determine in any technical way the source
of the musicality which he found to be so important. At

one point he does comment on English versification in his "Notes of a Translator":

The possibilities of English metrics are inexhaustible. The mono-syllabic nature of the English language opens the richest possible scope for English style. The compression of the English sentence is the guarantee of its pithiness, and pithiness is the friend of musicality, since the music of a word is constituted not by its sound, but by the relationship between its sound and meaning. In this sense English versification is musical to the highest degree possible. (III, 184)

He is never more specific in discussing the crucial matter of the relationship between sound and meaning in poetry, and he completely rejects formal analysis as a means of examining and inquiring into the nature of the music of verse. In his "Autobiographical Sketch," he writes of Andrei Belyi's concern with poetics during the early 1900's:

He gave a course in the practical study of the Russian classical iamb and by the method of statistical calculation analyzed, together with his students, its rhythmic figures and variations. I did not attend the studies of the circle because I have always considered, as I do now, that the music of the word is not an acoustic phenomenon and does not consist of the euphony of vowels and consonants, taken separately, but of the relationship between the meaning of speech and its sound. (II, 25)

Despite his avowed lack of interest in the purely formal study of poetry, Pasternak demonstrates in his translations of Shakespeare's plays a great sensitivity to structure and formal detail. The translations probably owe much of their interest and effectiveness to the sound of the verse, and to Pasternak's manipulation of structural elements which can, in some instances, be analyzed and described quite specifically. He demonstrates great ingenuity and inventiveness in re-creating some of the effects of the original texts, and despite the liberties he takes, his translations are, in many respects, remarkably faithful. I should like to examine here some passages which demonstrate his resourcefulness as a translator, his sensitivity to the sound, structure, and meaning of the original verse, and, on occasion, his idiosyncrasies.

Like most Russian translators of Shakespeare's plays, Pasternak preserves Shakespeare's blank verse. (One of the few exceptions comes in I.iii of *Romeo and Juliet,* where he translates the Nurse's long and very earthy speech into prose.) Rhymed couplets appear in translation where they were in the original text, and Pasternak often handles them with grace and unobtrusiveness, as may be seen in the speech of the King of France to Cordelia in *King Lear* (I.i.250–61), cited earlier on page 92. In handling songs and lyrics in the plays, Pasternak is equally careful to follow the basic rhyme and metrical pattern of the original, though he retains some flexibility and departs in some respects from the verse form of the original. In IV.iii of *Othello,* for example, Desdemona sings the "willow" song, not actually written by Shakespeare, but adapted by him from a popular ballad to suit the purpose of his drama.

> The poor soul sat sighing, by a sycamore tree,
> > Sing all a green willow:
> Her hand on her bosom her head on her knee,
> > Sing willow, willow, willow.
> The fresh streams ran by her, and murmur'd her moans,
> > Sing willow, willow, willow.
> Her salt tears fell from her, which soften'd the stones; — . . .
> > Sing willow, willow, willow. (IV.iii.40–48)

> Несчастная крошка в слезах под кустом
> Сидела одна у обрыва.
> Затянемте ивушку, иву споем.
> Ох, ива, зеленая ива.
> У ног сиротинки плескался ручей.

Ох, ива, зеленая ива.
И камни смягчались от жалости к ней.
Ох, ива, зеленая ива.

(P. 349)

Typical of Pasternak's translations of the songs is his tendency to clarify the meter and make the verse more regularly syllabo-tonic. It is not uncommon in English for the number of syllables in a verse foot to vary freely,[1] and in a number of instances in these plays, a regular metrical pattern can hardly be distinguished in the English text at all. In the willow song, the meter is not immediately recognizable in the opening line or even the second one, though the latter might be regarded as basically iambic, with a trochee in the third foot.

> The poor soul sat sighing, by a sycamore tree,
> Sing all a green willow.

Only in the third line does a regular ternary meter establish itself, anapestic (following an initial iamb) or amphibrachic:

> Her hand on her bosom her head on her knee.

In Pasternak's translation, the pattern of syllabic stress makes the amphibrachic meter obvious from the first words of the poem:

> Neschastnaia kroshka v slezakh pod kustom.

And this meter is maintained regularly throughout. The original "Sing willow, willow, willow," which might be described as an amphibrach followed by two trochees, is

1. See V. M. Zhirmunskii's comments on English tonic verse in *Vvedenie v metriku* (Leningrad: "Academia," 1925), pp. 208–12.

replaced by a refrain consisting of three regular amphibrachs: "Ŏkh ĭvă, zelĕnaia ĭvă" (O willow, green willow).

Pasternak was obviously sensitive to other factors of
sound patterning besides rhyme and meter. The refrain
was clearly chosen for its mellifluousness: in the English,
there is the repeated pattern of /l/ and /w/; in the nine
syllables of the Russian phrase, there are only six consonants, five of them voiced continuants, /v/, /z/, /l/,
/n/, /v/. It might be pointed out, however, that the refrain has been subtly altered. In the original, the line is
obviously part of a song ("Sing willow, willow, willow"),
the "willow" reduced almost to the status of a meaningless
word, a set of sounds. The translation seems more like a
direct address, even an invocation, with the adjective
"zelĕnaia" helping to establish the substantive reality of
the "iva": "Okh, iva, zelĕnaia iva" (O willow, green willow). Pasternak's Desdemona may seem to be actually
addressing something in nature; and the suggestion of a
turning to the natural world in the face of death, which
comes out in Pasternak's treatment of the figures of Ophelia and Desdemona in his early poem "English Lessons"
("Uroki angliiskogo"), is perhaps reflected in this translation as well. This may seem particularly likely in view of
another alteration made by the translator. The original
song contains a suggestion of nature's response to the
woman's grief:

> The fresh streams ran by her, and murmur'd her moans.

Pasternak introduces a stronger and more direct suggestion
of a compassionate response in nature, in translating a
following line:

> Her salt tears fell from her, which soften'd the stones

I kamni smiagchalis' ot zhalosti k nei.

(And the stones softened out of pity for her.)

Pasternak's sensitivity to Shakespeare's Ophelia is borne out in his handling of her songs as well. One of her last ones obviously refers to Polonius' death:

> And will he not come again?
> And will he not come again?
>   No, no, he is dead,
>   Go to thy death-bed,
> He never will come again.
>
> His beard was as white as snow,
> All flaxen was his poll;
>   He is gone, he is gone,
>   And we cast away moan;
> God ha' mercy on his soul!   (IV.v.184–93)

> Неужто он не придет?
> Неужто он не придет?
> Нет, помер он
> И погребен,
> И за тобой черед.
> А были снежной белизны
> Его седин волнистых льны.
> Но помер он,
> И вот
> За упокой его души
> Молиться мы должны.   (P. 283)

Here, too, Pasternak has regularized the meter, making it more strictly iambic, except for the first two lines: "Neuzhto on ne pridet?" As in the original, the third and fourth lines in each verse are shorter than the others, generally two feet in length. And the rhyme scheme (AABBA; CDEED) is generally followed in the Russian, most strictly in the first verse (AABBA; CCBACC). But other changes occur. In the first verse of the translation, where Pasternak has shortened lines 3 and 4 from five to four syllables in length, he creates an almost childish sing-song effect,

> Net, pomer on
> I pogrebën,
> I za toboi cheröd

(No, he died and is buried, and your turn is next)

which stands in ironic contrast to the subject of death and implication of grief and may suggest a means of distancing the insupportable fact of loss. When Pasternak's Ophelia reaches this point again in the second verse, she suddenly breaks off in the middle of the fourth line. She had just been singing of her father's white hair, and then recalls "no pomer on, / I vot" (but he died / And so). The suddenly shortened line, the break in the pattern at this point obviously suggests that for a moment she can go no farther. Then she collects herself, and Pasternak provides two lines instead of just one in which she remembers that "we must pray for the peace of his soul": "Za upokoi ego dushi / Molit'sia my dolzhny."

Pasternak's use of sound to underline or emphasize a certain mood, tone of voice or other effect is characteristic and important. The three Witches in *Macbeth*, for instance, are vividly presented in Pasternak's translation, and sound plays some part in the effectiveness of their portrayal. In the third scene of the play, the first Witch reports to the other two:

> A sailor's wife had chestnuts in her lap,
> And mounch'd, and mounch'd, and mounch'd: "Give me,"
>   quoth I:—
> "Aroynt thee, witch!" the rump-fed ronyon cries . . .
>
> (I.iii.4–6)

Со шкипершей сидела.
У той каштанов полон был подол.
Сама знай щелк себе да щелк!
«Дай погрызу»,—я попросила.
А эта тварь как гаркнет: «Вон отсюда,
Проклятая карга!»

(P. 427)

Pasternak's "shchëlk" is an obviously onomatopoetic counterpart for the English "mounch'd," but the effectiveness of its use is perhaps as much a result of timing as of the sound of the word itself. In Iurii Korneev's translation of the play, the line reads, "Shchëlk, shchëlk, da shchëlk. Ia govoriu ei: 'dai-ka!'"[2] In Pasternak's version, the repetitions of "shchëlk" are further separated and probably more suggestive of the timing of a real action: "Sama znai shchëlk sebe da shchëlk."

The translator's handling of "'Aroynt thee, witch!' the rump-fed ronyon cries" is particularly interesting. One can hardly miss the effect of sound repetition in *"aroynt,"* *"rump,"* *"ron*yon," with their pattern of /r/ + low vowel + nasal continuant + (in two cases) unvoiced stop. The Russian is quite different, but striking in its own right: "A eta tvar' kak garknet: 'Von otsiuda, / Prokliataia karga!'" (But that creature suddenly barks out: "Get out of here, you damned hag!"). Here the dominant vowel is /a/, coupled primarily with the back consonantal stops /g/ and /k/, which help to produce a suggestion of gutteral harshness. The vehemence of the effect, the prominence given to this cluster of phonemes may be heightened by the metathesis achieved in the final words of the two phrases: *"gark*net," *"karg*a."

2. William Shakespeare, *Polnoe sobranie sochinenii v vos'mi tomakh* (Complete Works in Eight Volumes), ed. A. Anikst and A. Smirnov (Moscow: Iskusstvo, 1957–60), VII, 11.

Pasternak's ability to manipulate sound and verse patterns may be further pointed up by contrasting another passage from *Macbeth* in his translation and Korneev's. In lines 12–19 of IV.i, Shakespeare's second Witch names nine ingredients which she contributes to the cauldron:

> Fillet of a fenny snake,
> In the cauldron boil and bake;
> Eye of newt, and toe of frog,
> Wool of bat, and tongue of dog,
> Adder's fork, and blind-worm's sting,
> Lizard's leg, and howlet's wing,
> For a charm of powerful trouble,
> Like a hell-broth boil and bubble.

If one includes the toad mentioned in the first line, Korneev also manages to name nine ingredients, and he is able for three lines to parallel the structure of the original, balancing two phrases in each line ("eye of newt, and toe of frog"), something which Pasternak does not attempt at all:

> Вслед за жабой в чан живей
> Сыпьте жир болотных змей,
> Зев ехидны, клюв совиный,
> Глаз медянки, хвост ужиный,
> Шерсть кожана, зуб собачий
> Вместе с пястью лягушачьей,
> Чтоб для адских чар и ков
> Был у нас отвар готов.[3]

(Following the toad, more quickly into the cauldron
pour the fat of the marsh snakes,
pharynx of viper, owl's beak,
eye of grass-snake [medianka], grass-snake's [uzh's] tail,
wool of bat, dog's tooth
together with a frog's metacarpus,
so that, for hellish charms and snares
our broth would be ready.)

3. Ibid., p. 64.

But his translation nonetheless may seem stiff and clumsy in comparison with the original, or even with Pasternak's translation:

А потом—спина змеи
Без хвоста и чешуи,
Песья мокрая ноздря
С мордою нетопыря,
Лягушиное бедро
И совиное перо,
Ящериц помет и слизь,
В колдовской котел вались!   (Р. 449)

(And then—the spine of a snake
without tail or scales,
the moist nostril of a dog
with the muzzle of a bat,
frog's thigh
and owl's feather,
lizards' dung and slime,
roll into the witches' cauldron!)

The necessity for coupling two nouns with modifiers in a single line leaves much of Korneev's passage cramped and inflexible, his lines tending to fall into a monotonous, heavily accented rhythm:

Zév ĕkhídnў, | klíuv sŏvínyĭ,
Gláz mĕdiánkĭ, | khvóst uzhínyĭ

In the original text, the syntactic pause comes after the first three syllables in most lines:

Éye ŏf néwt, | ănd tóe ŏf fróg,
Wóol ŏf bát, | ănd tóngue ŏf dóg.

The line is only seven syllables long; the two phrases in each line are not even in length, and both end with an

accented syllable, in effect on an upbeat. Korneev, however, is forced to use all eight syllables of the trochaic
tetrameter, the phrases in his lines are exactly even, and
both end on an unaccented syllable. There is a heavy
regularity about them. In contrast, Pasternak, like Shakespeare, employs a seven-syllable trochaic line, ending invariably on an accented syllable. He reduces the number
of ingredients for the cauldron from nine to six, making
no attempt to couple two phrases in a single line. There
are no such marked caesuras or syntactic pauses as in
Korneev's translation; those which may be found occur
invariably, as in Shakespeare's text, after the third syllable,
which is always accented:

$$\overset{\smile}{A} \overset{\smile}{po}\overset{/}{tom} \quad \Big| \quad -\overset{\smile}{spi}\overset{/}{na} \overset{\smile}{zme}\overset{/}{i}$$

and possibly:

$$\overset{(/)}{Bez} \overset{\smile}{khvo}\overset{/}{sta} \quad \Big| \quad \overset{\smile}{i} \overset{\smile}{che}\overset{\smile}{shu}\overset{/}{i}, \ldots$$
$$\overset{\smile}{Ia}\overset{\smile}{shche}\overset{/}{rits} \quad \Big| \quad \overset{\smile}{po}\overset{/}{met} \overset{\smile}{i} \overset{\smile}{sli}\overset{/}{z}'.$$

The line is more fluent, perhaps more vigorous than Korneev's, and in this respect comparable to the original.

The weightiness of the rhythm and the general harshness
of the sound in Korneev's translation are accentuated by
his frequent use of such consonants as /ž/, /z/, /č/, and
/x/, as in the first line,

Vsled za zhaboi v chan zhivei.

While this might seem appropriate for a witch's incanta-
tion, it does not really reflect the texture of the original.
Although there are more consonantal sounds in the Shakespearean original (about fourteen per line, as compared
to fewer than twelve per line in Korneev), those consonants mentioned above, common in Korneev's translation,

have few or no equivalents in the original (only four or
five /z/ sounds and one /č/ in lines 5–7), and the effect in
the English text is lighter, more fluent. In the opening line,
for instance, the dominant vowels are the unvoiced /f/
and the resonants /l/ and /n/: "Fillet of a fenny snake."
Pasternak used even fewer consonants than Korneev,
slightly over eight per line, and achieved an effect perhaps
closer to that of the original. He avoided the /ž/ altogether
(there are five in Korneev); he used only one sounded
/z/ (as opposed to four in Korneev); only one /x/ (three
in Korneev); only one /č/ (four in Korneev). The fluidity
of Pasternak's translation is further enhanced by his use
of elementary devices for internal rhyme and assonance,
such as the pattern of feminine endings in "pĕs'iá mokráiă
nŏzdría." The repetition of the /o/ sound in the first two
accented syllables helps to establish an even more consistent vowel pattern in the line. Similarly, in the lines "lia-
gushinoe bedro / I sovinoe pero" (frog's thigh and owl's
feather), there is not only a two-syllable repetition of
vowels at the line-ending, but an internal, three-syllable
repetition of a neuter adjectival ending, in the same position in the two lines.

                    _ _ ino-e bedro
                    _ _ ino-e pero

There is a vocalic correspondence in five out of seven
syllables.

   Another factor contributing to the stiffness of effect in
Korneev's text is his tendency to be generically and ana-
tomically specific in naming the animals and parts of
bodies which go into the cauldron: "ekhidna" (echidna,
or viper), "medianka" and "uzh" (two varieties of grass
snake), "zev" (pharynx), "piast'" (metacarpus). Pasternak

sticks to more commonplace terms and items, more easily identifiable and more horrifying when detached from their normal contexts—as the "pës'ia mokraia nozdria" (moist nostril of a dog). Although he has taken greater liberties than Korneev in some respects, his version of the passage is vigorous and effective and demonstrates considerable sensitivity to the original.

The sustained ingenuity and resourcefulness of Pasternak's handling of elements of verse are evident throughout his translations of the songs of Edgar and the Fool in *King Lear*. Part of the effectiveness of his versions of the songs comes from the fact that they are so thoroughly grounded in Russian idiom that they scarcely seem translations from a foreign language. This subtle russification extends sometimes even to verse form. In playing the role of Poor Tom, Edgar continually brings in snatches of English ballads and verse, such as

> Pillicock sat on Pillicock hill:
> Alow, alow, loo, loo! (III.iv.76–77)

Pasternak places this in a form more suggestive of a Russian folk ballad, with a line exactly repeated, except for one element in it:

> Сидел на кочке Пилликок,
> Сидел на бугорке. (P. 395)

(Pillicock sat on a hummock, he sat on a little knoll.)

At the end of the same scene, Edgar brings in some fragments from an old ballad:

> *Child Rowland to the dark tower came,*
> His word was still: *Fie, foh, and fum,*
> *I smell the blood of a British man.*
> (III.iv.186–88)

Pasternak maintains the absurdly disrupted effect caused by giving Child Rowland the words of the giant, through a juxtaposition of two jarringly different styles in his translation.

> Наехал на чёрную башню Роланд,
> А великан как ахнет:
> «Британской кровью пахнет».   (P. 396)

(Roland rode up to the black tower. And the giant suddenly exclaims: "I smell British blood.")

The original English is difficult to scan satisfactorily, but probably reads best as iambic, with minor variations: "Child Rówland tŏ thĕ dárk tówĕr cáme," etc. Pasternak's first line is in regular amphibrachs, four feet in length: "Năékhăl nă chërnŭiŭ báshnĭu Rŏlánd" (Roland rode up to the black tower). The movement of the line is graceful and fluent; it is composed primarily of continuants, with the resonant /n/ appearing most often. The following line marks an abrupt change, as the poet switches to iambic trimeter:

> Ă vĕlíkăn kák ákhnĕt,
> "Brĭtánskŏi krŏv'íu pákhnĕt."

(And the giant suddenly exclaims: "I smell British blood.")

A jerkiness of effect is created not simply by using a shorter foot and shorter line, but by the close repetition of dorsal stops and spirants in "velikan *kak akh*net," which tend to break up the rhythm of the line. Further, there is a change in tone which comes with the abrupt switch into a more colloquial vocabulary and phrasing, with "kak akhnet."

Pasternak is not drawing upon a familiar literary tradition here, as Shakespeare was, and the effect of his translation comes largely through an abrupt change in sound patterns and diction.

Another sudden change in rhythm and phrasing is used by both Shakespeare and Pasternak in one exchange between Edgar and the Fool in III.vi. Edgar begins the first line of a sentimental ballad by William Birche and is cut off by the Fool, who completes the verse with an unceremonious parody.

> *Edgar*: Come o'er the bourn, Bessy, to me, —
> *Fool*:   Her boat hath a leak,
>   And she must not speak;
>   Why she dares not come over to thee!
>
> (III.vi.26–29)

> *Эдгар*: Плыви ко мне, Бесси, через ручей.
> *Шут*: Но есть в лодчонке течь.
>   Завесть об этом речь
>   Нет смелости у ней.   (Pp. 397–98)

(*Edgar*: Sail to me, Bessy, across the stream.
Fool: But there's a leak in her boat. She doesn't have the nerve to bring it up.)

The English verse varies freely between iambs and anapests with perhaps one trochee in the opening line; the first line consists of four feet, the second and third are shortened to two, the fourth line lengthened to three:

$$\cup / \cup / \ / \cup \cup /$$
$$\cup / \cup \cup /$$
$$\cup / \cup \cup /$$
$$\cup \cup / \cup \cup / \cup \cup /$$

The sharpness of the transition in line length is heightened by the fact that the accented syllables in the first and last lines are followed by continuants, or are vowel-final (o'*er*, Be*ssy*, m*e*, da*res*, ov*er*, th*ee*), creating a fluent effect, while those in the second and third line are followed by stops in three out of four cases (boa*t*, lea*k*, spea*k*), suddenly abrupt and brisk by comparison. The change emphasizes the contrast between the sentimentality of the opening line and the flippant suggestiveness of the following ones.

In Pasternak's translation, the first line is in slightly irregular meter, perhaps also varying between iambs and anapests; but the last three lines are made into regular iambs, and the length of the line shortened from four to three feet, creating a comparable effect of sudden transition.

$$\cup/\cup\cup/\cup/\cup\cup/$$
$$\cup/\cup/\cup/$$
$$\cup/\cup/\cup/$$
$$\cup/\cup\cup\cup/$$

In other such passages in *King Lear*, the effectiveness of the translation comes largely through the patterning in sound. In III.iv, Edgar repeats a variant on a snatch of song:

> Through the sharp hawthorn blow the winds.   (45–46)

> Still through the hawthorn blows the cold wind.
>
>   (99–100)

This is translated consistently by Pasternak as,

> V ternovnike severnyi veter svistit.   (Pp. 394–95)

(The north wind whistles in the blackthorn bush.)

The accented vowels here are /o/, /e/, /e/, /i/, representing an unbroken rise in pitch. The unaccented vowels are all either /e/ or /i/, fairly high in pitch. The increasing use of the spirants /v/ and especially /s/ throughout the line also reinforce the effect of rising pitch, and perhaps of a whistling sound, which might be considered onomato-poetic.

Many of the lines sung by the Fool are evidently taken from old songs, and the relentless, but oblique, reference to Lear's foolishness in giving away his kingdom, through this indirect medium, serves to establish the peculiar mocking quality of the Fool. Like other Russian translators of Shakespeare, Pasternak was forced to condense and simplify the original Shakespearean text, and he sometimes points up sharply and directly the meaning of the verse, not incorporating all the original detail, or attempting to maintain the flavor of the song or the original indirectness of the jibe. This is to be seen, for example, in another song from the first act:

> Fools had ne'er less grace in a year;
> > For wise men are grown foppish,
> And know not how their wits to wear,
> > Their manners are so apish.   (I.iv.173–76)

> Приходит дуракам капут,
> Не спрос на них сегодня.
> Разумные себя ведут
> Безумных сумасбродней.   (P. 375)

In Shakespeare's English, the word "foppish" can evidently mean "foolish" in general, but the following lines indicate a foolishness in appearance, rather than in mind (as in their failure "to wear" their wits, and the "apishness" of their "manners"), which might encourage reading into the word its present connotations. The application of the passage to Lear is obvious, but comparatively indirect. In Pasternak's simple and compressed translation, on the other hand, the contrast between foolishness and wisdom is made through a play on the morpheme "um" (mind, wit, intellect) in words of contradictory meaning: wise men ("razumnye") are acting more madly ("sumasbrodnei") than fools ("bezumnykh"). The application is much broader, more closely connected with conceptual meaning. This verse has none of the obliqueness of the original song.

The effectiveness of Pasternak's translations of Shakespeare's works results in large measure from his extraordinary agility in manipulating a complex of linguistic elements to rhythmical, tonal, and dramatic effect. He manifests a remarkable sensitivity to uses of sound in language in his manipulation of vocalic and consonantal phonemes to support rhythmic patterns, to suggest a tone of voice or intonation. Equally remarkable is his ability not only to re-create a variety of metrical patterns and to achieve a sustained grace and mellifluousness in verse movement, but also to introduce rhythmical shifts and contrasts, which serve to stress the play of ironic and dramatic alterations in tone within the text. He is capable of producing onomatopoetic effects in some instances, but this represents only a minor part of his achievement in the expressive use of sound in poetry.

PASTERNAK'S CLASSICAL STYLE

IN COMMENTING on Shakespeare's use of metaphorical language in his "Notes on Translations of Shakespeare's Tragedies," Pasternak compared the dramatist to some of the great artists of Western Europe:

The stormy vitality of the brush of Rembrandt, Michelangelo and Titian is not the fruit of their considered choice. Possessed by an insatiable thirst to paint the entire universe, they had no time to paint any other way. (III, 194)

Pasternak recognized the "inward and outward chaos" of Shakespeare's blank verse and added that "the power of Shakespeare's poetry consists in its quality of sketchiness, powerful, unrestrained, and scattered about in disorder" (III, 195). The unrestrained and often chaotic turbulence of Pasternak's own early verse indicates a youthful affinity for the manner of creative expression described here, as suggested by Donald Davie in analyzing Pasternak's poem on the death of Mayakovsky in 1930:

The flow of association, from urban scenes to nursery-rhyme to geological to sporting metaphors and back to the geological volcanic metaphor of Etna in the last lines, is not, as in surrealist writing, the uncontrolled association of the unconscious in dreams. It may seem so, but this is an illusion brought about by the copiousness of the poet's invention, the rapidity and impetuosity of his transitions. It is the quality we associate with Shakespeare above all, and in a later poet such as Dryden only when we detect a Shakespearean note in him.[1]

Yet Pasternak's translations of Shakespeare's plays are relatively lucid, disciplined, controlled, betraying a closer affinity to the simpler, more classical style of Pasternak's later poetry. It is perhaps not wholly coincidental that the year 1940, which Pasternak himself repeatedly designated as the turning point in his stylistic development, was the year in which the first of his Shakespearean translations appeared in print. As Olga R. Hughes puts it, his translations may have "served as a laboratory of his new style."[2] There is some indication that Pasternak, whose

1. "Introduction" to *Pasternak*, ed. Donald Davie and Angela Livingstone (London: Macmillan, 1969), p. 28.
2. *The Poetic World of Boris Pasternak* (Princeton: Princeton University Press, 1974), p. 68.

own early writings were extremely difficult to grasp and comprehend, was making these translations with the needs of the theater and the general reading public in mind. In the early 1940s he wrote that "if fate is willing, I will occupy myself with a translation of *Antony and Cleopatra*, for a production planned by the Moscow Art Theater."[3] And at the beginning of his "Notes," he stated: "The demand of theaters and readers for simple, easily read translations is great and never ceases" (III, 193). Pasternak was not always pleased by the results of his simplification and clarification of the original Shakespearean texts. He wrote to Morozov about his *King Lear* in 1947:

The thought distresses, *kills* me that from that *distance* from which I reproduce Shakespeare ([the distance] is obligatory in my understanding), I completely *lay him bare*.[4]

In some instances he feels that the text "gains a great deal from this." "All that is called the content of the drama" is made more clear; "but for the less successful of his scenes, schematic, stilted, or rhetorical, it would be better if I translated them less clearly and comprehensibly."

However ambivalent his feelings were about doing so, Pasternak fairly consistently clarified obscure references and confusing ambiguities, and simplified involved and complicated syntactic structures in translating Shakespeare's plays. This undoubtedly resulted in much oversimplification or elimination of detail, but it would be virtually impossible to capture the full richness and complexity of the original Shakespearean text without eliminating or distorting any detail, nuance, or overtone. The

3. *Sochineniia*, III, 193. This is from "Moi novye perevody" (My New Translations), which first appeared in *Ogonek*, No. 47 (1942), p. 13.

4. *Masterstvo perevoda 1969* (Moscow: Sovetskii pisatel', 1970), p. 362.

problem is common to all translators of Shakespeare. Both English and Russian critics have noted with regret the almost inevitable impoverishment of Shakespeare's works at the hands of even the best of translators.[5] Russian translators of English poetry have always faced the additional problem of translating from a language which is largely monosyllabic into one which is highly inflected, constituted largely of polysyllabic words. E. Etkind cites a study which calculates the average length of English words as being 1.22 syllables, Russian words, 2.24 syllables.[6] Pasternak himself wrote of the "enviably laconic nature of English speech, which allows one to include an entire expression, consisting of two or more mutually contrasting clauses in a single English iamb."[7] If Russian translators attempt a close, literal translation, they run the risk of lengthening Shakespeare's plays inordinately, as has occurred on occasion.[8] If, on the other hand, they choose to

5. See for instance Iu. Gavruk, "Nuzhny li novye perevody Shekspira?" (Are New Translations of Shakespeare Necessary?), in *Masterstvo perevoda 1966* (Moscow: Sovetskii pisatel', 1968), pp. 93–104; and Reuben A. Brower, "Poetic and Dramatic Structures in Versions and Translations of Shakespeare," in *Poetics*, ed. D. Davie, K. Wyka, R. Jakobson, et al. (The Hague: Mouton, 1961), pp. 655–74.

6. *Poeziia i perevod* (Poetry and Translation) Moscow–Leningrad: Sovetskii pisatel', 1963), pp. 263–64.

7. "Notes on Translations of Shakespeare's Tragedies," *Sochineniia*, III, 196.

8. Mikhail Morozov, for instance, criticizes Peter Weinberg's scrupulously close translation of *Othello* into Russian in the mid-nineteenth century as being "much too long, much longer than the original; longer in fact by one fifth." And he points up that "this slows down the tempo of the action" (*Shakespeare on the Soviet Stage*, trans. David Magarshack [London: Soviet News, 1947], p. 19). The prominent critic and translator V. Levik comments in his essay "On Exactness and Faithfulness" ("O tochnosti i vernosti") that "one of the Russian translations of *Othello* is almost 2000 lines, that is nearly 60 per cent longer than the Shakespearean original" (*Masterstvo perevoda 1959* [Moscow: Sovetskii pisatel', 1959], p. 93).

make an equilinear translation, as Pasternak did, some of the original phrases may be cut, abbreviated, or telescoped to the point of incomprehensibility, a problem which Pasternak did not succeed in avoiding altogether.[9]

But simplicity of style in translation may have some virtues, despite the shortcomings, the textual distortions and losses which are all too readily evident. The most obvious advantage is clarity, particularly valuable in a work meant for stage presentation. Furthermore, while Pasternak could not and did not try to reproduce every detail of the original text, his translations were often characterized by a pithiness and aphoristic compactness and denseness. In reviewing Pasternak's translation of *Hamlet*, N. Vil'iam-Vil'mont commented that while "people talk about the greater brevity of the English language as compared with Russian . . . the poetic force of Pasternak's *Hamlet* showed already in the fact that his language is organically laconic . . . Reading his *Hamlet*, you are struck by the inexhaustible resources of *Russian laconicism.*"[10] Since Russian words are longer than English ones, a literal, word-for-word translation would be prohibitively

9. Iu. Gavruk points up some of the problems in the text of Pasternak's *Hamlet* in his essay "Nuzhen li novyi perevod *Gamleta* na russkii iazyk?" (Is a New Translation of *Hamlet* Needed in Russian?), in *Masterstvo perevoda 1966* (Moscow: Sovetskii pisatel', 1968), pp. 128–33. K. I. Chukovsky's works on translation contain a sharp and extensive criticism of the equilinear translations of his contemporaries and of their lone predecessor in the nineteenth century, A. A. Fet. He cites the telegraphic brevity and choppiness of expression characteristic of such translations, the truncated metaphors, and the elimination of crucial adjectives and epithets, references to gesture, terms of courtliness, etc. The culminating flaw is, of course, sheer incomprehensibility, resulting from one or a combination of the above factors. See *Vysokoe iskusstvo* (The High Art) (Moscow: Iskusstvo, 1964), pp. 169–201.

10. "*Gamlet* v perevode Borisa Pasternaka," *Internatsional'naia literatura*, No. 7–8 (1940), p. 290.

long and probably insufferably dull. But with their inflected endings and sometimes complex, multiple prefixes, single words in Russian often contain more information, highly condensed, than do their English counterparts, and some common grammatical constructions can be used to create effects not easily duplicated in English. Even in his translations, Pasternak could display the mastery of the resources of his own language which, as has been pointed out by Donald Davie, makes his own poetry so difficult to translate from Russian into English:

Five polysyllabic words can be ranged in two lines of Pasternak as massively as blocks of masonry—an effect available only in a highly inflected language, something that English, with its clutter of prepositions and participles, can hardly attain to.[11]

Within the simpler context of the translation, crucial words, phrases, or images may emerge very prominently and dramatically. And where these are essential to some aspect of psychological or thematic development, the translator may be able to achieve a remarkable faithfulness to the Shakespearean original, within the limits of a simpler stylistic framework. As Henry Gifford puts it,

The general effect of Pasternak's translations from Shakespeare is to thin out the original, so that it becomes an autumn wood with fewer leaves and with the outlines showing more clearly. . . . The verse Pasternak writes for his Shakespeare translations is taut and lucid; the sense has been winnowed out from the abundance of Shakespeare.[12]

As demonstrated earlier, the sense of the original is sometimes altered—above all when Shakespeare's work stands in conflict with Pasternak's own concepts and attitudes

11. Davie, "Introduction" to *Pasternak*, p. 17.
12. *Pasternak* (Cambridge: Cambridge University Press, 1977), p. 151.

toward human nature and imaginative creativity. But Pasternak reveals an ability at times to penetrate to the very essence of the original, particularly in bringing out the most elemental of contrasts, of visual, spatial, or temporal relationships. His handling of the latter is a major factor in the effectiveness of his terse and economical, "classical" style, and will be considered at length in this chapter.

Pasternak's tendency to simplify and clarify the original Shakespearean text might be illustrated by almost any passage, chosen at random, such as his version of III.i of *Antony and Cleopatra*, a minor scene in which Antony's officer Ventidius appears after a victory in Syria:

> *Ventidius*: Now, darting Parthia, art thou struck, and now
>   Pleas'd fortune does of Marcus Crassus' death
>   Make me revenger. Bear the king's son's body
>   Before our army. Thy Pacorus, Orodes,
>   Pays this for Marcus Crassus.
> *Silius*:   Noble Ventidius,
>   Whilst yet with Parthian blood thy sword is warm,
>   The fugitive Parthians follow. Spur through Media,
>   Mesopotamia, and the shelters whither
>   The routed fly. So thy grand captain Antony
>   Shall set thee on triumphant chariots, and
>   Put garlands on thy head.
> *Ventidius*:   O Silius, Silius,
>   I have done enough. A lower place, note well,
>   May make too great an act. For learn this, Silius;
>   Better to leave undone, than by our deed
>   Acquire too high a fame, when him we serve's away.
>   Caesar and Antony have ever won
>   More in their officer than person: Sossius,
>   One of my place in Syria, his lieutenant,
>   For quick accumulation of renown,
>   Which he achiev'd by the minute, lost his favour.
>   Who does i' the wars more than his captain can,

Becomes his captain's captain: and ambition,
The soldier's virtue, rather makes choice of loss,
Than gain which darkens him.
I could do more to do Antonius good,
But 'twould offend him. And in his offence
Should my performance perish. (III.i.1–27)

Вентидий: Стрелою в самое тебя попали,
О Парфия, метательница стрел![13]
Я избран мстить за гибель Марка Красса.
Убитого царевича нести
Перед войсками. Видишь, жизнью сына
Ты заплатил за Красса, царь парфян.

Силий: Пока твой меч дымится вражьей кровью,
Гони парфян. Преследуй беглецов,
Куда бы ни укрылись. Твой начальник,
Антоний, наградит тебя венком
И въездом на победной колеснице.

Вентидий: Я сделал много, Силий. Через край
Усердствовать не должен подчиненный.
Теряться перед старшими в тени
Умней, чем выделяться выше меры.
Антоний, как и Цезарь брали верх
Руками близких больше, чем своими.
Предшественник мой, Соссий, потерял
Его приязнь своей чрезмерной славой.
В войне затмить начальство—значит стать
Начальником начальника. Солдатом
Владеет честолюбье. Иногда
Урон милей невыгодной победы.
Я мог легко бы удесятерить
Завоеванья, но боюсь обидеть
Антония и этим погубить
Плоды стараний. (Pp. 493–94)

(*Ventidius*: We have struck you like a dart, o Parthia, hurler of
darts! I have been chosen to revenge the death of Marcus

13. In the 1944 edition, the opening line of the English text is translated by a single line: "Nu, Parfiia, teper' ty srazhena" (Well, Parthia,
now you have been struck down).

Crassus. To bear the murdered tsarevich before the troops. You see, king of the Parthians, you have paid for Crassus with the life of your son.

Silius: While your sword smokes with enemy blood, pursue the Parthians. Hunt down the fugitives, wherever they have hidden. Your superior, Antony, will reward you with a garland and an entry on a triumphal chariot.

Ventidius: I have done much, Silius. The subordinate should not be excessively zealous. To lose oneself in the shade before one's elders is wiser than to stand out inordinately. Antony has gained supremacy, as has Caesar, by the hands of his intimates more than by his own. My predecessor, Sossius, lost his favor through his own excessive glory. To eclipse one's commander in war means to become one's commander's commander. The soldier is ruled by ambition. Sometimes loss is sweeter than unprofitable victory. I could easily increase my conquests tenfold, but I am afraid of offending Antony and by that ruining the fruits of my endeavors.)

Throughout the translation there is an elucidation or elimination of obscure references. In line 4, "Orodes" and "Pacorus" are referred to as "tsar' parfian" (king of the Parthians) and "syn" (his son) rather than by name. The reference to "pleas'd fortune," a figure not as familiar to Pasternak's Russian audience as to one in Elizabethan England, is eliminated. The relatively obscure opening line, "Now, darting Parthia, art thou struck," is expanded and elucidated. "Darting Parthia" becomes "Parfiia, metatel'nitsa strel" (Parthia, hurler of darts). And the irony of the fact that Parthia itself has now been "struck," defeated by Ventidius' army, is clarified by referring to the army itself as "strela" (a dart, arrow):

> Стрелою в самое тебя попали,
> О Парфия, метательница стрел!

(We have struck you like a dart, o Parthia, hurler of darts!)

Also of importance in simplifying sentence structure is the reversal of syntactic inversions, as in the line,

> and now
> Pleas'd fortune does of Marcus Crassus' death
> Make me revenger

which becomes, "Ia izbran mstit' za gibel' Marka Krassa" (I have been chosen to revenge the death of Marcus Crassus). Similarly, in another long sentence in the original, the verb is withheld to the very end:

> Sossius,
> One of my place in Syria, his lieutenant,
> For quick accumulation of renown,
> Which he achiev'd by the minute, lost his favour.

This is translated:

> Предшественник мой, Соссий, потерял
> Его приязнь своей чрезмерной славой.

(My predecessor, Sossius, lost his favor, through his own excessive glory.)

A stronger balance in phrasing is also to be found in the translation. In lines 4–5 of the original, Ventidius gives the command: "Bear the king's son's body / Before our army." Pasternak has changed the verb to an infinitive, "nesti" (to bear), and the phrase becomes a second complement to the participle in the preceding sentence:

> Я избран мстить за гибель Марка Красса.
> Убитого царевича нести
> Перед войсками.

(I have been chosen to revenge the death of Marcus Crassus. To bear the murdered tsarevich before the troops.)

There is often a balance in form within the phrases:

> Теряться . . .
> Умней, чем выделяться . . .

(To lose oneself . . . is wiser than to stand out . . .)

> . . . брали верх
> Руками близких больше, чем своими.

(. . . gained supremacy by the hands of their intimates, more than by their own.)

Further, there is a breaking down of complex syntactic constructions into smaller units, as in

> and ambition,
> The soldier's virtue, rather makes choice of loss,
> Than gain which darkens him.

This is changed to two sentences:

> Солдатом
> Владеет честолюбье. Иногда
> Урон милей невыгодной победы.

(The soldier is ruled by ambition. Sometimes loss is sweeter than unprofitable victory.)

Finally, the entire second speech of Ventidius is constructed around a set of verbal contradictions and paradoxes, constituted by opposing phrases containing words of directly contradictory or of ironically similar meaning: "lower" / "great"; "undone" / "deed"; "captain" / "captain"; "loss" / "gain"; "offend" / "offence." In all but one case, Pasternak has reduced these to simple, direct statements. The opening line, for example, "A lower place, note well, / May make too great an act," is simplified to "cherez krai / Userdstvovat' ne dolzhen podchinennyi" (the subordinate should not be excessively zealous). Only the simplest word play, based on repetition of the same word or morpheme, is retained. The original "Who does i' the wars more than his captain can, / Becomes his captain's captain" is translated directly as "V voine zatmit' nachal'stvo—znachit stat' / Nachal'nikom nachal'nika" (to outshine one's commander in war—means to become one's commander's commander).

Something has obviously been lost. Shakespeare's more sophisticated Ventidius is aware of the paradoxical complexities of a world in which apparent gain turns to loss, and a man may be offended by another's attempt to enhance his greatness. This does not come through in translation, though in this exchange between two military commanders, clarity may be appreciated and a straightforward manner of speaking appropriate. Some might even prefer the relatively graceful translation, in which obscure allusions, syntactic complexities, inversions, and turbid paradoxes have been removed or simplified, and impediments to comprehension and the sense of movement within the passage have been reduced.

Pasternak's tendency to simplify has both advantages and disadvantages, and sometimes both are evident within a single passage. At the beginning of I.vii of *Macbeth*, for instance, Macbeth considers the prospect of Duncan's assassination:

> If it were done, when 'tis done, then 'twere well
> It were done quickly: if th' assassination
> Could trammel up the consequence, and catch
> With his surcease success; that but this blow
> Might be the be-all and the end-all—here,
> But here, upon this bank and shoal of time,
> We'd jump the life to come. (I.vii.1–7)

> Добро б удар, и делу бы конец,
> И с плеч долой! Минуты бы не медлил.

> Когда б вся трудность заключалась в том,
> Чтоб скрыть следы и чтоб достичь удачи,
> Я б здесь, на этой отмели времен,
> Пожертвовал загробным воздаяньем.   (P. 433)

(It would be good if there were a blow, and an end to the matter, and this were off my shoulders! I wouldn't hesitate a minute. If all the difficulty lay in hiding my tracks and attaining success, I would right here, on this bank of time, sacrifice any recompense beyond the grave.)

Macbeth expresses his apprehension that anxiety about the deed would not end with its completion, but would extend into the future, that retribution would come not merely in a future life beyond the grave, but in the future on earth. His statements, in the original, are based upon a paradox, the wish that an action might carry within itself the negation of its own consequences. His lines are turbid to the point of incomprehensibility, but perhaps because of this convey some sense of his agonized tension and mental turmoil at this moment. This is lost in Pasternak's clarified presentation, where the terms of the paradox are eliminated. Pasternak has brought the tone of the passage down to earth by syntactic simplification and colloquial usage. His Macbeth wishes this burden to be removed from his shoulders ("s plech doloi") or that his problem might lie simply in covering the traces of his crime ("chtob skryt' sledy"). He notes that if all would go as he wished, "minuty by ne medlil" (I wouldn't hesitate a minute). The translation may seem, by comparison with the original, overly simple and pedestrian. But there is a striking image which emerges in the fifth line:

> Я б здесь, на этой отмели времен,
> Пожертвовал загробным воздаяньем.

(I would right here, on this bank of time, sacrifice any recompense beyond the grave.)

The translation is quite direct, but the very change in the surrounding textual framework, the replacement of tortured abstractions with more straightforward, matter-of-fact detail, make this conjunction of time with the dimension of space, the image of Macbeth standing at a point in the vast expanse of time, emerge more strikingly. The final word, "vozdaian'e" (requital, recompense, retribution), is not colloquial but archaic, belonging to religious terminology, and this change in diction gives further prominence to the image. Macbeth's isolation is only emphasized by his readiness to reject what a future life might bring: "Ia b . . . / Pozhertvoval zagrobnym vozdaian'em" (I would sacrifice any recompense beyond the grave). The passage is typical of Pasternak's translations in both its weaknesses—oversimplification and loss of textual subtleties—and its strengths—the emergence of a central, striking image, in part because of the very simplicity and clarity of the textual framework.

Pasternak's techniques produced uneven results in other passages as well. In the opening scene of *2 Henry IV*, a man enters to bring Northumberland news of Hotspur's death at Shrewsbury:

> Yea, this man's brow, like to a title-leaf,
> Foretells the nature of a tragic volume.
> So looks the strond whereon the imperious flood
> Hath left a witness'd usurpation.
> Say, Morton, didst thou come from Shrewsbury?
>
> (I.i.60–64)

> Взгляните на него. Его лицо
> Как извещенье с траурной каймою.

> Такой бывает вид у берегов,
> Опустошенных бурею прилива.
> Ты в Шрусбери был, Мортон?   (P. 133)

(Look at him. His face is like a notice edged in black. There is
such a look on the shores ravaged by the storm of the flood.
You were at Shrewsbury, Morton?)

Pasternak's metaphorical references tend to be simpler
and more directly concrete than Shakespeare's. The result
is sometimes more trivial, even ludicrous. The comparison of the messenger's face to a notice with a black border ("izveshchen'e s traurnoi kaimoiu"), for example, is
rather insignificant beside the original comparison to "a
title-leaf, / [which] Foretells the nature of a tragic volume,"
and might even seem comically absurd if taken literally.
But the directness of the following lines gives them perhaps
a greater power than that of the original text:

> So looks the strond whereon the imperious flood
> Hath left a witness'd usurpation.

> Такой бывает вид у берегов,
> Опустошенных бурею прилива.

(There is such a look on the shores ravaged by the storm of the
flood.)

The indication of desolation is conveyed indirectly in the
original lines, the emphasis being on the personification
of the flood as a royal ravager ("the imperious flood /
[which] Hath left a witness'd usurpation"). In the translation, however, no such personification appears; nothing
is mentioned except the devastated shores themselves.
And the root morpheme "pust-" (empty) of the key adjective "opustoshennyi" (ravaged) suggests the spatial empti-

ness of the scene, heightening the suggestion of desolation
—the quality which Northumberland finds in the messenger's face.

This passage exemplifies a further tendency, typical of
Pasternak's usage in these translations. Although he retains or adds a few touches of personification in his
handling of Shakespeare's texts, he often presents the
natural world as inanimate and impersonal, a striking departure from his own work, where there is much personification and a suggestion of a vitality infusing the whole of
creation. The impressionism of his own early writing, the
lack of precise outline or clear definition in descriptive
passages, is generally not to be found in his translations
of Shakespeare's plays. On the contrary, descriptions of
landscapes and scenes, even visual images briefly alluded
to, often retain or acquire sharpness and clarity. Although
Pasternak's tendency to simplify the text could sometimes
result in impoverishment and loss, many passages have a
remarkable pictorial quality, despite, or perhaps because
of, the absence of a profusion of descriptive detail. This
sharpness and precision stand in curious contrast not only
to his practice in his own poetry,[14] but even to characteristics which have been pointed out in his other translations.
Etkind has noted, for example, the impressionism and lack

14. A. Lezhnev writes of Pasternak's own work that "his landscapes
can hardly even be called landscapes. They are not depictions of nature
but sense-perceptions of it. The objective datum vanishes behind the
subjective moment, is dissolved in it. If Pasternak's lyric work is that
of landscape, so too are his landscapes lyrical. More than that, they are
subjective, deformed, broken down into a series of sensation-atoms."
See "Boris Pasternak" in *Sovremenniki* (Contemporaries) (Moscow: Krug,
1927), p. 47; the translation is taken from *Pasternak*, ed. Davie and
Livingstone, p. 101 (note 1, above).

of visual clarity of a description of the Caucasus in Pasternak's translation of the "Zmeeed" (Zmee-ed = snake eater) by the Georgian poet Vazha Pshavela:

Pasternak's Caucasus is indistinct; typical of his description is the impressionistic image "in the mist of foliage." Pasternak does not seek clarity and hard lines; for him even the mountains merge into a certain world of "forbidding masses," which reigns "grandly and severely";—these adverb-epithets do not depict but suggest. He does not clarify his image; it seems that a many-faceted obscurity holds for Pasternak a special artistic value; it allows him to convey a common, yet inexpressible, impression of the world of the mountains . . . And, as always with Pasternak, this obscurity is unexpectedly combined with a simple, familiar, down-to-earth intonation,—the poet turns out to be on familiar terms with a grandiose and yet completely domestic nature.[15]

In contrast to this may be noted the visual clarity which Pasternak has maintained and perhaps heightened in translating Edgar's description of the supposed view from the cliffs at Dover to the blind Gloucester in *King Lear.*

> Come on, sir; here's the place: stand still. How fearful
> And dizzy 'tis to cast one's eyes so low!
> The crows and choughs that wing the midway air
> Show scarce so gross as beetles; half way down
> Hangs one that gathers sampire, dreadful trade!
> Methinks he seems no bigger than his head.
> The fishermen that walk upon the beach
> Appear like mice, and yond tall anchoring bark
> Diminish'd to her cock, her cock a buoy
> Almost too small for sight. The murmuring surge,
> That on th' unnumber'd idle pebble chafes,
> Cannot be heard so high. I'll look no more,
> Lest my brain turn, and the deficient sight
> Topple down headlong.   (IV.vi.11–24)

15. Etkind, *Poeziia i perevod,* pp. 97–98 (note 6, above).

Вот это место. Стойте, господин.
Какая жуть—заглядывать с обрыва
В такую глубь! Величиной с жука,
Под нами вьются галки и вороны.
Посередине кручи человек
Повис и рвет морской укроп, безумец.
Он весь-то с голову, а рыбаки
На берегу—как маленькие мыши.
На якоре стоит большой корабль.
Он сверху шлюпкой кажется, а шлюпка
Не больше поплавка—едва видна.
О камни ударяют с шумом волны,
Но их не слышно с этой высоты.
Довольно. Голова б не закружилась!
Еще слетишь. Нет, лучше не глядеть.   (Р. 408)

(Here is the place. Stand here, sir. How horrible—to peer from
a cliff into such a depth! Below us hover daws and crows, the size
of a beetle. A man hangs in the middle of the steep slope and picks
samphire, the madman. In all he seems the size of his head, and
the fishermen on the shore—like little mice. At anchor stands a
large ship. From above it looks like a ship's boat, and the ship's
boat no bigger than a float—scarcely visible. Waves strike against
the rocks with a roar, but they cannot be heard from this height.
Enough, or my head will start to spin! A person could fall! No,
it's better not to look.)

In both original and translation there is a suggestion of
visual perspective, the smallness of common objects and
persons below conveying an indication of the dizzying
height of the cliff. Pasternak's translation is quite close,
detail for detail. But the very compression of phrasing in
the Russian passage, the bare designation of the objects
seen, and of the indicators of size, heightens the starkness
of contrast and perhaps creates a stronger suggestion of
actual dimension. Constructions establishing comparisons
of size in the original ("no bigger than his head"; "so gross

as beetles") are reduced in Russian to the stark brevity of "s golovu," "s zhuka" ([the size] of a head, of a beetle). All incidental detail is omitted. "The fishermen that walk upon the beach" become "rybaki / Na beregu" (the fishermen on the shore). Further, Pasternak has been more precise than the original author in placing everything in the scene, indicating contrasts in apparent size and relative position. Where the original Edgar notes how fearful it is "to cast one's eyes so low," Pasternak's translation recalls the relationship between the cliff and the abyss below: "zagliadyvat' s obryva / V takuiu glub'" (to glance from the cliff into such a depth). He indicates the position of the viewers in relation to the birds below; the phrase "the crows and choughs that wing the midway air" becomes "pod nami v'iutsia galki i vorony" (below us hover daws and crows). The man gathering samphire on the cliff does not hang "half way down," but "poseredine kruchi" (halfway down the cliff). In connecting the two sentences

> Methinks he seems no bigger than his head.
> The fishermen that walk upon the beach
> Appear like mice

into one,

> Он весь-то с голову, а рыбаки
> На берегу—как маленькие мыши

(In all he seems the size of his head, and the fishermen on the shore—like little mice)

Pasternak emphasizes the comparison of apparent sizes, and thus strengthens the suggestion of perspective.

In the comparison of items in the following lines, one smaller than the other, Pasternak follows the original text closely:

> and yond tall anchoring bark
> Diminish'd to her cock, her cock a buoy
> Almost too small for sight.

> На якоре стоит большой корабль.
> Он сверху шлюпкой кажется, а шлюпка
> Не больше поплавка—едва видна.

(At anchor stands a large ship. From above it looks like a ship's boat, and the ship's boat no bigger than a float—scarcely visible.)

Pasternak makes the allusion to the "tall anchoring bark" longer (in terms of the line length, if not of the number of words, or details), while the last expression is reduced to two words. The progression from great to small in the size of objects is reflected in the phrasing. Pasternak's description of the scene is extremely clear and objective, and a suggestion of vast spatial dimension is captured perhaps more strongly in the translation than in the original.

Pictorial clarity and balance are brought to another passage, which is strikingly changed in Pasternak's translation. In the third act of *2 Henry IV*, King Henry asks why sleep has deserted the king himself, though it visits his humblest subjects:

> Wilt thou upon the high and giddy mast
> Seal up the ship-boy's eyes, and rock his brains
> In cradle of the rude imperious surge,
> And in the visitation of the winds,
> Who take the ruffian billows by the top,
> Curling their monstrous heads, and hanging them
> With deafing clamour in the slippery clouds,
> That with the hurly death itself awakes?
> Canst thou, O partial sleep, give thy repose
> To the wet sea-boy in an hour so rude,
> And in the calmest and most stillest night,
> With all appliances and means to boot,
> Deny it to a King?   (III.i.18–30)

Но нет, смотри. Вот мачта корабля,
Высокая до головокруженья,
А юнга спит на кончике ее.
Мальчишку убаюкало волненье.
Он спит, а по морю гуляет смерч,
И вьет веревку из обрывков пены,
И ловит море за седой хохол,
И вздергивает на небо, а буря,
Похоже, мертвых может разбудить.
О сон, пристрастный сон, на мачте юнга
Тебя вкушает в этот грозный час,
И ты отказываешь в утешенье
Средь тишины полночной королю,
Где все для отдыха к его услугам!   (P. 155)

(But no, look. There's the mast of the ship, so high it makes your head spin, but a ship's boy sleeps at its tip. The roughness of the sea has lulled the boy. He sleeps, and a waterspout wanders about the sea, and twists a rope from scraps of foam, and catches the sea by its grey tuft, and snatches it up to the heavens, but the storm, it seems, could wake the dead. O sleep, partial sleep, the ship's boy on the mast tastes you in that terrible hour, and you deny comfort to a king amidst the silence of midnight, where everything for repose is at his disposal.)

Perhaps the most immediately noticeable difference in the translation is that Pasternak presents a much milder version of the storm. "The rude imperious surge" becomes simply "volnen'e" (agitation, roughness, choppiness), and all the following images are modified. He localizes the violence of the storm in the "smerch" (waterspout) which wanders about the sea:

                    а по морю гуляет смерч, . . .
          И ловит море за седой хохол,
          И вздергивает на небо . . .

(and the waterspout wanders about the sea, . . . and catches the sea by its grey tuft and snatches it up to the heavens . . .)

The epithets and details which gave the suggestion of powerful violence to the original lines—"the ruffian billows," "their monstrous heads," "the slippery clouds"—are reduced to "more" (the sea), "sedoi khokhol" (a grey tuft), and "nebo" (the sky). The winds "who," in the original text, "take the ruffian billows by the top, / Curling their monstrous heads, and hanging them / With deafing clamour in the slippery clouds," are left out altogether. No mention is made of the "deafing clamour" of the storm, and instead of building up to the climactic declaration "that with the hurly death itself awakes," Pasternak's King Henry comments more modestly that the storm would *seem* to be able to wake the dead:

> а буря,
> Похоже, мертвых может разбудить.

(but the storm, it seems, could wake the dead.)

Where the original passage was constituted of a series of interlocking clauses and phrases building up to a question, the translation consists of a series of balanced phrases, all indicative statements:

> И вьет веревку из обрывков пены,
> И ловит море за седой хохол,
> И вздергивает на небо.

(And twists a rope from scraps of foam, and catches the sea by its grey tuft, and snatches it up to the heavens.)

The effect is much more even, calm. In the opening lines Pasternak makes no allusion to movement at all, but rather suggests a fixed picture. He departs from the original text in calling on his audience to view the scene: "No net, smotri. Vot machta korablia" (But no, look. There's the mast of the ship), and he captures attention not by portraying a scene of great turbulence, but by emphasizing the dizzying height of the mast ("Vot machta korablia, / Vysokaia do golovokruzhen'ia," There's the mast of the ship, so high it makes your head spin), and then placing the ship's boy at its tip: "A iunga spit na konchike ee" (But a ship's boy sleeps at its tip). The use of the diminutive "konchik" (little tip, end), emphasizing the apparent smallness of the far end of the mast, may heighten the suggestion of perspective. There is no sign of movement at all until the fourth line, and even at this point Pasternak suggests a more benevolent storm, substituting "mal'chishku ubaiukalo volnen'e" (the roughness of the sea has lulled the boy) for the more sharply ironic "and rock his brains / In cradle of the rude imperious surge." The translation may even provide a suggestion of a soothing presence in the natural world, rocking the ship's boy to sleep on his lofty perch. The lines which follow might even seem lulling, setting forth a wondrous tale ("On spit, a po moriu guliaet smerch . . . ," He sleeps, and a waterspout wanders about the sea . . .), rather than a harsh and threatening reality.

Throughout the passage, the tone is fundamentally altered. Instead of harsh irony, and an implicit expression of envy of the boy who could sleep amidst the violence and savage turmoil of the storm (obviously parallel to the civic turmoil besetting King Henry's own strife-ridden kingdom), there is almost a suggestion of nostalgia for the calm and sense of peace, possibly for the soothing presence, which makes it possible for the ship's boy to sleep on his awesome perch. Whatever losses have been incurred, the translator's use of pictorial elements and balanced phrasing serves to make the translation effective and evocative in its own way.

Another marked change in scenic description occurs in
Antony and Cleopatra, in Enobarbus' account of Antony's
circumstances at the time of the first approach of Cleopatra.

> From the barge
> A strange invisible perfume hits the sense
> Of the adjacent wharfs. The city cast
> Her people out upon her; and Antony,
> Enthron'd i' the market-place, did sit alone,
> Whistling to the air; which, but for vacancy,
> Had gone to gaze on Cleopatra too,
> And made a gap in nature.   (II.ii.211–18)

> Как я сказал, с баркаса долетал
> Пьянящий запах. Он привлек вниманье
> На набережных. В городе в тот миг
> На главном рынке, пред толпой, на троне
> Сидел Антоний. Город опустел.
> Все высыпали на берег. Антоний,
> Насвистывая, продолжал сидеть
> Один на площади, но даже воздух
> Сбежал, казалось, на реку глазеть
> На Клеопатру, обокрав природу.   (P. 483)

(As I said, an intoxicating scent flew from the boat. It attracted
attention on the embankments. In the city at that moment, in
the main market place, before a crowd, on a throne, sat Antony.
The city became deserted. Everyone poured out to the shore.
Antony, whistling, continued to sit alone in the square, but even
the air, it seemed, ran down to the river to look at Cleopatra,
thus robbing nature.)

Pasternak presents a striking picture which is only indirectly alluded to in the original text. Shakespeare begins with
Antony alone in the market place and the city already
deserted; Pasternak begins earlier, with the city still peo-
pled, and Antony facing a crowd. He adds details which
emphasize Antony's position of prominent grandeur at this
moment, placing him dramatically in the center of the

238 *The Style of the Translator*

scene. He first defines a large area around Antony ("v gorode v tot mig," in the city at that moment), then gradually works in ("na glavnom rynke, pred tolpoi, na trone," in the main market place, before a crowd, on a throne), until he centers on the figure of the man himself ("sidel Antonii," sat Antony). When he makes the city's desertion occur at this point ("gorod opustel," the city became deserted), the immediate contrast heightens the suggestion of Antony's sudden and rather ludicrous isolation:

> Антоний,
> Насвистывая, продолжал сидеть
> Один на площади.

(Antony, whistling, continued to sit alone in the square.)

Even the word "alone" ("odin") occurs not inconspicuously, at the end of the line (". . . did sit alone"), but prominently, at the very beginning: "Odin na ploshchadi."

Pasternak frequently makes effective use of scenes and landscapes in these translations, often creating a sharply defined perspective, suggesting spatial dimension, and clearly, sometimes dramatically, positioning his central figures. The scenes often appear unmoving, fixed; movement or development in time or space is itself usually carefully and coherently defined; and indications of direction, position, and gesture are given, often unobtrusively, throughout the translations. In I.iii of *Othello*, various reports reach the Venetian Council concerning the movements of the Turkish fleet, and all are carefully translated by Pasternak, who often uses Russian verbs of motion with their directional complements. In his version of

> yet do they all confirm
> A Turkish fleet, and bearing up to Cyprus   (I.iii.7–8)

he employs the construction "plyvet na" (is sailing to):

> Но что турецкий флот плывет на Кипр,
> На этом сходятся все сообщенья.　　(P. 306)

(But all reports agree that a Turkish fleet is sailing to Cyprus.)

A sailor brings word that "the Turkish preparation makes for Rhodes"; and the translator employs the same verb of motion with a different directional preposition "k": "Turetskii flot / Plyvet k Rodosu" (p. 307) (the Turkish fleet is sailing toward Rhodes). When Othello receives word that he must attend the council meeting, he delays only to take leave of Desdemona:

> I will but spend a word here in the house,
> And go with you.　　(I.ii.48–49)

In translation the movement into the house and back again is indicated:

> Я только в этот дом зайду и выйду.　　(P. 305)

(I will just stop in at the house and come out again.)

In Russian, the use of "v" meaning "in" or "into," followed by the accusative case, as here in "v etot dom," implies movement, "into the house."

Preventing a fight between Brabantio's followers and his own, Othello gives the command,

> Hold your hands,
> Both you of my inclining and the rest.　　(I.ii.81–82)

Unlike the original, Pasternak's translation virtually demands a gesture, at the very least a glance toward first one, then the other, of the warring parties:

> Подальше руки. Отойдите прочь!
> И вы, и вы.　　(P. 306)

(Get your hands away. Move back! Both you, and you.)

Pasternak not only indicates gesture, direction, and movement in space, he also emphasizes the coherent, step-by-step unfolding of events in time. When Othello asks Brabantio, the outraged father of Desdemona, "where will you that I go, / And answer this your charge?" Shakespeare's Brabantio answers

> To prison, till fit time
> Of law, and course of direct session,
> Call thee to answer.   (I.ii.85–87)

Pasternak's Brabantio specifies, step by step, that he will go "first into prison. You will sit there awhile. The time will come, they will call you out—you will answer":

> Сперва в тюрьму. Немного посидишь.
> Настанет время, вызовут—ответишь.   (P. 306)

As in Enobarbus' description of Antony in the passage cited above, scenes are often clearly presented, positions and movements of characters defined, and the course of events unfolds coherently, often with considerable dramatic effect. Shakespeare's Othello tells the Venetian Council of his wooing of Desdemona, of his response to her request

> That I would all my pilgrimage dilate,
> Whereof by parcel she had something heard,
> But not intentively: I did consent,
> And often did beguile her of her tears,
> When I did speak of some distressed stroke
> That my youth suffer'd.   (I.iii.153–58)

In translating the last three lines, Pasternak has Othello speak not of something which "often" happened, but of a

particular event, taking place at a certain time, a scene
with two participants, one observing the other:

> Я начал. И когда
> Дошел до первых горьких столкновений
> Моей незрелой юности с судьбой,
> Увидел я, что слушавшая плачет. (P. 309)

(I began. And when I came to the first bitter clashes of my
unripe youth with fate, I saw that my listener was weeping.)

In *2 Henry IV*, Northumberland confronts the messenger
who will confirm news of his son's death at the battle of
Shrewsbury:

> How doth my son, and brother?
> Thou tremblest, and the whiteness in thy cheek
> Is apter than thy tongue to tell thy errand.
> Even such a man, so faint, so spiritless,
> So dull, so dead in look, so woe-begone,
> Drew Priam's curtain in the dead of night,
> And would have told him half his Troy was burnt:
> But Priam found the fire ere he his tongue,
> And I my Percy's death ere thou report'st it. (I.i.67–75)

> Что сын и брат мой?
> Но ты дрожишь, и бледность щек твоих
> Все выдает мне раньше, чем твой голос.
> Так, верно, именно пришел гонец
> Сказать Приаму о пожаре Трои,
> Так бледен был, растерян и убит.
> Но прежде чем он выговорил слово,
> Из-за откинутой полы шатра
> Приам увидел сам огонь пожара.
> Так точно гибель Перси я прочел
> В твоих глазах. (P. 133)

(How are my son and brother? But you tremble, and the pallor
of your cheeks reveals everything to me, before your voice.

Probably just like this came a messenger to tell Priam about the burning of Troy, as pale as this, confused and crushed. But before he had uttered a word, from beyond the opened flap of the tent Priam himself saw the flames of the conflagration. Just so I read the ruin of Percy in your eyes.)

In some respects the passage is more spare and taut than the original. The catalogue of adjectives used to describe the messenger, "so faint, so spiritless, / So dull, so dead in look, so woe-begone," is narrowed down to three: "tak bleden byl, rasterian i ubit" (was as pale, confused and crushed). But the account of Priam's discovery of the burning of Troy, parallel to Northumberland's discovery of his own son's death in battle, is extended. Instead of saying that the messenger "drew Priam's curtain in the dead of night / And would have told him half his Troy was burnt," Pasternak's Northumberland goes further back in time and tells first of the man's entry: "Tak . . . imenno prishel gonets . . ." (Just like this . . . came a messenger . . .). Then in a completely separate sentence he turns to Priam's discovery; the single line "but Priam found the fire ere he his tongue" is expanded to three, and Pasternak builds up a certain tension by holding back the moment of discovery until the third line:

> Но прежде чем он выговорил слово,
> Из-за откинутой полы шатра
> Приам увидел сам огонь пожара.

(But before he had uttered a word, from beyond the opened flap of the tent Priam himself saw the flames of the conflagration.)

There is a suggestion of dramatic progression, and Pasternak has made the image more visually striking by providing a framework for the view of the fire: "Iz-za otkinutoi poly shatra . . ." (From beyond the opened flap of the tent . . .).

The succession of events in time, the very passage of time itself has grim implications in *Macbeth*, as already suggested in the earlier chapter on that play. In Pasternak's translation, the slow passage of time is sometimes emphasized by adjectives or adverbs introduced into the text. As Macbeth tries to convince two men that Banquo is the cause of their suffering and should be murdered, he asks,

> Are you so gospell'd,
> To pray for this good man, and for his issue,
> Whose heavy hand hath bow'd you to the grave,
> And beggar'd yours for ever?   (III.i.87–90)

In the next to last line, Pasternak's Macbeth speaks not of a completed destruction effected by Banquo, "whose heavy hand hath bow'd you to the grave," but of one slowly ("medlenno") taking place; he "medlenno vgoniaet vas v mogilu" (is slowly driving you to the grave). Macbeth says to his wife shortly afterward:

> Better be with the dead,
> Whom we, to gain our peace, have sent to peace,
> Than on the torture of the mind to lie
> In restless ecstasy.   (III.ii.19–22)

In translation, the original "restless ecstasy" is replaced by a "medlennaia pytka" (slow torture), something experienced with the passing of time. In Pasternak's *Macbeth* the use of verbs and verbal constructions is crucial in conveying a suggestion of a process occurring in time, and the approaching end of that process. In the original lines beginning Macbeth's speech in V.iii,

> I have liv'd long enough: my way of life
> Is fall'n into the sere, the yellow leaf   (V.iii.22–23)

there is a metaphorical reference to the autumn of life with its signs of withering, and the implication of approaching death. In the translation, verbal constructions play a more vital role in communicating this, though the first verb, "pozhil," has a positive connotation (lived well, lived it up) not to be found in the original text.

> Я пожил на своем веку. Я дожил
> До осени, до желтого листа.   (Р. 460)

(I have seen life in my day. I have lived until autumn, till the yellow leaf.)

Pasternak uses the perfective verbs "pozhil" and "dozhil," both prefixed forms of "zhit'" (to live), indicating that a process has come to an end. The construction "dozhil do . . ." (lived until . . .) in particular indicates that the final point in a progression has been reached; and the metaphorical implications of "autumn" and the "yellow leaf" simply reinforce the significance of this. The close parallelism in form ("Ia pozhil . . . Ia dozhil") also serves to give the two verbs emphatic prominence in the sentence.

Such use of verbal particles, and emphasis on the element of time, are to be seen again in the speech in V.v which begins "To-morrow, and to-morrow, and to-morrow," expressing Macbeth's sense of the futility of life and the implacability of time. The passage has been analyzed earlier in the chapter on *Macbeth,* but a few details might be emphasized again. In translating "out, out, brief candle" as "konets, konets, ogarok dogorel" (the end, the end, the candle has burned out), Pasternak again uses a verb with the "do-" prefix, indicating that a process has come to an end; "goret'" by itself would mean simply "to burn." Earlier in the passage, Pasternak's Macbeth speaks of life creeping not "to the last syllable of recorded time," but "k poslednei nedopisannoi stranitse" (toward the last, still uncompleted page). The key word in the translation is the complex participle "nedopisannyi," which is constructed from another verb with the "do-" prefix, "dopisat'" (to finish writing), "pisat'" meaning simply "to write." In this instance, the "page" is "nedopisannaia," not completely written, but the suggestion is that the end is inexorably approaching, has been all but reached.

There is a sense of fatality hanging over the latter scenes of *Antony and Cleopatra* as well, as Antony faces his final defeat at the hands of Caesar, and both he and Cleopatra confront death. This is often conveyed in Pasternak's translation by verbal usage similar to that in his *Macbeth*. Upon removing his armor after his last battle, for example, Antony exclaims, "No more a soldier: bruised pieces, go" (IV.xiv.42). Pasternak uses a verb indicating that Antony's past fighting has now come to an end:

> Я отвоевал,
> И больше не солдат. Прощайте, латы!   (P. 518)

(I have come to an end of fighting, and am no longer a soldier. Farewell, armor!)

(The verb "otvoevat'" could, ironically enough, also mean "to win," which is obviously not its meaning here, though the irony might not be altogether inappropriate.) His determination to end his life is expressed in the original text:

> So it must be, for now
> All length is torture: since the torch is out,
> Lie down and stray no farther.   (IV.xiv.45–47)

Pasternak replaces the adverb in the statement "the torch
is out" with a verb indicating the end of a process: "fakel
dogorel" (the torch has burned out). The same verb, the
same alteration of the text is found in Cleopatra's speech
after the death of Antony:

> Our lamp is spent, it's out.   (IV.xv.85)

> Угас наш свет, лампада догорела.   (P. 522)

(Our light is extinguished, the lamp[16] has burned out.)

The exclamation of the guards on finding Antony's
body in an earlier scene reflects the cosmic imagery used
throughout the play in describing Antony, and suggests
that time has come to an end altogether:

> *Second Guard*:   The star is fall'n.
> *First Guard*: And time is at his period.
> *All*:   Alas, and woe!
>   (IV.xiv.106–07)

Pasternak has translated, again using perfective verbs:

> *Второй часовой*:   Звезда скатилась.
> *Первый часовой*: Великая пора пришла к концу.
> *Все*: О горе, горе нам.   (P. 519)

(*Second sentry*: The star has fallen.
First sentry: The great time has come to an end.
All: O woe, woe to us.)

Sometimes the sense of finality is conveyed through a
visual image. Iras says to Cleopatra, shortly before her
death:

---

16. The Russian word "lampada" generally refers to an icon-lamp;
here, as elsewhere, Pasternak introduces religious overtones into his
translation.

> Finish, good lady, the bright day is done,
> And we are for the dark. (V.ii.192–93)

Pasternak has made the last phrase less figurative:

> Кончай царица. День наш миновал.
> Смеркается. (P. 527)

(Finish, Empress. Our day has passed. It is growing dark.)

At some points in the play, however, there is a suggestion of the overcoming of time and death itself, as is prefigured even in an early scene, where Cleopatra attempts to prevent Antony from leaving for Rome, reminding him of his earlier tributes to her:

> Eternity was in our lips, and eyes,
> Bliss in our brows' bent; none our parts so poor,
> But was a race of heaven. (I.iii.35–37)

Pasternak's version is close, but even here he has captured a suggestion of process, of transition, of becoming, which contributes to the effectiveness of his translation.

> Вечность
> Была в моих глазах и на губах,
> Ты видел меж бровей моих блаженство,
> Я вся была небесною. (P. 474)

(Eternity was in my eyes and on my lips, you saw bliss between my brows. I was entirely celestial.)

In the first phrase, "vechnost' / Byla v moikh glazakh i na gubakh" (eternity was in my eyes and on my lips), "eternity" is the subject, and the personal reference to "my eyes" occurs within a prepositional phrase ("v moikh glazakh"), suggesting a degree of personal passivity or receptivity. Eternity is invested in her person. In the second phrase, "blazhenstvo" (bliss) is relegated to the position of object itself, and loses the position of dominance within the sentence. In the third, "ia vsia byla nebesnoiu" (I was entirely celestial), the personal pronoun becomes the subject for the first time; the adjective "nebesnoiu" (heavenly, celestial), here in the instrumental case, serves merely an attributive function. The sequence strongly suggests the emergence of an individual identity which subsumes the infinite. Pasternak has in his own way recaptured the suggestion of individual transcendence.

As Cleopatra envisions Antony after his death, he assumes transcendent proportions; and Pasternak's translation of this passage, too, is close, simple, balanced:

> *Cleopatra*: I dreamt there was an Emperor Antony.
>   O such another sleep, that I might see
>   But such another man!
> *Dolabella*:   If it might please ye, —
> *Cleopatra*: His face was as the heavens, and therein
>   stuck
>   A sun and moon, which kept their course, and lighted
>   The little O, the earth.
> *Dolabella*:   Most sovereign creature, —
> *Cleopatra*: His legs bestrid the ocean, his rear'd arm
>   Crested the world: his voice was propertied
>   As all the tuned spheres, and that to friends:
>   But when he meant to quail, and shake the orb,
>   He was as rattling thunder. For his bounty,
>   There was no winter in 't: an autumn 'twas
>   That grew the more by reaping: his delights
>   Were dolphin-like, they show'd his back above
>   The element they lived in: in his livery
>   Walk'd crowns and crownets: realms and islands were
>   As plates dropp'd from his pocket.   (V.ii.76–92)

> *Клеопатра*: Мне снилось, был Антоний государь.
>   Еще один бы сон такой, чтоб снова
>   Такого человека увидать!

Долабелла: Позволь сказать...
Клеопатра: Его лицо сияло,
    Как лик небес, и солнце и луна
    Свершали оборот и освещали
    Кружок земли, как маленькое «о».
Долабелла: Венчанная красавица...
Клеопатра: Ногами
    Переступал он океан. Рукой
    Он накрывал вселенную, как шлемом.
    Казался голос музыкою сфер,
    Когда он разговаривал с друзьями,
    Когда ж земной окружности грозил,
    Гремел, как гром. Он скупости не ведал,
    Но, словно осень, рассыпал дары
    И никогда не превращался в зиму.
    Забавы не влекли его на дно,
    Но выносили наверх, как дельфина.
    Двором ему служил почти весь свет.
    Как мелочью, сорил он островами
    И царствами.   (P. 525)

(*Cleopatra*: I dreamed that Antony was emperor. One more such dream, that I might again see such a man!
Dolabella: Allow me to say...
Cleopatra: His face shone, like the face of the heavens, and sun and moon were completing their orbit and illumined the little circle of the earth, like a little "o."
Dolabella: Crowned beauty...
Cleopatra: With his legs he stepped over the ocean. With his hand he covered the universe, as with a helmet. His voice seemed like the music of the spheres when he spoke with friends, but when he threatened the circumference of the earth, it crashed like thunder. He knew no stinginess, but, like autumn, scattered gifts and never turned into winter. His amusements did not draw him to the bottom, but bore him aloft like a dolphin. Almost all the world served him as a court. He squandered islands and kingdoms like small change.)

The effectiveness of this towering image of Antony lies in part in its simplicity and compression, in the fact that the most far-flung elements—"the heavens," "sun," "moon," "the ocean," "the world"—are all brought into direct, simple relationship with one another and with the lineaments of the man whose dimensions they designate. In the translation, relationships and parallels in identity are only strengthened. In translating "his face was as the heavens" as "ego litso siialo, / Kak lik nebes" (his face shone like the face of the heavens), Pasternak has closely identified the elements of the simile, using the morphemically related "litso" and "lik." (Although both words mean "face," the latter could refer to the image on an icon, and its use strengthens the possible religious overtones of the allusion to the heavens.) As Shakespeare's Cleopatra continues, "His face was as the heavens, and therein stuck / A sun and moon," she is apparently referring not to "the" sun and moon in the heavens, but to something she observes in the face of Antony. She is expressing herself figuratively. Pasternak maintains a complete ambiguity as to whether "sun and moon" are to be seen in the face of Antony, or in that of the heavens; no real distinction is made between them:

> Его лицо сияло,
> Как лик небес, и солнце и луна
> Свершали оборот.

(His face shone like the face of the heavens, and sun and moon were completing their orbit.)

Through stating that the face of Antony shone ("siialo"), rather than simply "was," Pasternak indicates another active resemblance to the sun and moon, which "osveshchali / Kruzhok zemli" (illumined the little circle of the earth). And in commenting that the sun and moon "svershali oborot" (were completing their orbit), rather than "kept their course," he indicates more directly the shape of their course, and establishes a more direct contrast between the great circle completed by them, and the small circle of the earth ("kruzhok zemli").

At the beginning of the following speech, there is another parallel.

> His legs bestrid the ocean, his rear'd arm
> Crested the world.

> Ногами
> Переступал он океан. Рукой
> Он накрывал вселенную, как шлемом.

(With his legs he stepped over the ocean. With his hand, he covered the universe, as with a helmet.)

The immense size of the limbs of this Antony is emphasized in the Russian translation by the use of verse and sentence structure, isolating "nogami" (with his legs) and "rukoi" (with his hand), making them stand out forcefully within the verse phrasing.

This is indeed a Renaissance image of man, expressed in terms of the dimensions of the universe; and Pasternak has managed to suggest an immensity of size and dimension, largely through references to far-flung heavenly bodies and through structural parallels and relationships within the text.

In general, the unavoidable reduction of detail in imagery and phrasing in translations of Shakespeare's plays, which Reuben Brower has demonstrated to result in an important loss of meaning and dramatic force, nonetheless makes it possible to bring out some sequential relationships, visual contrasts, and internal dramatic developments with stark effectiveness. Pasternak has heightened the effects which can be attained within the limits of translation in such a manner that his work attains its own force without distorting greatly the meaning of the original.

Throughout these translations, Pasternak's use of simple balance and parallelism in phrasing, as well as his tendency toward clarification and simplification in the handling of obscure references, syntactic complexities, paradoxical statements, and conflicting sets of images, help to establish a stylistic framework of classical terseness, grace, and lucidity. Pasternak does not attempt to recapture the baroque richness of imagery and allusion of the original text, but is highly selective, presenting a few essential details and images, often related to crucial recurrent themes, which stand out distinctly and powerfully in the translations because of the very starkness of the setting in which they appear. The limitations of translation are sometimes converted into virtues in his rendition.

Pasternak brings to Shakespeare's imagery considerable plasticity, pictorial sharpness, and a suggestion of spatial dimension, using a minimum of descriptive detail. There is a tautness and coherence in his handling of dramatic sequence, the unfolding of events in time, as well as in his portrayal of scenes and landscapes, the arrangement of elements in space; and he uses all these elements to powerful effect. In this, as well as in the lucidity and balance of phrasing in these translations, there is some evidence of similarity to classical Pushkinian style,[17] a point which

17. Gifford repeatedly alludes to the Pushkinian nature of Pasternak's translations of Shakespeare: "The Shakespeare of Pasternak has become inevitably the fellow countryman of Pushkin" (*Pasternak*, p. 150) (note 12, above). Pasternak's "orderliness, clarity, and precision [in translating Shakespeare] derive conceivably from their [Schlegel-Tieck's] example, but more certainly from that of Pushkin, which anyone writing blank-verse drama in the Russian language cannot avoid" (p. 158).

may be clarified by turning briefly to the poetry of Pushkin himself. Maurice Baring comments, in comparing Russian to Greek poetry:

Pushkin at times has the simplicity and the power of evoking a whole picture in one line without ornament or epithet, such as we find only in Homer.[18]

To exemplify this he quotes a line from *The Covetous Knight*: "I more, gde bezhali korabli" (And the sea, where ships were scudding). He attributes its effectiveness to "the perfect lilt and appropriateness of his words and his rhythm, and . . . the movement and accent of the particular verb employed." But the fact that the line refers in a simple way to an expanse of space and a movement across that space cannot be ignored in evaluating its pictorial force. This line is only part of a longer descriptive passage from the Baron's soliloquy:

> Читал я где-то,
> Что царь однажды воинам своим
> Велел снести земли по горсти в кучу,
> И гордый холм возвысился—и царь
> Мог с вышины с весельем озирать
> И дол, покрытый белыми шатрами,
> И море, где бежали корабли.

(I read somewhere, that a tsar once ordered his warriors to pile handfuls of earth into a heap, and a proud hill arose—and the tsar could view with gaiety from its summit both the valley, covered with white tents, and the sea, where ships were scudding.)

The Baron refers to the rising of the hill—not simply to its height, but to the movement by which it attained that height—and places the Tsar at its summit, making this the

18. "Introduction" to *The Oxford Book of Russian Verse* (1925; rpt. Oxford: Clarendon Press, 1958), p. xliii.

vantage point for his view of the valley and the sea beyond. He establishes the dimension of height and then of distance, suggesting a coherent development in time and space. The line "i dol, pokrytyi belymi shatrami" (and the valley, covered with white tents) conveys a picture through the simple reference to a broad space covered with patches of white. And this adds to the suggestion of spatial immensity. The indication of vast space and the suggestion of its control by the man who created the hill and then dominated the landscape from its height illustrate the enormity of power experienced by the Baron upon the growth of his wealth to immense proportions.

Two more brief examples may be used to illustrate the effect of pictorial, spatial representation in Pushkin's work —the opening lines from "Anchar":

> В пустыне чахлой и скупой,
> На почве, зноем раскаленной,
> Анчар, как грозный часовой,
> Стоит один во всей вселенной

and from *The Bronze Horseman*:

> На берегу пустынных волн
> Стоял *он*, дум великих полн,
> И вдаль глядел.

In each case, Pushkin begins with a reference to a vast, unbroken space: "V pustyne chakhloi i skupoi, / Na pochve, znoem raskalennoi" (In the stunted and miserly desert, on the earth, parched with heat); "Na beregu pustynnykh voln" (On the shore of the deserted waves). In the first poem, all epithets contribute to the suggestion of a wasted, lifeless desert ("chakhloi," "skupoi," "znoem raskalennoi"; stunted, miserly, parched with heat) as well as to the further implication of the poisoning of life by the

tree. In the second, the famous oxymoron of the "pustyn-
nye volny" (deserted waves) indicates the similarly empty
waste of the sea. In both, the morphemic particle "pust-"
(empty) is prominent.

Against each background appears a single imposing
figure: "Anchar, kak groznyi chasovoi" (The anchar, like
a terrible sentry); "Stoial *on*, dum velikikh poln" (*He*
stood, filled with great thoughts). The contrast is emphasized by turning again to the vast perspective of the surrounding area: "Stoit odin vo vsei vselennoi" (Stands alone
in all the universe); "I vdal' gliadel" (And looked into the
distance). There is a strong suggestion of isolation and of
power exerted in isolation implicit in these passages, and
in the second particularly, a sense of the individual's confrontation with vastness.

Pasternak's capacity, then, for maintaining a clear suggestion of spatial dimension and perspective in descriptive
passages in these translations, making them revelatory of
broader aspects of characterization and experience, indicates an affinity in these works to the classical Pushkinian
style, which extends beyond simplicity and balance in
syntax and phrasing. Equally important to the poet's effect
is the suggestion of coherence of development and movement—in time as well as space—and the emergence of the
dimensions of the world of the dramatist, temporal as well
as spatial, in the translations.

Conclusion

PASTERNAK's translations of Shakespeare's plays reflect the paradoxical contradiction which Pasternak attributed to Shakespeare's "realistic" art: "on the one hand there is the miracle of objectivity," on the other, the "self-willed" "outpourings of his own genius." Pasternak was often highly sensitive to the structure, form, tone, and meaning of the Shakespearean original and remarkably faithful in reproducing it. In some respects he was a self-effacing translator, using his own artistic gifts to reproduce in his language the work of another writer. Yet he was often conscious of making the translations his own, of departing from the original text in order to create an original Russian work, imbued with his creative vitality, reflecting the shaping power of "his own genius," revealing his own views on reality, on human psychology, on the nature of art. Because of this, Pasternak's translations cannot ultimately be separated from the rest of his creative work. They reflect many of his own predilections and tendencies as an artist; but they also reveal his capacity for self-effacement and for change. Undoubtedly they affected Pasternak himself and his own writing. Some of the characteristics of Pasternak's own work are evident in them, of course. His very ability to approximate the effect of the original in his handling of prosodic elements—meter, verse structure, patterns in sound—demonstrates his own linguistic inventiveness and ingenuity, his feeling for sound and rhythm in verse, his mastery as a poetic craftsman.

The regularity and clarity of meter in his versions of the songs from the plays accords with Lydia Pasternak Slater's assertion that Pasternak's poems "are without exception strictly rhythmical and written mostly in a classical metre."[1] But elements which are relatively new to Pasternak's work also appear in these translations. Whether the style he employed reflects the demands of translation, or his own growing desire for simplicity of poetic expression, it is simple, spare, lucid, diametrically opposed in some respects to the style of his own earlier writings. There is rarely a suggestion of the transforming power of personal emotion, the dynamic relationship between object and perceiver which seems to be implied by Pasternak's early statement that "focussed on a reality which feeling has displaced, art is a record of that displacement." The impressionism, the fluidity, the lack of personal definition or identification, the animation of the natural world, the suggestion of a vitality infusing all of creation and reflected in the dynamic interaction of its component elements—all of which are characteristic of Pasternak's early poetry— are rarely to be found in his translations of Shakespeare's plays. On the contrary, placement, movement, and development in time and space are given sharp and coherent definition. Positions of objects and persons are clearly identified, and sometimes they appear in dramatic isolation. Landscapes and scenes described in the texts appear fixed and stable, clearly drawn. The translator's style suggests not the displacement of reality by feeling, but an effort to define reality sharply and objectively.

This sparse, "objective" style was undoubtedly developed for many reasons, some of them purely technical,

1. Boris Pasternak, *Fifty Poems*, trans. Lydia Pasternak Slater (London: Unwin Books, 1964), p. 11.

having to do with the structure of the language and the mechanics of translation. Yet it cannot be considered a purely mechanical or formal phenomenon. Pasternak's own works often suggest a consciousness of an energy, a vital power infusing everything that exists, breaking down the discrete "categories of being" and at times the very barriers of individuation. Isaiah Berlin writes in "The Energy of Pasternak" that

there is [in Pasternak's work] . . . a sense of unity induced by the sense of the pervasiveness of cosmic categories, (perhaps derived from the poet's neo-Kantian days in Marburg) which integrate all the orders of creation into a single, biologically and physiologically, emotionally and intellectually, interrelated universe.[2]

And Andrei Siniavsky finds that

metaphor in the poetics of Pasternak plays above all a connecting role. It instantly and dynamically draws into a single whole the separate parts of reality, and thus embodies the great unity of the world, the interaction and interpenetration of phenomena.[3]

The frequent allusions to resurrection and rebirth in Pasternak's work reflect an ultimate assurance that life itself will be sustained and continually renewed, and the sense of life, of an elemental vitality investing all things, emerges throughout his writings. Even in the translations, there are a few instances of personification of the natural world, with evidence of its sympathy for human suffering. And it is perhaps significant that in Cleopatra's triumphant affirmation of the grandeur of Antony as she envisions him after his death, he merges almost indistinguishably with

2. *Partisan Review*, 17, No. 7 (Sept.–Oct., 1950), 749.
3. From "Poeziia Pasternaka," the introductory essay to *Stikhotvoreniia i poemy* (Poems), by Boris Pasternak (Moscow–Leningrad: Sovetskii pisatel', 1965), p. 17.

the elements of the cosmos for a moment, and that Pasternak maintains an ambiguity of expression in comparing
the "face of Antony" and the "face of the heavens," as if
the relationship were not simply a figurative one. It is all
the more striking, therefore, that in his translations of
Shakespeare's plays, so many natural scenes are described
as barren, desolate, devoid of signs of life or vitality, and
that Pasternak has sometimes altered the original text to
achieve this effect. He often weakens or eliminates altogether allusions to an inherent savagery and destructive-
ness in the natural world; yet the scenes he describes may
appear bleak or even threatening precisely because of their
emptiness, the absence of life; and individuals may seem
isolated in a bare and comfortless setting, virtually a void.
As recreated by Pasternak, the central tragedy lies in the
absence or extinction of life—not simply that of an individual, but of something which exists beyond him and
encompasses far more than himself.

Yet it seems ultimately impossible for Pasternak to
maintain an unremitting pessimism. The stubbornly affirmative impulse underlying his own writing is still evident on occasion. Not only has he weakened expressions
of pessimism, cynicism, bitterness, and cruelty, modifying
suggestions of the impossibility of retaining innocence or
integrity, and evidence of the prevalence and power of evil
in man; but he also retains and strengthens signs, particularly in *Antony and Cleopatra*, of a human potential for
overcoming inherent baseness and for attaining a transcendent personal grandeur, touching upon the eternal
and infinite.

Appendix

PASTERNAK'S translation of *Hamlet* first appeared in its
entirety in *Molodaia Gvardiia* in 1940, and was repub-
lished during Pasternak's lifetime in 1941, 1942, 1947,
1951, 1953, 1956, and 1957. Individual scenes were published as well in a number of journals. Major cuts and
revisions appeared in the editions of 1942, 1947, and 1953;
minor changes are to be found in the others as well. Evgenii
Pasternak has commented in personal correspondence
(Nov. 10, 1973) that when he prepared the edition of his
father's translation of *Hamlet* for publication in a volume
of Shakespeare's tragedies and sonnets (*Tragedii, Sonety*)
which appeared in Moscow in 1968, he had twelve variant
versions to work with, as well as manuscript corrections
made by Pasternak himself in a late edition of the translation. He has commented also that of all the different
versions, Pasternak himself preferred the initial one, which
appeared in 1940. Evgenii Pasternak used this early edition
of the play as his basic text, and there would appear to be
good reason for doing so in this study. Yet I have chosen
not to for a number of reasons. In the first place, there is
the sheer convenience of using a single edition, the *Izbrannye proizvedeniia* (Moscow, 1953), which contains all of
Pasternak's translations of Shakespeare's plays, as a basic
text in making citations and references. Second, the passages I have chosen to work with were, for the most part,
relatively stable, changing little even when the text was

extensively revised; it would matter relatively little which
edition I used in working with them. Third, where major
changes did occur in the passages under consideration,
there is some reason to believe that they were made freely
and without coercion by Pasternak himself and represent
his own preference and point of view. For example, a
number of bawdy or indelicate speeches, most of them by
or about Ophelia, were cut for the 1942 edition and never
restored. It may not be surprising, of course, that such
measures were taken in preparing the text for publication
by the Children's Publishing House (Detgiz). Writing later
to the editor of Detgiz, A. O. Naumova, about Morozov's
criticism of cuts made in his translation of *Romeo and
Juliet,* Pasternak reminded her that "you yourself call for
the elimination of improprieties."[1] But there is some evidence that Pasternak did not make these changes unwillingly or under duress. In a letter to Naumova, dated
May 23, 1942, Pasternak discussed the forthcoming publication of his translation of *Hamlet* by Detgiz. Angered and
discouraged by the criticism of Morozov, and by his
insistence that Pasternak make his translation more literal,
Pasternak asserted that he could not assent to Morozov's
suggestions, even if this meant that the work would not
be published again, and he stated finally of his translation,
"Either it is suitable, or it isn't; in the latter instance, there
is nothing to say, and in the former, then my concern is
whether or not the galleys should be touched. Then the
improprieties could be eliminated, this is a five-minute
matter."[2] The editor comments that he is referring here to
"abridgements made for the Detgiz edition of 1942" which
"remained in all following editions." Pasternak wrote here

1. *Masterstvo perevoda 1969* (Moscow: Sovetskii pisatel', 1970), p. 358.
2. Ibid., pp. 342–43.

as if he had made the cuts himself and were not sure that the editor would accept them; and it seems unlikely that he would make such changes if he did not approve of them, considering his stubborn refusal at this point to make other requested alterations. It might be pointed out also that these cuts remained even in later editions which were not published by Detgiz; Pasternak made many revisions in his translation for the 1953 edition, but did not restore these cut passages, even though many of the bawdy passages in his translation of *Romeo and Juliet* (such as those in Mercutio's speeches in II.i) were restored. Further, the one play not translated by Pasternak in the 1953 *Izbrannye proizvedeniia—Much Ado about Nothing*, translated by Tat'iana Shchepkina-Kupernik—is very literal, even in the handling of bawdy and indecent allusions and, perhaps most telling, in Claudio's brutal accusations of Hero in IV.i, when he refuses to go through with their wedding. It would seem that the cuts in *Hamlet* reflect Pasternak's own preferences, and not those of a puritanical censor or editor.

Many of the changes Pasternak made in the closet scene (III.iv) for the 1947 edition also had the effect of bowdlerizing the text. But this was not true in all instances, and some changes serve to alter the character of Hamlet himself in a way that is difficult to account for, except as a matter of choice and personal interpretation. It is indeed ironic that in spite of the criticism Pasternak received for translating *Hamlet* so freely, in spite of Morozov's efforts to have the translation brought closer to the original in revised editions and Pasternak's grudging concessions and compromises, the later editions of the translation are actually further in many respects from the original text than the first one was. The edition of 1947 is probably the freest, most audacious of all, and it would seem highly improbable that in all the changes he made Pasternak was simply yielding to editorial demands. It was in the 1947 edition, for example, that Pasternak produced the version of the "to be or not to be" soliloquy which Vladimir Markov found to be so freely translated, so personal and topical, as to constitute a potentially dangerous means of self-expression.[3] To give a brief example of the liberties Pasternak took, the line "Or to take arms against a sea of troubles, / And by opposing end them" acquires a rather militant, even inflammatory, ring: "Il' nado okazat' so-protivlen'e, / Vosstat', vooruzhit'sia, pobedit' / Ili pogib-nut'?" (p. 86) (Or is it necessary to show resistance, to rise up, to take arms, to conquer or to perish?), which is lost in the more literal translation of the passage in 1953: "Il' nado okazat' soprotivlen'e / I v smertnoi skhvatke s tselym morem bed / Pokonchit' s nimi?" (p. 263) (Or is it necessary to show resistance and in mortal combat with a whole sea of troubles put an end to them?). Numerous other departures from the still relatively literal first edition appeared in 1947, most with no political or topical bearing whatever. It would be interesting to explore the peculiarities of this edition further, but I confine myself in this study to those passages which survived in the altered, and somewhat more conservative, 1953 edition.

3. See "An Unnoticed Aspect of Pasternak's Translation," *Slavic Review*, 20, No. 3 (Oct. 1961), pp. 503–08.

Bibliography

PASTERNAK'S TRANSLATIONS OF SHAKESPEARE'S WORKS

Sonnets and Songs from the Plays

Sonnet 73. *Novyi mir*, No. 8 (1938), p. 9.

"Muzyka" (Music), from *Henry VIII* (III.i) and "Zima" (Winter), from *Love's Labour's Lost* (V.ii). *Krasnaia nov'*, No. 8 (1938), p. 131.

"Muzyka," "Zima," and Sonnets 66 and 73. In Pasternak, Boris. *Izbrannye perevody* (Selected Translations). Moscow: Sovetskii pisatel', 1940. Pp. 112–14.

"Zima." *Ballady i pesni angliiskogo naroda* (Ballads and Songs of the English People). Moscow–Leningrad: Gosudarstvennoe izdatel'stvo detskoi literaturoi [Detgiz], 1942. P. 48.

"Zima," monologue of Mercutio (from *Romeo and Juliet*, I.iv), Hamlet's monologue (from *Hamlet*, III.i), the prayer of the King (from *Hamlet*, III.iii). In *Priglushennye golosa: poeziia za zheleznym zanavesom* (Muffled Voices: Poetry behind the Iron Curtain), ed. Vladimir Markov. New York: Chekhov, 1952. Pp. 393–99.

Sonnets 66 and 73, "Zima," and "Muzyka." *Zvezdnoe nebo: stikhi zarubezhnykh poetov v perevode B. Pasternaka* (The Starry Heavens: Poems of Foreign Poets in the Translation of B. Pasternak). Moscow: Progress, 1966. Pp. 25–27.

Sonnet 74. In "Pis'ma o *Gamlete*" (Letters about *Hamlet*),
    ed. Evgenii B. Pasternak and Valentina Kozintseva.
    Voprosy literatury, No. 1 (1975), pp. 219–21. This
    correspondence contains a rough draft and later
    corrections of a translation of Sonnet 74, made by
    Pasternak at Grigorii Kozintsev's request.

Hamlet

Gamlet, "Predstavlenie vo dvortse" (The Presentation in
    the Court) (III.ii.145–213). *Ogonek*, No. 18 (1939),
    p. 8.
Gamlet, "Akt III, stsena iv." *Tridtsat' dnei*, Nos. 3–4
    (1940), pp. 70–73.
Gamlet, prints datskii (Hamlet, Prince of Denmark). *Mo-
    lodaia gvardiia*, Nos. 5–6 (1940), pp. 15–131.
Stseny iz tragedii Gamlet (Scenes from the Tragedy *Ham-
    let*). Moscow, 1941.
Gamlet, prints datskii. Moscow: Gosudarstvennoe izda-
    tel'stvo khudozhestvennoi literaturoi, 1941.
Gamlet, prints datskii. Moscow–Leningrad: Detgiz, 1942.
Gamlet, prints datskii. Moscow–Leningrad: Detgiz, 1947.
Gamlet, prints datskii. Moscow: Iskusstvo, 1951.
Gamlet, prints datskii. Moscow: Detgiz, 1956.
Gamlet, prints datskii. Moscow: Iskusstvo, 1957.
Gamlet, prints datskii. Moscow: GIKhL, 1964.
Gamlet, prints datskii. Moscow: Pravda, 1976.

Romeo and Juliet

Romeo i Dzhul'etta, "Prolog i otryvok iz pervogo akta"
    (Prologue and an Excerpt from Act I [i.153–231]).
    Tridtsat' dnei, No. 4 (1941), pp. 41–42.
Romeo i Dzhul'etta, "Otryvok" (An Excerpt) (Prologue
    and I.i). *Internatsional'naia literatura*, No. 5 (1941),
    pp. 147–51.

Romeo i Dzhul'etta. Moscow: Izdanie vsesoiuznogo upravleniia po okhrane avtorskikh prav, 1943.

Romeo i Dzhul'etta. Moscow: GIKhL, 1944.

Romeo i Dzhul'etta. Moscow–Leningrad: Detgiz, 1944.

Romeo i Dzhul'etta. Moscow: Uchebno-pedagogicheskoe izdatel'stvo, 1950.

Romeo i Dzhul'etta. Moscow: Iskusstvo, 1951.

Antony and Cleopatra

Antonii i Kleopatra. Moscow: GIKhL, 1944.

Othello

Otello, IV.iii. *Literaturnaia gazeta*, Dec. 9, 1944.

"Iz novykh perevodov B. Pasternaka" (From the New Translations of B. Pasternak): *Otello*, IV.iii.40–56 (Desdemona's "willow" song), and V.ii.1–84, 260–83, 331–57. *Leningrad*, Nos. 13–14 (1945), p. 17.

Otello—venetsianskii mavr (Othello, the Moor of Venice). Moscow: Izdanie vsesoiuznogo upravleniia po okhrane avtorskikh prav, 1945.

Otello—venetsianskii mavr. Moscow: GIKhL, 1945.

Otello—venetsianskii mavr. Moscow: Iskusstvo, 1951.

Otello—venetsianskii mavr. Moscow: Uchebno-pedago-gicheskoe izdatel'stvo, 1951.

Henry IV, parts 1 and 2

Korol' Genrikh Chetvertyi (King Henry IV), *part 1*, I.ii, II.ii, II.iv, III.iii; *part 2*, I.ii, II.i, V.iii, V.v. *Zvezda*, Nos. 2–3 (1946), pp. 118–44.

Genrikh Chetvertyi: istoricheskaia khronika v 2-kh chas-tiakh (Henry IV: A Historical Chronicle in 2 Parts). Moscow–Leningrad: Detgiz, 1948.

Korol' Genrikh Chetvertyi. Moscow: GIKhL, 1949.

King Lear

Korol' Lir. Moscow: GIKhL, 1949.
Korol' Lir. Moscow–Leningrad: Detgiz, 1949.
Korol' Lir. Moscow: Iskusstvo, 1965.

COLLECTIONS OF SHAKESPEARE'S WORKS

Vil'iam Shekspir v perevode Borisa Pasternaka (William
      Shakespeare in the Translation of Boris Pasternak).
      Ed. M. M. Morozov. 2 vols. Moscow–Leningrad:
      Iskusstvo, 1949–50. Volume 1 contains *Romeo and
      Juliet, King Henry IV, parts 1 and 2,* and *Hamlet;*
      volume 2, *Othello, King Lear,* and *Antony and
      Cleopatra.*
Tragedii (Tragedies). Ed. M. M. Morozov. Moscow–Len-
      ingrad: Detgiz, 1951. Contains *Romeo and Juliet,
      Hamlet, Othello, King Lear,* and *Macbeth.*
Izbrannye proizvedeniia (Selected Works). Ed. M. M.
      Morozov. Moscow: GIKhL, 1953. Contains *Ro-
      meo and Juliet, King Henry IV, parts 1 and 2,
      Hamlet, Othello, King Lear, Macbeth,* and *Antony
      and Cleopatra* in Pasternak's translation; also
      Much Ado about Nothing in the translation of
      T. Shchepkina-Kupernik, and the Sonnets in the
      translation of S. Marshak.
Polnoe sobranie sochinenii v vos'mi tomakh (Complete
      Works in Eight Volumes). Ed. A. Smirnov and A.
      Anikst. Moscow: Iskusstvo, 1957–60. Contains
      Othello and *King Lear* in Pasternak's translation
      in VI, 281–568.
Tragedii, Sonety (Tragedies, Sonnets). Moscow: GIKhL,
      1968. Contains *Romeo and Juliet, Hamlet, Othello,
      King Lear, Macbeth,* and *Antony and Cleopatra*

in Pasternak's translation; the Sonnets in the translation of S. Marshak.

BASIC EDITION OF PASTERNAK'S WORKS USED IN THIS STUDY

Sochineniia (Works). Ed. G. P. Struve and B. A. Filippov. Ann Arbor: University of Michigan Press, 1961.

Vol. I: *Stikhi i poemy 1912–1932* (Poems, 1912–1932).

Vol. II: *Proza 1915–1958. Povesti, rasskazy, avtobiograficheskie proizvedeniia* (Prose, 1915–1958. Short stories, autobiographical works).

Vol. III: *Stikhi 1936–1959. Stikhi dlia detei. Stikhi 1912–1957, ne sobrannye v knigi avtora. Stat'i i vystupleniia* (Poems, 1936–1959. Poems for children. Poems, 1912–1957, not included in the books of the author. Essays and speeches).

Vol. IV: *Doktor Zhivago*.

WORKS ON PASTERNAK'S TRANSLATIONS OF SHAKESPEARE

Akhmanova, Olga and Zadornova, Velta. "The Present State of Shakespeare Translation in the USSR (Russian Translations of Shakespeare)." *Shakespeare Translation*, No. 2 (1975), pp. 38–47 (40).*

Alekseev, M. *"Gamlet* Borisa Pasternaka" (Boris Pasternak's *Hamlet*). *Iskusstvo i zhizn'*, No. 8 (1940), pp. 14–16.

*Where only part of the work deals with Pasternak's translations, exact page numbers are given in parentheses.

Borovoi, L. "Dvadtsat' chetvertyi *Gamlet*" (The Twenty-fourth *Hamlet*). *Literaturnaia gazeta*, Apr. 20, 1940.

Brower, Reuben A. "Poetic and Dramatic Structure in Versions and Translations of Shakespeare." In *Poetics*, ed. Donald Davie, Kazimierz Wyka, Roman Jakobson, et al. The Hague: Mouton, 1961. Pp. 655–74 (665–67).

Etkind, Efim. "Ob uslovno-poeticheskom i individual'-nom" (On the Conventional-poetic and the Individual). *Masterstvo perevoda 1966*. Moscow: Sovetskii pisatel', 1968. Pp. 134–60 (142–47).

F., E. "Pechat' o *Gamlete* v perevode B. Pasternaka" (The Press on *Hamlet* in B. Pasternak's Translation). *Literatura v shkole*, No. 6 (1940), pp. 93–95.

Finkel', A. "66-i sonet v russkikh perevodakh" (Sonnet 66 in Russian Translation). *Masterstvo perevoda 1966*. Moscow: Sovetskii pisatel', 1968. Pp. 161–82 (172–74).

Gavruk, Iu. "Nuzhen li novyi perevod *Gamleta* na russkii iazyk?" (Is a New Translation of *Hamlet* Needed in Russian?). *Masterstvo perevoda 1966*. Moscow: Sovetskii pisatel', 1968. Pp. 119–33 (128–33).

Gifford, Henry. *Pasternak*. Cambridge: Cambridge University Press, 1977. "Pasternak as Translator," pp. 147–61.

Iakobson, A. "Dva resheniia" (Two Solutions [concerning Sonnet 66]). *Masterstvo perevoda 1966*. Moscow: Sovetskii pisatel', 1968. Pp. 183–88.

"K perevodam shekspirovskikh dram" (On Translations of Shakespeare's Dramas). Ed. Evgenii B. Pasternak. *Masterstvo perevoda 1969*. Moscow: Sovetskii pisatel', 1970. Pp. 341–63. Contains correspondence of Boris Pasternak, Mikhail Morozov, and others, concerning Pasternak's translations.

Kiprenskii, A. "Pervyi russkii perevod *Gamleta*" (The First Russian Translation of *Hamlet*). *Literaturnaia gazeta*, June 5, 1940.

Krzhevskii, B. "Iz novykh perevodov B. Pasternaka" (From the New Translations of B. Pasternak). *Leningrad*, Nos. 13–14 (1945), p. 17.

Levik, V. "Nuzhny li novye perevody Shekspira?" (Are New Translations of Shakespeare Necessary?). *Masterstvo perevoda 1966*. Moscow: Sovetskii pisatel', 1968. Pp. 93–104 (97–100).

Levin, Iu. "Russkie perevody Shekspira" (Russian Translations of Shakespeare). *Masterstvo perevoda 1966*. Moscow: Sovetskii pisatel', 1968. Pp. 5–25 (24).

Lozinskaia, L. "Novyi perevod *Romeo i Dzhul'etty*" (A New Translation of *Romeo and Juliet*). *Ogonek*, No. 46 (1942), p. 13.

Markov, Vladimir. "An Unnoticed Aspect of Pasternak's Translations." *Slavic Review*, 20, No. 3 (Oct. 1961), 503–08.

Morozov, Mikhail M. "*Gamlet* v perevode Borisa Pasternaka" (*Hamlet* in the Translation of Boris Pasternak). *Teatr*, No. 2 (1941), pp. 144–47.

Morozov, Mikhail M. "Novyi perevod *Antoniia i Kleopatry* Shekspira" (A New Translation of Shakespeare's *Antony and Cleopatra*). *Pravda*, Oct. 2, 1944, p. 3.

Morozov, Mikhail M. "Novyi perevod *Romeo i Dzhul'etty*" (A New Translation of *Romeo and Juliet*). *Literatura i iskusstvo*, Nov. 21, 1942.

Morozov, Mikhail M. *Shakespeare on the Soviet Stage*.

Trans. David Magarshack. London: Soviet News, 1947. Pp. 20–21.

Morozov, Mikhail M. "Shekspir v perevodakh B. Pasternaka" (Shakespeare in the Translations of B. Pasternak). *Literaturnaia gazeta*, Aug. 7, 1943.

Ozerov, L. "Zametki Pasternaka o Shekspira" (Pasternak's Remarks about Shakespeare). *Masterstvo perevoda 1966*. Moscow: Sovetskii pisatel', 1968. Pp. 111–18.

Pasternak, Boris. "Moi novye perevody" (My New Translations). *Ogonek*, No. 47 (1942), p. 13. Rpt. in *Sochineniia*, III, 191–93.

Pasternak, Boris. "Novyi perevod *Otello* Shekspira" (A New Translation of Shakespeare's *Othello*). *Literaturnaia gazeta*, Dec. 9, 1944. Pasternak's comments on the play are followed by his translation of IV.iii.

Pasternak, Boris. "O p'ese Shekspira *Korol' Genrikh IV*" (About Shakespeare's *King Henry IV*), introductory remarks to a reading of passages from *1 Henry IV*, II.iv and III.iii. Originally recorded in 1947. Released on side two of "Vil'iam Shekspir v perevodakh S. Marshaka i B. Pasternaka: chitaiut avtory perevodov" (William Shakespeare in the Translations of S. Marshak and B. Pasternak: The Authors of the Translations Read) (Moscow: Melodiya, 1976). M40-38965-66

Pasternak, Boris. "Ot perevodchika" (From the Translator). Preface to Pasternak's translation of *Hamlet*. *Molodaia gvardiia*, Nos. 5–6 (1940), pp. 15–16. Rpt. in *Sochineniia*, III, 190–91.

Pasternak, Boris. "Zametki k perevodam shekspirovskikh tragedii" (Notes on Translations of Shakespeare's Tragedies). *Literaturnaia Moskva*. Moscow: GIKhL, 1956. Pp. 794–809. Rpt. in *Sochineniia*, III, 193–

211. This essay was written during the early 1940s. A slightly different version appeared in English translation under the title "Some Remarks by a Translator of Shakespeare" in the Moscow journal *Soviet Literature*, No. 9 (Sept., 1946), pp. 51–57.

Pasternak, Boris. "Zametki o perevode" (Notes on Translation). Ed. E. B. Pasternak. *Masterstvo perevoda 1966*. Moscow: Sovetskii pisatel', 1968. Pp. 105–10. This was based on a manuscript which survived from the early 1940s; only one part of it had been published previously, under the title "Novyi perevod *Otello* Shekspira" (see above).

Pasternak, Boris, and Kozintsev, Grigorii. "Pis'ma o *Gamlete*" (Letters about *Hamlet*). Ed. Evgenii B. Pasternak and Valentina Kozintseva. *Voprosy literatury*, No. 1 (1975), pp. 212–23. A few short passages from this correspondence are contained in the Appendix to Kozintsev, Grigorii, *Nash sovremennik Vil'iam Shekspir* (Our Contemporary William Shakespeare), 2nd ed. (Moscow: Iskusstvo, 1962).

Reztsov, L. "Prints datskii v novom osveshchenii" (The Danish Prince in a New Light). *Literaturnoe obozrenie*, No. 20 (1940), pp. 52–55.

Rowe, Eleanor. *Hamlet: A Window on Russia*. New York: New York University Press, 1976. "Pasternak and *Hamlet*," pp. 147–66.

Siniavskii, Andrei. "Poeziia Pasternaka." Introductory article to *Stikhotvoreniia i poemy* (Poems), by Boris Pasternak, ed. L. A. Ozerov. Moscow–Leningrad: Sovetskii pisatel', 1965. Pp. 9–62 (50–53).

Solov'ev, B. "V poiskakh *Gamleta*" (In Search of *Hamlet*). *Literaturnyi sovremennik*, No. 12 (1940), pp. 140–48.

Tizengauzen, V. *"Gamlet* v perevode B. Pasternaka"
        (*Hamlet* in the Translation of B. Pasternak).
        Sovetskoe iskusstvo, Apr. 30, 1940.
Vil'iam-Vil'mont, N. N. *"Gamlet* v perevode Borisa Pas-
        ternaka" (*Hamlet* in the Translation of Boris Paster-
        nak). *Internatsional'naia literatura,* Nos. 7–8 (1940),
        pp. 288–91.

Index